RIGHT *from the*
START

Care and Training for the Life of Your Dog

RACE FOSTER, DVM
MARTY SMITH, DVM

Howell Book House

New York

Dedication

This book is dedicated to our wives and children, who have always supported us. They have always been understanding with us when we were away from home because of our profession, and patient when we were home but involved in the writing of our books.

Macmillan Publishing books may be purchased for business or sales promotional use. For information please write: Special Markets Department, Macmillan Publishing USA, 1633 Broadway, New York, NY 10019.

Howell Book House
A Simon & Schuster Macmillan Company
1633 Broadway
New York, NY 10019

MACMILLAN is a registered trademark of Macmillan, Inc.

Library of Congress Cataloging-in-Publication data

Foster, Race; Smith, Marty

　Right from the start: care and training for the life of your dog
/Race Foster, Marty Smith.
　　　p. cm
　Includes index
　ISBN 0-87605350-9
　Dogs—Training.　2. Dogs.　I. Smith, Marty, 1947–
II. Title.
SF431.F675　1998
636.7'0887—dc21

Manufactured in the United States of America

Table of Contents

Acknowledgements

We want to thank all of our customers, employees and friends who have made the Drs. Foster and Smith company a reality.

The two of us have enjoyed working for and with our customers over the last fifteen years. They have challenged us to learn more and to provide them with better products and services every year.

Our employees have continued to take on greater and greater responsibilities, and see their sole responsibility as serving the needs of our customers and their animals.

Many people helped us with this book. We want to thank Dr. Holly Frisby, Dr. Joe Bodewes, Beth Grasser, Pam McFarland, Pat Heery and Candi Besaw for providing expertise in assembling and proofing the book. And nothing would have been possible without Beth Adelman at Howell Book House, who provided the professional direction and guidance that was needed throughout the book.

We also want to thank the many instructors and teachers we had in veterinary college. They gave us a foundation of knowledge that we were able to continually build on throughout our careers.

We also want to thank the many trainers we have known over the years. But especially we want to thank Rick Smith and Delmar Smith, who have both dedicated their lives to dog training. Their books, seminars and untiring willingness to answer questions have been instrumental in developing our training philosophies.

Introduction

This book was written by two veterinarians. Our main goal is to enable dog owners to recognize, understand and deal with the problems they are most likely to encounter with their pet over the course of its life. We will discuss the relationship that forms between people and their dogs and how these two very different animals interact with each other. We will try to help readers select the dog that is right for them, and then guide them through the various stages of their pet's life. This includes the care and training of the dog, along with the medical and behavior problems most dog owners encounter.

What we see as important and how we deal with these issues is affected by our professional and personal experiences. We work with professional breeders and trainers every day. This experience, along with breeding and training our own animals, has guided us on the issues covered in the book. Individuals from these or other professions might handle these topics differently, because of their backgrounds. They might also see different issues as more important to discuss. We each must work from our own unique perspective.

While some might think we are specialists because we limit our practice to dogs and cats, we would consider ourselves generalists. In the course of a typical day at our clinic, we will deal with the problems of many different breeds of dogs, and of dogs of unknown lineage. Their owners could be individuals who have only one dog or breeders with 40 or 50 animals. We've also donated numerous hours of our time working at local animal shelters where none of the animals had a human companion.

From day to day, it is common for us to work with everything from routine preventive medical care to serious and even life-threatening diseases. An increasing portion of our time is also spent dealing with behavioral problems and training issues. Most of our clients suffer through more behavior problems with their pets than they do medical ones, and we often become their first stop for information or a solution.

With this background, it is our goal in this book to work our way through the life of the dog, from puppyhood through old age. We will try to deal with the various stages of the animal's life, explaining the care and training required and tackling the problems you may encounter. We will help you with the time-consuming problems of puppyhood, the trials of adolescence, the principles of keeping an adult dog healthy and happy, all the way through to deciding when it may be time to say good-bye to a treasured friend.

This may seem like a lot of ground to cover. In veterinary school, we are taught about what seems to be millions of medical and behavior problems. But soon after graduation we quickly learn that although dogs can be affected by all of these conditions, most are afflicted by only a very few. The vast amount of our professional time is spent dealing with the same problems over and over again. In any stage of their lives, 90 percent of all dogs suffer from the same 10 or 12 medical or behavioral problems. From our experience, we believe this book will fulfill the needs of most clients that pass through our clinic's doors.

The book is arranged to follow the aging process of the dog. It starts with choosing a puppy and ends with the old dog. In between there are descriptions of the various life stages and the corresponding training, behavioral and medical issues. You may choose to read straight through the book, or move back and forth according to what concerns you and your dog. If you're concerned about a specific problem, the Index will help you find where that topic is discussed.

Chapter 1

WHY OWN A DOG?

We often talk about "owning a dog." In our minds, we may think we own them, but in reality, we don't. In most situations it would be better to describe what happens between a person and a dog as a relationship. Typically, it is a two-way street: we train (or attempt to train) a dog to fit into our world, and the dog trains us to adapt to its lifestyle and needs. Most dog "owners" will adjust their daily schedules to be home at a certain time to feed the dog or let it out. They soon find themselves buying the pet's favorite food, along with a wide assortment of treats and chew toys, dressing themselves in the appropriate breed sweatshirt, and either buying a dog bed or sharing their own.

WHAT MUST YOU DO?

It is important to understand that, as with any relationship, for it to be truly successful we must invest a significant amount of time and effort and be willing to accept numerous responsibilities. Whether the dog we end up with acts and behaves the way we want it to will probably depend on how much time we spend with it, either in active training or in simple companionship—preferably both. Regardless of the animal's age when it comes into our lives, the first few months to a year together will be the most demanding on our time. This is the stage of active training, in which we mold the animal behaviorally into the pet we want. Done correctly, this should be a fun time for both parties, but the need for you to allot enough time is very important. Minutes and hours invested during this period will lead to years of enjoyment.

Yet even with this task successfully completed, you must remember that throughout the entire life of your pet, changes will need to be made in your daily schedule to ensure that the dog can get outside at appropriate times, be fed regularly and given the one-on-one attention it deserves. If you go on vacation, you'll either need to make plans for boarding at a commercial kennel, arrange for a dog sitter or make sure that wherever you go, they are also willing to accept your canine friend.

Finances must also be taken into consideration. Even after you buy or adopt your pet, there will be significant expenses. There will be veterinary bills at least once a year for annual vaccinations, physical examinations and preventive flea and heartworm medications. In all probability, there will also be occasional trips to the animal clinic to treat various medical problems and emergencies. And there will always be day-to-day expenses for everything from dog food to toys to the grooming and boarding bills.

WHAT MUST YOUR DOG DO?

The relationship also makes demands on your canine counterpart. The dog will be forced to alter many of its natural or instinctive behavior patterns. For millions of years, dogs have enjoyed living naturally as wild pack animals, and they have had few restraints placed on them concerning when and where they can eliminate, how much they bark or whether they jump up on or bite another member of their immediate family unit. In fact, most of these activities have real meaning for them and are part of maintaining their proper place within the hierarchy of the pack. For dogs, all of these activities play a role in the dominance game that rules their day-to-day existence. Living with us in a fashion that most of us appreciate means that they give up any hope of being dominant over anything except the family cat—and even that is not a sure bet. Now they are not supposed to even dig a hole to lie in or breed with other dogs, unless we say it's permitted.

Whether we examine this human–dog relationship through the eyes of either participant, we should recognize the numerous compromises that both parties are required to make. For both it is hard work. So then why do so many "owned dogs" and their "masters" seem to be having so much fun? Why do people actively seek out dogs, and what keeps most dogs from reverting to their wild behaviors? The answer is simple. In most cases, for both parties, the rewards of the relationship far outweigh the disadvantages.

The relationship between a person and their dog brings a lifetime of companionship, enjoyment and love for both parties.

THE PAYOFF

For the dog, these rewards may seem obvious. Longer life, better health, a constant uninterrupted food supply, a warm and dry place to live and protection from larger predators would be just a few. However, the dog does not think in these terms. What our canine counterparts enjoy most from this recently developed human bond is simply the companionship. Dogs respond to affection and respect probably more than any other animal. In fact, there is something within their personalities that causes most of them to actively seek out this type of symbiotic relationship. A portion of this characteristic that we see in most of today's dogs has been brought about or accentuated through selective breeding, but this same trait is easily recognized in wild coyote puppies, which can be domesticated to live with humans. Treated with respect, dogs truly enjoy life with us.

For us, the rewards are also obvious. They far outweigh all responsibilities and expenses. There is no other way, no other place in the world today, that a person can so easily get all the love, devotion and respect that comes so automatically from having a dog in their life. We regret that we cannot give the writer credit, but years ago we read in a book about dogs, "Whoever said you can't buy love never heard of puppies!" That statement is so true.

Said simply, having a dog is a lot of work. It will be demanding in terms of money, time and responsibilities. However, for most people it will pay dividends far in excess of their investment. Anyone who brings a dog into their life and truly makes an effort to make that animal their friend will be rewarded with unquestioning loyalty and love.

Chapter 2

WHICH DOG IS RIGHT FOR YOU?

You've decided that you want to bring a dog into your life. You realize the extent of the commitment you are making. You are willing to invest the time, energy and money necessary to make this relationship work for you and your dog. With those decisions behind you, there are still plenty of questions left to answer. After all, the American Kennel Club recognizes more than 140 breeds, and there are just about that many different shapes and sizes of mixed breed dogs. So which one should you get?

In some instances, your individual needs or lifestyle may guide you to your choice. In other cases, your situation may be more flexible and you can choose from a wide range of dogs without making a mistake. And then, do you really want a purebred? There may be advantages to choosing a prince or princess from the "Heinz 57" clan.

Which will be better for you, a male or female? Does it make any difference once they're spayed or neutered?

You also need to consider whether you want to start with a puppy or an adult. Both have advantages and disadvantages. Usually the time you have available, combined with what you want in a dog, will help you make this last decision.

IS THERE A "RIGHT" DOG FOR YOU?

The dog you select should be one that closely fits your lifestyle and what you perceive your needs to be. Dogs come in all sizes and shapes, and which one is best for one person may not fit into another's life at all. As veterinarians

5

we have over 35 years of experience dealing with a wide range of dogs, and an even wider range of owners. To say that there is one and only one "right" dog for an individual just isn't true. We have seen thousands of human-canine "odd couples" that were perfectly happy.

A person's size or age means very little when it comes to choosing a dog.

There are traits, be they physical or behavioral, that in a general sort of way can be applied to any breed or type of dog. It would therefore seem that it's easy to match appropriate people with appropriate dogs. It isn't! The problem arises because in any single breed of dog there is a very, very wide variety of physical and behavioral characteristics. Not all adult male Golden Retrievers weigh between 68 and 72 pounds. They could be much smaller or much larger. They can also vary in color, how much they shed, their overall physical conformation and whether they are afflicted by any of a wide range of medical conditions. Neither are they all mellow, low-key pets (typical of the Golden Retriever) that lie near the fireplace all day. Their personalities can vary greatly because of genetically transmitted variables, and as a result of early interactions with people or littermates. Some Golden Retrievers will be great hunters. Others may have no interest in birds, while a few may be gun shy and therefore terrified of the hunting experience. Every dog of every lineage (whether purebred or mixed) is an individual, and no one can look at a puppy and predict with consistent accuracy what it will be as an adult.

The same can be said of dog owners. In our practice we have as a client an 80-year-old, 110-pound woman. Some might say that when choosing a canine companion, because of her physical stature she should restrict herself to a lap dog. In her case, nothing could be further from the truth. Although she has no background as a professional dog trainer, she and her 100-pound male Rottweiler get along perfectly and she is always in control. At the other end of the spectrum, we have 220-pound men who have difficulty handling their 15-pound mixed breed dogs. People vary greatly in their ability to train and care for dogs. A person's physical size, age, intelligence, financial worth or occupation mean very little when it comes to deciding which dog they should have.

What follows in this chapter are generalities; they are certainly not hard and fast rules. We will not attempt to be too specific or try to lead you through all the endless choices available to you. We haven't covered all of the possibilities, but have only tried to indicate the questions you should ask. You need to consider your own situation and make an honest effort to determine if there is a specific dog or type of dog that would be right for you. You will probably have a wide range to choose from, but the more effort you put into your decision, the happier both you and your new canine companion will be.

WHAT WILL YOUR NEW DOG'S ROLE BE?

The first and most important question you must ask yourself is what purpose your new canine companion will serve in your life. Before you try to decide which dog is right for you, you need to understand exactly what you want. Some people may acquire a pet to satisfy very specific needs. Do you want a hunting partner in the field, a guard to protect your home by barking or with its aggressive appearance or behavior, a playmate and learning experience for children, or something else? There are numerous specific roles that animals can fill. In most homes, however, the dog's role will simply be that of companion. That is, it will be a four-legged friend that you enjoy being with, regardless of your activity.

The Labrador Retriever is an excellent hunter in upland fields
or over water.

Every specific use or role for a dog comes with another subset of choices. If you want a dog as a hunting partner, you must choose an animal that is best suited for your type of hunting. Will it be for the upland field, where a dog will be moving through cover all day? Some of these breeds (such as the Pointer) will point with their body to indicate the approximate location of the game; others (such as the Springer Spaniel) will attempt to flush the bird into flight; while still others (such as the Labrador Retriever) may be along only for the retrieve. Some breeds (including the Chesapeake Bay Retriever) may spend long hours in a duck blind and then be asked to swim through cold water to perform a retrieve. A few are commonly asked both to hunt for birds in the upland fields and to retrieve over water. Different breeds have been selectively bred for different types of fieldwork. The one that is right for you will depend on your hunting style.

Some animals used to guard a home or business from intruders only need to bark, and a Poodle or Bichon Frise may suffice. They are telling whoever might be out there that it is impossible to enter the building without being detected. Other dogs in the protection field need an intimidating appearance. Few breeds fill this bill better than a Doberman Pinscher or a Rottweiler with lips curled back exposing their teeth. Others dogs that work in actual law enforcement must sometimes be able to defend and protect with their physical abilities. This will probably mean a large dog that has the ability to knock a man off his feet.

Combining what you want of your dog with an understanding of the traits of the various breeds or types of dogs, you can make an intelligent decision about which dog is best for you. A wide range of literature is available that portrays the traits, attributes, abilities, activity levels and personalities of the different breeds. An excellent book that describes the various breeds in detail is *The Complete Dog Book* by the American Kennel Club.

If the dog is acquired simply for companionship, almost any member of the canine species, regardless of its lineage, would be acceptable. But they come with an infinitely wide range of characteristics pertaining to size, coat, general appearance and behavior, so there's still a lot more to think about.

YOUR LIFESTYLE AND SURROUNDINGS

Your activity level dictates to a certain degree what type of dog will be best for you. A jogger can handle almost any breed, provided the dog can keep up with them. A backpacker who hopes their four-legged friend can carry part of the weight needs a strong but not necessarily large companion. An elderly person who wants a lap dog certainly wouldn't choose a Saint Bernard. While all of this may seem like little more than common sense, in our clinics we frequently see human-canine "odd couples."

You need to choose a dog that is physically and temperamentally able to join you in your favorite activities.

The amount of space available should also be considered, as it relates to the activity level and overall size of the dog. Someone who has a rural home surrounded by 80 acres can probably accommodate any breed, while the person living in a fifth-floor, one-room apartment may not want an exercise-demanding Border Collie.

Please understand that more than 60 percent of the dogs owned by Americans today are housedogs, that is, they spend the vast majority of their life in their owner's home. If this will be your situation, look at your home and yard and be realistic about the amount of exercise your pet can get within those confines. (Time alone in the yard does not count as exercise—dogs seldom play by themselves.) Remember that before they partnered with us, dogs in their natural state spent all of their time outside interacting with other dogs and searching for food. They lead very active lives, and only a few of those living with us today have given up much of their natural desire for exercise.

As you start looking at different breeds or types of dogs, you will learn that some are much more active than others. The activity level, or how "hyper" an individual dog or breed is, must be taken into account when you are choosing a dog.

A small, active dog is obviously easier to accommodate than a large, active one, but sometimes size does not correlate with behavior. A Yorkshire Terrier may seem to go 90 miles per hour all day long (and probably does). However, adults of one of the giant breeds, such as the Saint Bernard, typically sleep 16 to 18 hours a day. Does this mean you need a huge yard to keep a Yorkie? Of course not. But it does mean if you have limited space and want a very active dog, a Yorkie might be right for you. It also explains why some larger breeds often do so well in apartments or smaller homes.

This large Rhodesian Ridgeback is relatively calm, while the Pomeranian is usually on the move.

Other facets of a dog's physical makeup, besides its size and activity level, also need to be considered. One of the most important is the haircoat. Most dogs with longer coats need more care. This may mean special grooming techniques, such as frequent trimming, brushing or baths. Some owners enjoy keeping their pet looking its best, while others consider it a burdensome chore. In either case, this may not be a problem with a puppy, which usually has not yet developed its full adult coat. So remember, what you see on a pup will probably not be what you will live with for years. Later in life your longhaired dog will require additional time and/or expense to keep its coat in good condition. This is also true of some shorthaired breeds, such as the Poodle. Longhaired dogs are usually a disaster if they are outside in tall grass, weeds or brush. Their coats become matted and filled with everything they can snare.

DOES SEX MATTER?

Many future pet owners give little thought to whether they get a male or female dog. They may plan to spay or neuter the dog, and assume that the care and problems for either sex will therefore be the same. But female and male dogs have unique differences in their personalities, and these should be taken into consideration. Again, we will admit there are probably as many exceptions to the rules as there are generalities about the two sexes. Still, it's worth looking at the typical differences.

In their wild state, dogs are members of packs and constantly compete with one another for position within a dominance hierarchy. Many domestic dogs also challenge their human packmates, trying to work out where the boundaries are and, in some cases, even vying for actual dominance. This behavior is usually much more pronounced with male dogs, especially those that have not been neutered. This kind of dog usually needs an owner with more of a "take charge" attitude during training and thereafter.

If the owner of any dog, male or female, remains in control, these dominance issues rarely become a problem. (This will be discussed later in greater detail.) Still, for future owners who perceive themselves to be of a more timid nature, selecting a female dog can lessen the chances of encountering dominance problems.

Another trait of male dogs, whether they are neutered or not, is their habit of lifting their rear leg while urinating. In both wild and domestic dogs, this is part of territorial marking. They deposit their urine on raised or vertical objects, leaving their scent for other dogs to note. For most owners, this causes little or no problem. However, some gardeners don't like it, as their bushes and shrubs suffer from the high nitrogen levels found in dog urine. Some believe that neutering will prevent the dog from lifting his leg—not true!

Unneutered male dogs also tend to roam—sometimes great distances—seeking out females in heat. Leashes, fences, kennels or cable tie-outs curb this, but there must be a lot of frustration bottled up in a restrained male dog that senses a nearby female in season that is ready to breed! Neutering, especially if done before one year of age, will usually prevent roaming behavior from developing. However, if an adult dog has made a habit of roaming in search of prospective mates, it may continue even after it's been neutered.

Female dogs are typically easier to train, especially during the housebreaking phase, and usually grow up to be calmer pets. This statement, of course, is an over-generalization, as there are many exceptions.

The major problem with female dogs, if they are not sterilized, is their once or twice yearly heat cycles, and all the problems associated with them. If these are not dealt with correctly, the animal may become pregnant!

PUREBRED OR MIXED?

Should your new dog be a purebred or a mixed breed? For many, this is not even a question—they've been thinking about a specific breed all along, and nothing else even enters their mind. When they were growing up their parents had English Setters, for example, so they automatically look for an English Setter. For others, they simply want a purebred, and nothing else will do.

It is ironic that many future dog owners seek out a purebred without any idea of what breed they might want. They never consider a mixed breed dog—affectionately known as a Heinz 57. It's not that they have anything against mixed breeds; they simply never think about them. Before you start trying to choose from among the more than 140 breeds officially recognized by the American Kennel Club, you need to understand the differences and pros and cons of a canine blueblood versus a humble mongrel.

When it comes to the blood, a dog is simply a dog. Purebred dogs carry no greater premium on health or temperament than their mixed breed cousins. As a matter of fact, when looking at the results of blood tests done at our veterinary clinic, we can't tell if the sample in question came from a particular breed or a mongrel. Remember, all dogs, whether Chihuahua, Saint Bernard or a cross, are the same species. Biologically there is little difference and behaviorally there is even less.

There are differences between purebred and mixed breed dogs, but they are mostly in what the buyer wants or perceives. Several thousand years ago humans brought wild or free-roaming canines into their lives. Originally, they were used to help us with our work. In various parts of the world, different basic shapes and sizes of dogs were used for these initial transformations to domestication.

Regardless of their role, from the very start we have continually tried to alter the dog's abilities, behavior, size, shape, color, conformation and so on to fit some purpose or goal we had. This was done through selective breeding. Those wanting a bigger, stronger dog for carrying goods or protection bred only the largest dogs to each other, and kept only the biggest puppies. Those that wanted highly effective herding dogs or better hunters bred only those showing the greatest abilities in these areas. And of course, there were others that wanted a specific appearance, color or type of coat.

At some point in time, a standard is established and these animals are designated a unique breed. With the stroke of a pen on an official looking document, they are transformed from mixed breed to purebred.

If you are seeking a dog and need it for a specific purpose, you may be better off choosing a purebred that has been selectively bred with those traits in mind. Through generations of selective breeding, these traits have been refined and strengthened well past those found in the general population of dogs. While it is often said that any dog can be trained to do anything, you may be wiser to use the years of experience and efforts of others than to start on your own. For example, if you really want a dog to help you work your livestock, you're better off with a herding breed such as a Border Collie or an Australian Cattle Dog.

However, as we've mentioned before, most people want a dog for companionship. In that case, the breed of dog is not as important as the general size and activity level. Sometimes, people have specific needs that dictate their choice of dog. For example, if a respiratory condition or allergy means you should not be around dogs that shed a lot, you should select a breed that's appropriate for your own health. The advantage of a purebred here is that you know exactly what you're getting.

Most people want a dog simply for companionship.

Certain kinds of dogs are well known for the fact that they shed much less than most dogs. Examples are Poodles and Schnauzers. In these situations in which a specific physical trait is important in your dog, it is probably better to choose a purebred. It would be very difficult, if not impossible, to predict how much a mixed breed puppy will shed as an adult.

Some dog owners find certain dogs more attractive than others, and simply must have a dog with a certain look. It would be foolish for them to choose a different breed or one of mixed lineage. If someone knows what they want their dog to look like as an adult, but are starting with a puppy, they need to choose a specific breed so they'll be sure to have what they want a year later.

Some dog breeds are known for generally having certain personalities or behavior patterns. You can select one that matches yours, or what you would prefer to see in your pet. For example, Golden Retrievers are often thought of as having gentle, friendly personalities. To some that is the perfect dog. Others would prefer a more outgoing, excitable dog. Still others might want an animal to protect their home, and this role would be best fulfilled by a dog less tranquil than most Golden Retrievers. However, while choosing a purebred will give you some degree of certainty about the dog's looks, its temperament is a very different matter. There are laid back Doberman Pinschers and vigilant Golden Retrievers. Individual dogs can vary a great deal.

Often your choice of breed may have to be the result of compromises. Maybe you want a dog with the calm personality of the Golden Retriever, but you want it to have short hair. Then you need to choose another breed. With all the breeds available today, you should be able to find one that closely matches your needs.

Choosing to get a purebred is saying that you have specific desires or needs for your pet. Although you can find books written on every breed that describe its behavior patterns and physical abilities, remember that what is written describes only what the writer believes is the norm for the breed. The individual dog you get may differ greatly from that norm. Buying a purebred dog may increase your chances of finding exactly what you want, but it is not a guarantee.

This puzzle shows the breeds currently recognized by the American Kennel Club.

Keep in mind when thinking about purebred dogs that many manmade alterations in the basic structure and behavior of the original canine model have brought along some disadvantages. Some dogs, especially those with short noses and flat faces, may have difficulty breathing or giving birth to their puppies naturally. Very large or giant breeds usually have shorter life spans, often by several years. Breeds with excessive skin folds are generally more prone to bacterial skin infections.

In some purebreds, harmful or unwanted characteristics have arisen. Because so many physical characteristics are passed on by a subtle interaction of many genes, whenever breeders select for one trait, they may unknowingly select for many others. Hip dysplasia is a degenerative and often severely debilitating disease of the hip joints of dogs. It is transmitted genetically from one generation to the next. This condition is rare in wild dogs, because any condition that decreases the overall ability of a wild animal to compete in their world is quickly eliminated through natural selection. However, through human-engineered selection, hip dysplasia has become common in several breeds.

Today, concerned and ethical breeders work very hard to eliminate undesirable traits from their breeds. They truly care about the animals they produce and their future. But when they are working with limited gene pools, the task is not easy and the results are not quick.

So, purebred or mixed? Remember exactly what you are expecting out of this relationship. Most dog owners are not looking for a dog that can perform specific tasks. They are simply looking for a companion for themselves and their family. They don't care if the dog can retrieve ducks from an ice cold lake, carry a 50-pound load of camping gear up a mountain trail, or protect them from three attackers simultaneously. They want a well-disciplined and loving companion that is enjoyable to be with. For people who have no preconceived ideas of the exact size, color or hairstyle, a mixed breed may be perfect.

When considering your choice between a purebred and mixed breed, don't forget the cost. Purebred puppies frequently sell for anywhere from $300 to $3,000, depending on the particular breed and the lines involved. Mixed breed models are usually free or go for only a small adoption fee. In some households this can mean the difference between getting a dog or not getting one. And for some dogs, it can mean the difference between life and death. We promise you that the child who receives their first puppy will rarely care about its color, coat, size or the price you paid.

A Puppy or an Adult Dog?

For most people, getting a dog means bringing home a two-month-old puppy. Most people don't even think about an adult dog, but they probably should. For some first-time dog owners, a puppy is the worst possible choice.

While there's nothing cuter than a puppy, they present some definite disadvantages. It is always more difficult to determine the personality of any dog when it is evaluated in the first few weeks of life. Later in this book we'll discuss some guidelines you can use in selecting a puppy, but that is all they are. Remember that a seven-week-old puppy you may be looking at is approximately a year old in human terms. Anyone would admit that it is nearly impossible to judge how a human's personality will turn out from watching them in their crib!

Many experienced dog fanciers and trainers would remind us that this is a two-edged sword. While we may not be able to predict the future personality of the puppy, by starting with a young dog we will be able to have a greater effect on its development and behavior. Dogs are just like people in that many aspects of their personality are a result of their genetic background. However, also like us, they are also a product of their surroundings. A puppy that finds itself in a loving home with lots of attention will probably turn out much differently than a littermate that was tied to a tree in the backyard and whose only exposure to humans came in a once-a-day feeding. By choosing a puppy, you have the potential to have a much greater effect on its personality than if you start with an adult.

This, of course, assumes that you have time to carefully shape your puppy into the dog you want it to be. Selecting a puppy means you will spend a lot more time in training. That includes everything from housebreaking to leash training to basic commands. Additionally, puppies have to grow through some less-than-delightful phases, such as chewing on everything in sight, imperfect bladder control, whining at night, frequent trips to the veterinarian for vaccinations and wormings, the expense of neutering and more. Without exception, dogs take a lot more of your time during their first year of life. To many, this is the best part and they love the involvement. Other dog owners struggle to find the extra time.

Puppies, even with all their additional requirements, are usually more expensive to buy. There simply is a greater demand for them. They are cute, very appealing bundles of joy, and most Americans want their new dog to be a pup. Many breeders have a long waiting list of prospective puppy buyers. Adult dogs, on the other hand, are often given up because their owners discovered they couldn't give them the time required or realized having a dog wasn't for them. Adults aren't as cute as puppies and the market for them is much smaller. Typically, they do not command high prices. In fact, many go "free to a good home."

The value of an adult dog is often overlooked. One plus is that you know exactly what you're getting, in terms of size, coat, color, activity level and overall personality. The model you will have for the next several years is standing right in front of you. Additionally, with the help of your veterinarian, you can determine if the dog has any medical problems, such as hip dysplasia. With a puppy we can sometimes only guess if conditions such as these will develop later in life but with an adult we know, even if the animal is not yet showing signs of a problem.

SO IS THERE A RIGHT DOG FOR YOU?

The dog you bring home will be a part of your life for many years. For this partnership to be the best it can be for both of you, it's important that you make the right choice.

If you feel you still don't have the knowledge to make the decision, talk to dog breeders, trainers, veterinarians and other pet owners. All people, whether they are specialists or not, love to talk about their pets and there is a wealth of information available just for the asking. You could also attend a local dog show to get a better understanding of the various breeds and their characteristics. Read as much as you can about the different kinds of dogs. We've been brief here, but 99 percent of the breeds listed by the American Kennel Club have had several books devoted just to them. Today there are also hundreds and hundreds of good books and magazine articles dealing with every phase of pet ownership.

Sometime in this process, take time to consider the needs of the dog. Consider your surroundings and lifestyle. Make sure the dog fits into the environment you will be able to provide. Remember the word *relationship* and that it's a two-way street, with each party making both commitments and compromises. In this case, the majority of these commitments will fall on your shoulders. And that's fair, because you are the one who gets to make all the choices.

Chapter 3

WHERE TO GET YOUR NEW DOG

So far you've decided whether or not you want a purebred, and the age dog you would prefer. You've taken the time to make some very important decisions—ones that most prospective owners never take into consideration. Now you have to find that dog. There are lots of different sources, and some are much better than others. In other words, you still need to do some homework.

BUYING FROM A BREEDER

Buying from a breeder means you have selected a specific breed of dog. If you are starting out with a particular breed in mind, breeders are listed by breed in magazines such as *AKC Gazette, Dog World, Dog Fancy, Gun Dog* and others. You can also find breeders listed in newspaper ads, telephone books, veterinary clinics, grooming parlors, local dog clubs, hunt clubs, the Internet and lots of other places. However, the best way to select a breeder is through a referral that comes directly from people you know. They, or someone they know, should have experience with the breeder and be happy to pass the name along.

Dog breeders, just like dog breeds, come in all varieties. There are those that devote their lives to producing better and better puppies with fewer and fewer problems. Many of these care little about the money they earn for their pups, but honestly strive with every new litter to produce puppies that conform to a higher standard for their abilities, behavior and physical attributes.

The breeders of this English Setter litter worry more about producing
top-quality pups than about making money.

Today we know that genetics affect most characteristics in all living things.
The dedicated breeder works constantly to accentuate the good and eliminate
the bad. These are the highly ethical breeders, and they're the people you
need to search for when you're shopping for your new dog.

Some full-time breeders, on the other hand, have made a very good
financial living out of breeding as many puppies as they can possibly sell,
with little regard to the potential problems they may be passing on to new
owners. Some are large-scale breeding operations, known as puppy mills,
where several animals of the same breed are placed in a single enclosure and
no one even knows which dogs are the parents of a particular litter. In actuality,
these large-scale operations don't care. They just want to churn out as many

puppies as possible. All the stories about used car salesmen are nothing compared to the lack of ethics that this group lives by. These are the people you need to avoid.

Someplace between these two extremes falls an intermediate group of breeders. Most of these people only occasionally breed a litter. They do it for a variety of reasons. For some, they really believe that they have a great dog and they want one of its pups. There is nothing wrong with that. Most of these people want the best for the puppies they produce and will work hard to find them good homes.

Other occasional breeders aren't very selective about choosing which dogs to mate with theirs. They use whatever is available—any dog with papers will do. Neither are they very particular about where the puppies will go. They produce the litter solely to make money, and they usually fail both in producing good puppies and in making money. Usually, raising a single litter produces many more expenses than they ever thought possible. There are food and veterinary bills, toys, equipment and more. The time spent working with and cleaning up after a litter of puppies could be more profitably spent in most part-time jobs.

There is no national registry that ranks breeders as to their ethics or the quality of puppies they produce. It is possible for you to get a truly great puppy from any one of them. Your chances are just much better when you deal with a conscientious, reputable breeder. The responsibility therefore lies on your shoulders to make a good decision. You have to do your homework and ask lots of questions.

Remember, genetics play an important role in how your puppy will turn out, so learn as much about its parents as you possibly can. Spend as much time considering them as you do the pup. They probably are very similar to what your puppy will someday be. Every time you visit the kennel, before any decision is made, spend time with them. The appendix lists most breeds and the most common medical problems affecting them. You probably aren't able to diagnose or recognize these just by looking at the parents, but you should ask the breeder about these conditions and if the parents or related dogs have had problems.

Take plenty of time evaluating the behavior and disposition of the parents, too. Many of these traits are also controlled by genetics. In Chapter 5 we will also outline some of the physical abnormalities to look for or be aware of when you're picking a puppy.

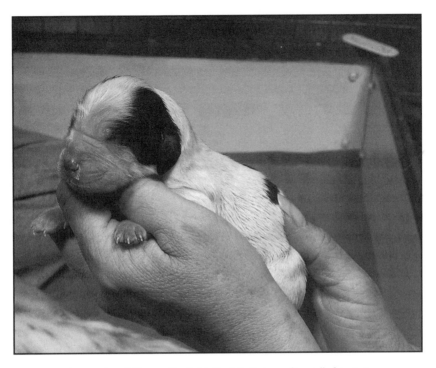

At one day of life, much of this English Springer Spaniel's future is determined by its genetics.

Don't take a puppy from parents that display behavioral patterns you don't want to live with for the next 10 to 15 years. Problems with aggression, excitability or shyness can be brought on by how a dog is treated, but they can also flow from generation to generation through genetic pathways. You want to start out with a puppy that has the very best possibility of becoming the dog you want, so don't make any compromises at this point.

If you are unable to spend time with the parents of the puppy you are interested in, don't be afraid to ask for references. (The male partner in the breeding may live thousands of miles from the kennel.) Most good breeders love to talk about other puppies they've bred, where they have gone and how they have developed. And most owners of good dogs are ecstatic to talk about their animals, so there should be no scarcity of information if the quality is there. Also, talk to your veterinarian about the breeder or the parent dogs to see if he or she can offer any insights. Do everything you can to determine if there are any potential problems that might affect your decision to purchase a puppy from a particular source.

BREED RESCUE ASSOCIATIONS

Another excellent source of purebred dogs is the breed rescue associations. These are made up of people who have a strong interest in a specific breed. They are dedicated to ensuring that puppies and dogs of their breed find their way into good homes. They are constantly on the lookout for dogs that are up for adoption for various reasons. Large breeds may have outgrown the family's home, the owner may have died, a divorce may have split up a home, but usually the simple fact is that the dog is no longer wanted. Upon learning of these animals, rescue league members will typically take these pets into their homes and then work very, very hard to find them new owners.

Rescue groups are an excellent source of both puppies and adult dogs. You will probably be surprised at how diligent rescue members are at assessing whether you are qualified to take on one of their charges. Remember, their interests are totally with the animal and ensuring that this time it gets a good home. Breed rescue associations can be found by contacting the American Kennel Club at (919) 233-9767 (or on the Internet at www.akc.org).

PUPPIES FROM PET SHOPS

It is impossible for most people to walk through a mall and not stand and look at the puppies in the window of a pet shop. They are usually at an age when they recognize people and are striving for attention. They either jump at you against the glass or cage, or sleep in big adorable balls of fur. Let's face it, they're cute and therefore the natural impulse is to take one home.

While many pet shops diligently try to provide top-quality puppies, the main disadvantage for people buying their pets from these facilities is that it is almost impossible to learn anything about the breeder or the animal's parents. You'll know the breed, age and sex, but that is about all the information you'll have. You won't have any idea if the particular line of dogs has a high incidence of hip dysplasia, epilepsy or whatever. Regretfully, a lot of puppies from the puppy mills end up in pet shops.

If you can't resist, at least try to have the animal examined by your veterinarian before you buy it. This will give you an idea if the animal is currently in good health. However, the problem with an evaluation at this age is that it is impossible to diagnose or predict the occurrence of many serious medical or behavior disorders that might show up later in the animal's life.

BREEDING YOUR OWN PUPPY

Many dog owners have a dog they love and think it is exactly what they want. It has a great personality, is excellent with children, easily trained, may be a fabulous hunter, and has had few or no serious medical problems. If they are going to get another dog, they want it to be as much like the one they already have as possible. They decide to breed their animal and keep a puppy from that litter. In their minds, this is the closest they can come to duplicating the dog they own.

This seems logical, but genetics doesn't work that way. The way to get a puppy that is as close as possible to your own dog is to repeat your dog's breeding—that is, to mate your dog's sire and dam again—and take a puppy from that litter. Unfortunately, this isn't always possible.

If you have the female, breeding a litter at home can be a great experience or it can be a disaster. It is usually a lot of fun for the entire family to watch new puppies come into the world, grow and then play for hours and hours. In the end, some profit may be shown when the remaining littermates go to their new homes at seven to eight weeks of age. But before you start off, understand that a tremendous amount of work is involved and rarely is there much profit. In fact, most first-time breeders actually lose money.

Whether you own the female or male, if you do it correctly there will be expenses even before the breeding occurs. We never recommend breeding dogs before they are 24 months of age. It takes at least that long to determine if the animal has any significant health or behavioral problems. Regretfully, some health problems don't show up until the animal is even older.

Both animals should be examined by a veterinarian to see if they are carrying any significant medical disorders that can be passed on to future generations. We aren't saying this because we are veterinarians trying to drive more business to our doors. If you are going to breed a litter, it is your responsibility to ensure to all future owners that the puppy they pay for is and will be as healthy as possible. Think how you would feel when the owners and their children find out the pet they bought from you has a disease that will limit its life or may cost more than they could afford to treat or correct. Please believe us, this frequently happens.

To use a very, very common example, let's assume you mate two young dogs of the same breed. They seem healthy, have great personalities and have been easy to train. The puppies are born, all goes well, and at seven weeks every pup goes to a new home. Unfortunately, in about eight to 15 months the calls begin to come in from the new families that their pups have started showing a painful lameness in their hindquarters. Their veterinarians, through X-rays, have diagnosed hip dysplasia. Briefly, this is a genetically transmitted disease that usually results in severe and painful degenerative arthritis in the hip joints of dogs. Most cases can be treated through medical or surgical means, but the animals may never be able to exercise normally or do what they were purchased for, and should never be bred. Additionally, these treatments will probably be expensive and there is no guarantee they will help the condition or even eliminate the discomfort the animal is in.

What are you going to do? What are your responsibilities? You bred the puppies, you took the money and told the buyers how great the parents were. You never lied. You just didn't know what you were doing. Now several other families have to deal with a problem that could have been avoided. If you only have one dog to breed and now you know it is carrying the disease, you can't give them another puppy from a future breeding. Are you prepared to give them their money back? Are you willing to help with the medical bills they are going to incur if they decide to try treatment? As veterinarians, we have been involved in cases just like this thousands of times!

If you still want to breed your own dogs but want to bypass the above horror story, here are some recommendations. Don't breed your dog unless you honestly believe it is really something special and can contribute to the overall quality of the breed. Wait until it's at least 24 months of age. By that age, you and your veterinarian will have a better chance of recognizing any serious behavioral or medical problems.

Before breeding, take both dogs to a veterinarian and have a thorough examination done. In addition to the usual tests, this will probably include, but not be limited to, X-rays and certification that the dog is free of hip dysplasia, an eye exam and blood tests for sexually transmitted disease. The animals will probably be brought up to date on all vaccinations and wormed if necessary. If your veterinarian sees any problem that might preclude breeding, he or she will discuss it with you. Remember, this should be done with both prospective parents.

A dog that has been bred several times and seems to be producing healthy dogs could still be carrying problems that never came forward because the dogs it was bred to did not have those problems. If you are going to breed your dog with a supposedly "proven" mate, you still must make sure both are checked for breeding soundness and certified free of things like hip dysplasia. And make sure you ask about the diseases listed in the appendix.

When you've been through all of this and done the best job you can, you'll understand why good breeders charge what they do for their puppies, and why they are so careful about the homes the pups end up in.

There are a few more questions you need to answer before you breed your dog. If you cannot sell or in some way find good homes for the puppies you don't want to keep, what will you do with them? If there are four remaining pups, it is the rare family that can absorb them into their family. What are your choices? In case it enters your mind, remember that most puppies delivered to a humane society do not find homes. They are euthanized after seven to 10 days, due to economics and lack of space. For most people, that thought is an extreme burden for their conscience.

SHELTERS AND POUNDS

Today it is tragic how many dogs start and end their lives in animal shelters. Americans produce more puppies than there are homes for them, especially good homes. That pound dog could be a purebred, but unless the previous owners dropped off its papers, you'll never know. And unless you intend to breed an animal, the registration papers have little meaning except to satisfy your curiosity about your pet's parents and background.

Once you've decided to look in a shelter, you should still ask as many questions as possible about your prospective pet. Take your time and try to determine what you can about its personality and behavior. Most shelters vaccinate and worm all animals as they pass through the door. Find out what has been done with the dog you're interested in. Have your veterinarian give it a good health exam. Know as much about it as you can.

If it was dropped off by the previous owner, try to contact them to learn if there was any known behavioral problem or medical condition that influenced their decision. They may have given it up for adoption after it bit the neighborhood children. Is that a problem you really want to take on? Remember, however, that these situations are fairly rare, and humane society employees do not unload dogs on new families without explaining everything they know. At most shelters, they have more good dogs than they'll ever find homes for.

In the vast majority of cases, getting a puppy or adult dog from a shelter does not come with any perceivable disadvantages. There may be very little difference between the dog you get at a pound and the one you choose at a breeding kennel. And you have given a home to an animal that may not have even been alive in seven days.

Dogs from animal shelters provide just as much love and companionship as dogs from anywhere else.

TAKE YOUR TIME

Whether your choice is a puppy or an adult, take your time in choosing your dog. This animal will be your best friend for many years to come, and all the time and effort you spend before the final selection will greatly increase your chances of getting the dog that's right for you.

Chapter 4

THE FIRST SIX MONTHS— BEHAVIOR AND BASIC CARE

You've decided you want to start with a puppy. You already know whether you want a purebred dog or a mix. Now the fun part comes: Selecting the one for you. This may be from a litter at the breeder's home or kennel or a group at the humane society. Preferably, this selection doesn't have to be accomplished in a single trip, and you can make several visits over the course of one to two weeks. Puppies, just like people, have good days and bad days, and their behavior can vary from one visit to the next.

Avoid the impulse to pick one because of its size or color. You should be trying to understand something about their individual personalities. Stop and think; years from now the dog's personality and abilities will be more important than its overall appearance. Before you choose, it's important to understand what has affected the puppy's development through its early life.

HOW A PUPPY'S PERSONALITY FORMS

Let's assume you are looking at a puppy that is between four and seven weeks of age. At this point, its behavior is a product of genetics and how the breeder has managed the pup's activities and environment. These activities are known as socialization—developing interactive skills with members of its own and other species and learning to be comfortable in different situations and environments. The personality and behavior of a mature dog will be strongly affected by how it interacts with littermates, its mother, people and various external stimuli that it encounters during the first 12 weeks of life. The breeder will control a portion of this period, and you the rest.

From its mother, a puppy receives the first stimulation to breathe, nurse, urinate and defecate. She trims the umbilical cord, cleans the pup several times a day, keeps it warm and makes sure the environment is safe and secure. She supplies everything needed. She also provides discipline when the pup's behavior exceeds limits that only she understands.

Orphan puppies require significant amounts of care just to ensure their survival through seven weeks of age. People who become their surrogate mothers find that the frequent feedings are the least of their worries. Puppies before 10 to 14 days of age do not pass stool or urine without external stimulation, nor are they able to maintain their body temperature. Without some sort of external coaxing, their intestinal tracts shut down. Left by themselves, they often become chilled, which can lead to their death. In addition to providing a balanced diet, their human mothers must induce them to eliminate their wastes, keep them clean and somehow maintain their body temperature at approximately 100°F.

From their littermates, puppies acquire additional knowledge about how to interact with members of their own species. Through their play, they learn about dominance and submission, get an introduction to mating behavior and receive a wide range of stimulation that helps develop their senses and physical abilities. Puppies that have no littermates, or come from litters that were split up at too young an age, typically have difficulty interacting with dogs later in life. Not knowing how to react when confronted by a member of their own species, they tend to be either overly shy or aggressive. Usually they fail miserably in multi-dog households.

Through handling and play with humans during their first seven weeks of age (which all good breeders encourage), the puppy learns to trust and interact with people. Without this involvement in their lives they tend to have difficulty forming relationships with or being comfortable around people. Dogs isolated from humans at an early age tend to become one-person dogs. They usually do not fit well into homes that have children or several adults. Obviously, these traits can sometimes be overcome, but it is not always easy.

In most situations, breeders provide what the puppies need for correct socialization with little effort expended. They keep the puppies with their littermates until they are seven weeks old. The mother is left with the puppies throughout most of this period. After four or five weeks, she will be allowed to spend time away from the pups, but she'll still be with them for several visits each day. Good breeders love children, if for no other reason than to have them around to play with their developing puppies.

Good breeders often have children help with their puppies' socialization.

In our own experiences of raising litters, we have our children start holding and petting the puppies when they are only a few days old. At three to four weeks of age, we let them play together in outdoor situations for an hour or more every day. And, like most breeders, we try to expose the pups to many different stimulating environments or situations. They shouldn't be confined to a whelping box or pen until they depart for their new home. They need to learn to respond to many different situations to develop confidence in themselves. Their curiosity needs to be stimulated. If you ever decide to breed your own litter, all these same things will become your responsibility.

PICKING YOUR PUPPY

Let's assume you're picking your dog from a group of puppies. They could be within the confines of a large cage at a shelter, or in a room, kennel or yard at the breeder's home. Remember, as you try to make your selection, that just as every person is different, so is every dog. Your goal is to select a particular puppy that matches your image of the perfect dog.

Many authors and dog fanciers emphatically believe that it is impossible to judge an adult dog's personality or abilities from its behavior as a puppy. One of our close friends, Delmar Smith, is a very famous dog trainer. He once visited the Queen of England's kennel. It is renowned for producing numerous field and obedience champions. Delmar asked the senior resident trainer, responsible for the majority of these wins, about how he consistently picked puppies that would be future winners. The old gentleman smiled and simply replied that he let everyone else pick the pups they wanted and then worked with whatever was left. He believed that through seven to 10 weeks of age, all puppies were equal.

We would agree that picking a puppy is far from an exact science, but most people who are involved with dogs believe there are better methods than random selection. Most of us do not want a puppy that will mature into an overly aggressive animal. Neither do we want one that is excessively timid or shy. We want a dog that will be reasonably easy to train, cause little damage to our home and friends and adapt well to our family and household.

Spending a little time with a group of puppies and observing them carefully can usually help to isolate those with good, outgoing personalities. They'll be in the midst of puppy play, being neither overly dominant nor submissive. If you crouch down, friendly pups will usually run to your feet. When picked up and supported well, they normally won't fight or struggle to get down.

Ask yourself some obvious questions. Does the puppy seem to enjoy being with people? Is it overly afraid of stimuli such as sounds or sudden movement? Most of this is common sense and can be assessed by anybody who has no preconceived ideas. Anything is better than saying simply, "I want a brown one with lots of spots."

There have been books written on puppy selection. Some are very good, while others seem to lead readers down a long and difficult path. Most good methods use a test that measures the puppy's responses to some sort of stimuli. This attempts to eliminate most subjectivity. We believe there are two very good and useful books on this subject. They are straightforward and easy to use. One is written by the Monks of New Skete and is titled *The Art of Raising a Puppy*. The other is Clarice Rutherford and David Neil's book, *How to Raise a Puppy You Can Live With*. They both explain and guide you through a system of evaluating the individual animal's personality. Both books also give an excellent discussion of the behavioral development of dogs through their first year of life. We would strongly recommend them to any prospective puppy owner.

Although we endorse these puppy selection methods, remember that they only judge the puppy on that particular day during one stage of its life. Tests done on another day could yield very different results.

Keep in mind that the environment the animal lives and matures in will also greatly affect its behavior and personality as an adult. This means you will have an opportunity to affect the puppy after it is living with you. The more time you spend with your new friend, the better chance you have of it growing into the animal you want. Regardless of the test or selection method you use, you cannot expect the animal to continue to develop without your guidance.

THE MAGIC SEVEN-WEEK MARK

You've picked out your puppy and paid the bill. It is six weeks of age and you want the puppy now! However, the breeder says you can't take it home for seven more days. They say they always keep the puppies with the mother and littermates until they are 49 days of age. Exactly seven weeks! While you may be angry or disappointed, in our opinion you are very lucky. You are dealing with a breeder who is worried more about doing what is right for the dog than about getting out of an additional week of puppy cleaning duties.

It may seem very subjective, but it has been shown by several animal behaviorists that this is what's best for the puppy. They should stay within their litter until they are 49 days of age, and then immediately go to their new homes. Through seven weeks of age, the pups are still learning much from their interactions with their mother and littermates. This will help them later in life when they are confronted by other dogs. Being in the presence of its littermates gives a puppy more confidence when it encounters new experiences. These could be anything from a loud noise, fences that need to be climbed over or through, a large object like a tree or the sound and sensation of the wind in its face.

The puppy still needs to be around people. That will never change. In fact, it's very important for a six-week-old puppy. If the breeder is out of neighborhood children or is running short on time, you should plan on spending time at the kennel during the next few days, if it's at all possible. Remember, your responsibilities started the day you said you wanted that puppy.

PREPARING FOR YOUR NEW PUPPY

This last week will also give you a chance to prepare your home for the puppy's arrival. When parents find out they are going to have a child, they make all sorts of preparations. A room is set aside and the walls may be redone with an appropriate wallpaper or paint, a supply of formula fills the pantry, baby bottles and diapers are purchased in huge quantities, toys and pacifiers are picked out, etc.

You need to make the same preparations for your puppy. It is going to need a room, or at least a place it can call its own. A wire pen or crate will fill this bill. You are better off getting an adjustable one that will be big enough for the dog to use as an adult. The pup will also need food and water bowls, toys to chew on and play with, a collar and leash, a bag of a top-quality dry puppy food, and plenty of newspapers or training pads. The bills are adding up!

Take some time to puppy-proof your home. Pick up or protect items you don't want chewed, and block off areas that will be off limits to the puppy. If your children are young or are not familiar with puppies, you should spend some time with them during these last few days explaining common sense rules on how to handle and play with the pup.

THE BIG DAY

The big day arrives and it's off to pick up the puppy. Many people worry that this is a traumatic event for the puppy, but it probably isn't as bad as you might think. Leaving its mother and littermates will probably bring about some separation anxiety. However, this can be greatly diminished if everyone in the family plans their schedules so someone is with the puppy constantly for the first three to four days.

Some authors suggest leaving the puppy alone and giving it time to itself to adjust to the new surroundings. We disagree. In our homes, we plan for this introductory period by keeping the puppy involved with plenty of attention from children and other family members through every waking moment. When we aren't with the puppy, it is eating or sleeping. You'll be amazed how time spent in this manner will speed up the housebreaking process, but we'll come back to that later.

Coming home will start out with a car ride from the shelter or breeder's home. Try to keep this from being a terrifying experience for the pup. The main problem dogs have with car rides usually isn't what we humans refer to as motion sickness, but rather simple anxiety about the vibrations, sounds and, to a lesser degree, the movement of the car. Many dogs that have developed problems with car rides get nervous or even nauseous before the engine is even started. It's important that this first trip not be a bad experience that turns into a pattern of behavior. Before you leave the kennel, try to get the pup to go to the bathroom, so there are no floods or surprises stimulated by all the excitement of the ride.

On this first trip home we break a cardinal rule about traveling with pets. We do not put the puppy in a crate. Remember they are small and easy to hold. Rather, we have someone other than the driver hold the puppy in a blanket or towel and talk or in some way try to distract it from the ride. If you've got a long way to go and need to stop for the puppy to relieve itself, do not use a highway rest stop! At this age the puppy has very little, if any, protection from common dog diseases, and these areas can easily be contaminated with the organisms causing these conditions. We never recommend these facilities for pets of any age, but if you must use them, wait until your puppy has completed its vaccination series.

One of the first things you need to do is get the puppy to a veterinarian for an initial examination. You'll want to make sure it is in perfect health, free of any congenital problems or other medical conditions. (But remember, this visit is not a guarantee that congenital or genetic diseases, such as dysplasia, seizures or allergies will not surface later.) Also, find out exactly what the breeder (or humane society) has done for the puppy. In all probability, the puppy has had some vaccinations given by the breeder or shelter. It probably has also been wormed and may even be on a heartworm preventive. Depending on the breed, the tail may have been docked and the dewclaws removed. It is common for all or some of these to have been done. This helps explain some of the cost of your puppy, regardless of where it was obtained. Your veterinarian will need all of this information, along with the actual or an approximate birth date.

Pick a location in your home, hopefully within a crate or pen, where the puppy will sleep. The first few nights, it will whine and possibly bark. That's normal, and if you ignore this refrain it will soon end.

Continuing the Socialization Process

We talked about how the breeder must provide the puppy with an environment that prepares it for life among humans and occasional encounters with other animals, and teaches it to be comfortable in a wide range of situations and environments. This is called socialization. Even though the puppy is now in its permanent home, socialization must continue, as the pup is still developing behavioral patterns. In fact, these first few weeks in your home are some of the most important in the socialization process.

We talked about keeping the puppy's schedule full for the first few days in your home, in an effort to limit any loss it might feel from being separated from its littermates and mother. However, between seven and 10 weeks of age there is an additional problem. At this time, most puppies go through a period in which they lose some of their self-confidence. Trust comes harder for them and things that we would expect them to be comfortable with suddenly elicit anxiety or fear. Where before they would boldly charge into a new situation, now they seem apprehensive. Problems could be caused by almost anything—loud noises, new people, play that's a little too rough, going to a new place, and so on.

Behaviorists have found that this loss of confidence has little to do with the change in where they are living or the separation from their siblings and mother. Even when the litter remains together, this behavioral pattern is noted. Don't overreact; your puppy will mature through this and be just fine if you do your part. You do not want to become overly protective and isolate it from the outside world. We think it's better during this two- to three-week period to increase the range of your puppy's experiences by small steps, not giant leaps and bounds. Choose activities that can be controlled. Introduce the puppy to new people, including children, but don't let 30 kids come screaming at it from all directions. Let it meet the neighbor's nice dog, just not the rowdy one down the street. At approximately 12 weeks of age this period comes to an end, and most owners will see their puppies become bolder around new people, animals and experiences.

From this point through at least one year of age, it is imperative that you make every effort to expand the puppy's environment and expose it to new things. During this stage of their lives dogs should be around as many different people and animals as possible. Take them with you when you go for a walk, shopping or even to work. Get them used to loud noises, such as vacuum cleaners. Encourage your children to bring their friends over to meet the new pet. Take an obedience or training course where you'll meet other dogs. All of this is important.

Dogs that are isolated during their first year of life develop many problems. A few will become aggressive, but the majority are more likely to become overly shy or timid. They lack confidence around new people and situations. They cower in the presence of strangers. They jerk at their leash to get away from children or other pets. Forced to be in a new place, they may sit shaking behind you, drooling and panting rapidly. In the worst cases, they may become fear biters. This is when dogs encounter new people or pets they are afraid of and don't know how to react; they end up biting the stranger out of sheer panic. Once this behavior develops, it can be very difficult to overcome. It's much better to avoid it altogether with lots of positive socialization.

GENERAL PUPPY CARE

If you've never had a dog before, your head should be filled with questions about what you should be doing, and not doing, with or for your new puppy. The breeder, employees of the animal shelter, veterinarian, friends and neighbors are all there as information sources. There are also numerous books, magazines, videos, television shows and the Internet.

Remember, just like this book, some of what you hear may only be opinions, and sometimes these can be wrong. Just as you may someday seek a second opinion about a veterinary medical case, don't ever be afraid to ask the same question of different people. No matter what you ask about dogs (unless it's something like how many legs do they have), you will get widely differing views. There is a lot of bad or misguided information about canines. There are ridiculous myths and fables about dogs and how to raise and care for them. Often it's best to let common sense be your guide. We humans who are parents brought home our first baby when it couldn't feed itself, walk or even get a drink on its own, but somehow, most of us succeeded.

Feeding becomes a major issue on the first day. Many new owners worry that without its mother's milk, their pup is going to have a hard time adjusting to its new home. They may be surprised at how well puppies make it through this transition, because they don't understand how far along dogs are in their development at seven weeks of age. At seven weeks your puppy should be completely weaned to solid food.

Through our clinics and catalog business we work with hundreds of breeders and animal shelters. It's common practice for most of these individuals to start feeding their puppies a commercial food at 21 days of age. Some of the toy breeds may start three to four days later. Even though their eyes didn't open until 11 to 13 days old, just 10 days later puppies are ready to start on something in addition to mom's milk. Most breeders take dry puppy food, soak it in warm water for 30 minutes and then give it to the litter when they are 21 days old. The first day they may only stick their noses in it and try to lick some of the liquid. But after that, they eat—and they eat very well.

After a week or so of offering the softened food, the pups are still nursing but they also get this puppy food twice a day. This takes a huge burden off the mother, especially when she has a large litter. As soon as possible, the amount of water mixed in the food is decreased and then finally eliminated. This depends on how fast the pups' teeth are coming in and is based on the judgment and experience of the breeder. Puppies fed on this sort of a schedule grow rapidly and with fewer problems.

When you pick up the puppy, be sure to ask what it has been eating. It is a good idea to continue feeding the same type and brand of food for at least a few days. If you decide to switch brands, mix the two together for a few days.

We always tell all new puppy owners to use a dry food formulated for puppies. Most seven-week-old dogs can eat this as it comes from the bag without any problem. A few, especially the toy breeds, may need it moistened for one to two additional weeks, but that is all. Today there are many top-quality brands of dry puppy foods, even ones formulated specifically for large and giant breeds.

These 30-day-old Cocker Spaniel puppies are already eating dry food.

We generally do not recommend canned food or the semi-moist fake meat burgers. Canned foods are typically higher in calories and fat and are usually 80 to 83 percent water. That makes them pretty expensive if you squeeze out the top four-fifths of the can. The semi-moist foods are about 55 percent water and use high levels of salt for preservation. Again, you are paying too much for water and puppies don't need the salt.

Dry foods are only 9 to 11 percent water and are made of the same quality ingredients as the other types of foods. They are more economical, easier to use and, in our opinion, are better for your dog. Dogs on dry foods typically have fewer intestinal upsets, either diarrhea or constipation. They also have fewer problems with unwanted weight gain. We see no advantage as far as coat or skin quality is concerned with canned foods. Probably the most important advantage of using dry foods and feeding them dry is that the abrasive action of eating them is good for the dog's teeth and gums. Dogs that regularly eat any of the softened foods always have more dental problems, ranging from tartar and plaque build-up to abscesses, tooth loss and gum disease. Any or all of these cause bad breath.

The only thing we dislike more than canned or pre-moistened foods for dogs is table scraps. We strongly recommend never starting to feed these, because once you do, it never stops. Most nutritionists believe dogs that are on a good quality, commercially prepared dry food are nutritionally better off than their owners. This has been proven in many studies. Table scraps are usually higher in calories and certainly aren't balanced nutrition. Neither are they fortified with the vitamins and minerals that dogs require.

By the way, when it comes to pets, we consider milk just another table scrap. Cow's milk contains sugar in the form of lactose, which requires the enzyme lactase to digest it. Most humans produce this digestive enzyme. Most dogs do not produce it at adequate levels. That is why they often develop diarrhea or softer stools when they eat milk or milk products. When you see milk or milk by-products listed as ingredients in pet foods, lactose bacteria have been used to break down the sugar into more easily digestible forms. Dogs do not need fresh milk!

The puppy's feeding schedule will be dictated by your own personal schedule. You don't want to leave food out for the puppy so that it can eat whenever it wants. You need to be there for the feedings, because you want the puppy and its entire body on a set schedule. This is best accomplished by feeding the pup what it will eat in a specific period of time on a specific schedule. The dog's entire system will be on a predictable timetable, and it will then go to the bathroom on a more specific schedule. This will make housebreaking much easier and faster.

Typically, puppies between seven weeks and six months of age are fed three times a day, with water given with or soon after the meal. From six months to a year, they generally eat twice a day. Then, at approximately a year of age (except for the giant breeds), they cut themselves back to a single daily feeding.

Make it a habit to give the puppy some quiet time after the meal. The puppy may need to go to the bathroom, but don't let the children romp and play with it for the first hour to hour and a half after eating. This can lead to stomach upsets that can sometimes be very serious.

The amount of food given with each meal should never be dictated by what is on the back of the dog food bag. From our experience, the manufacturers obviously want to sell a lot of food. With our own pups, we place an ample amount of food down for them, and then after 10 to 15 minutes it is picked up. You'll soon learn to judge how much they need and, depending on how fast they clean their dish, when they need more. Remember to have water available with or immediately following the meal.

One of the biggest complaints veterinarians hear from dog owners, especially those with animals younger than 18 months, is that they never eat enough. The owners feel the dog isn't putting on weight or growing as fast as they think it should. They are tempted to somehow encourage their animals to eat more. Don't do it. The growth rates and appetites of young animals on a good-quality food are dictated primarily by their genetics. Don't try to make your dog grow faster than it should, or into something it isn't. This will only cause problems. Artificially accelerated growth leads to bone and joint disorders. Feed your pup the amount it wants and let the dog's body dictate its needs.

Puppies may seem to drink large quantities of water. They need it and cannot be deprived. For dogs of any age that eat dry food, water will be needed to rehydrate it in their stomachs for digestion. Puppies also need more water per pound than adults, because they are growing. Growth comes through very active metabolism at the cellular level. These processes produce many wastes and by-products that are excreted through the blood. This requires plenty of water to carry these substances to and through the kidneys. As we will see, it is okay to schedule when your puppy drinks, but every day you must make sure the pup is able to consume what it wants and needs.

Grooming can start right away with a new puppy. Many owners think it's a mistake to bathe or brush dogs under six months of age. They worry that bathing will dry out the coat or that brushing may be too rough on a puppy at this age. The opposite is actually true. Many puppies will come from their breeder or the humane society with a dirty or smelly coat. These dogs need to be bathed and it will do no harm. There are numerous shampoos on the market designed to be gentle on a puppy's skin and coat, and most of these will not burn or irritate the eyes. Puppies do not need regular baths, but whenever a puppy gets dirty, it's okay to bathe it.

Brushing the coats of young pups will feel just as good to them as it does older dogs. It has similar benefits for puppies in that it cleans the coat, removes loose hair and stimulates the oil glands of the skin. Our favorite kind of brush for young dogs is the pin and bristle brush. These brushes have metal pins on one side and soft bristles on the other. They can therefore be used on any kind of dog. At this age the puppy will see brushing as just another form of petting. Get your pup used to it now so it will let you brush it without fuss as an adult.

Puppies should have their nails trimmed, if this was not done by the previous owner. Puppy nails have tiny, sharp points and these can easily scratch you, the children or your furniture. After this initial trimming, puppies are usually active enough to keep their nails worn down for four to six weeks. After that, check them and trim them just as you would the nails on older dogs.

Get your puppy used to being touched on all parts of its body: mouth, ears, tail and feet. This will make it easier for both the dog and veterinarian during future examinations or medical treatment.

Many new puppy owners are not sure if their pets should be allowed to go outside. While we agree that it is a good idea to keep them away from high-traffic dog areas until they have the complete protection provided by their vaccination series, it's fine for them to go outside in your yard or immediate area.

We live in the far northern reaches of Wisconsin, where it is rarely very warm and never hot. It is usually cooler than the rest of the United States, with winter temperatures going well below zero. Obviously, puppies shouldn't be left outside in cold weather, but they can tolerate very cold temperatures for the time it takes to go to the bathroom. Additionally, being outside is good for them, exposing them to new sights and sounds and helping them gain confidence and adjust to their growing world. Remember what we said about socialization and isolation.

HOUSEBREAKING

If your dog is going to live inside your home, and in America more than 60 percent of our pets do, you are going to have to go through the housebreaking process, unless you have grossly different hygiene standards than most people. It isn't hard, it needn't be messy and it needn't be a struggle. It doesn't have to take a long time. Remember that it is a training issue and you'll need to have more than casual input. It will take some of your time, but the more involved you get, the shorter that time will be.

We want to get into general training principles in more detail in Chapter 6, so we will keep it simple here. There are some key issues to deal with when it comes to housebreaking. Housebreaking Rule Number One and also The Most Important Rule: If you don't catch your puppy doing something, don't punish it! We don't care what someone else may tell you or what you've read—if you find a mess that was left when you weren't there, clean it up and forget it.

If you didn't see the dog make the mess, clean it up and forget it.

Discipline won't help, because unless you catch the puppy in the act, it will have no idea what the scolding is for. Your puppy has urinated and defecated hundreds of times before it met you. Mom or the breeder always cleaned it up. Nobody made a fuss before and the pup will not relate the punishment, regardless of its form, to something it has done without incident numerous times before—especially if they did it more than 30 seconds ago! Puppies are just like our children. Unless something was really fun (and a repetitive act like going to the bathroom isn't), they are not thinking about what they did in the past. They're thinking about what they can do in the future. At this point in its life, a puppy's memory is very, very poor.

Anyway, let's be honest: It was your fault, not the pup's. If you had been watching, you would have noticed the puppy suddenly walking or running around in circles with his nose down, smelling for the perfect spot to go to the bathroom. It's just as consistent as the taxi driver behind you honking the horn the instant the traffic light changes. The puppy will show the same behavior every time. It may vary a little from pup to pup, but they always show their own "pre-potty pattern" before the act.

If you actually catch the puppy in the act of urinating or defecating, it's still your fault; you weren't watching for or paying attention to the signals. Don't get mad. Quickly but calmly pick the pup up, and without raising your voice sternly say "no." Carry it outside or to its papers. It will help to push the tail down while you are carrying the dog, as this will often help them to stop urinating or defecating any more.

This is the proper way to pick up a puppy when you catch it making a mess.

The pup is going to be excited when you get it outside or to the papers, but stay there with it a while. When the dog finishes its job, reward it with simple praise such as "good dog."

Puppies may spontaneously urinate when excited. This may be when they first see you, at meeting a new dog or when they are scared. It's is often referred to as submissive or involuntary urination. Do not discipline puppies for this, as it is something they cannot control. Simply ignore it and clean up the mess. If you don't overreact, they will usually outgrow this behavior between four and seven months of age. This topic will be discussed in more detail in Chapter Eight.

In the disciplining of dogs, just like in physics, every action has a reaction—and, for training purposes, these may not be beneficial! If you overreact and severely scold or scare the heck out of a puppy for making what is, in your mind, a mistake, your training is probably going backwards. Scolding for a housetraining accident is especially difficult for puppies to understand, as they are carrying out a natural body function. Carried one step farther is the idea of rubbing a puppy's nose into a mistake it made, whether you caught it or not. In the limits of a puppy's intelligence, please explain to us the difference between rubbing its nose in the current mess in your kitchen versus the one the neighbor's dog left in the park two weeks ago. If your puppy were smart enough to figure all this out, the only logical choice would be to permanently quit going to the bathroom. Punishment rarely speeds up housebreaking. Often it makes the dog nervous or afraid every time it needs to go to the bathroom.

We'll give you a perfect example of how this kind of discipline causes long-term problems between a dog and its owner. A client makes an appointment to discuss a housebreaking problem. They're hoping that on physical exam or through some testing we can find a medical reason for their dog's inability to successfully master housebreaking. They readily admit their frustration with the dog. The fecal and urine tests reveal no problem.

In the exam room the pup is showing a lot more interest in the veterinarian than it is in its owners. The animal's eyes are almost saying, "Please kidnap me from them." When the owner reaches down to pet the dog on its head, the pup reflexively closes its eyes and turns its head to the side. The dog reacts as if it were going to be hit. The classic line that usually goes with this is, "When we get home we know he has made a mess because he always sulks or runs and hides." The owner clearly does not understand the dog. The dog isn't thinking about some mistake it may have made. Rather, the pup has learned that when the people first get home, for some reason it has yet to figure out, they are always in a bad mood and the dog gets punished. The puppy has decided that maybe it would be better off avoiding them for awhile, so it tries to hide.

What this tells us is that the dog has been punished for making messes in the owners' absence. During this punishment the puppy is not, absolutely *not* thinking about what it might have done two hours ago. It isn't thinking that it shouldn't make messes in the house. The animal isn't even thinking about the messes. In this particular case, the discipline, misunderstood by the puppy, has caused it to fear its owners, and this will probably affect their relationship throughout the life of the dog.

If you want housebreaking to go quickly, regardless of the method you use, spend as much time as possible with your puppy. In an exam room, one of us once listened to a client complain about how he had to take some time off from work for his own mental health and also, but unrelated, how the puppy wasn't doing too well in the housebreaking department. For us this statement was just too good to be true. It was the perfect set-up for our pitch. This gentleman, a bachelor, truly loved his puppy. We saw them together everywhere. Still, the problem was that he worked in a downtown office and the pup was home alone. His work allowed him to get home frequently, but not always on a consistent schedule. There would be accidents when he was gone, and sometimes he was gone longer than the abilities or the attention span of the puppy.

It was an easy problem to fix. We simply suggested his health and the puppy's training would both do better if he stayed home for a week or so. It worked. The man kept a watchful eye, and was always there when he was needed. In less than seven days, the 10-week-old puppy was housetrained. We aren't saying there was never another accident, but they were few and far between. The man realized his dog could be trusted and from then on they spent their days together at the man's office.

There are several ways to housebreak a puppy. With the first, you can put down papers or pretreated pads, encouraging the dog to use these areas for going to the bathroom. The pads are scented with a chemical that attracts the puppy. Whenever you see the dog starting into its "pre-potty pattern," you gently pick it up without talking and carry it over to the papers or pad, and then offer praise when it goes to the bathroom.

This brings us to Housebreaking Rule Number Two: Praise the pup when things go right. Don't let this turn into a situation where your only action is saying "no" when the dog is caught using the wrong area. If your pup gets it right, let it know!

When all goes well and the dog is using the papers consistently, the papers are either moved closer to the door or another set is placed outside. The transition is made from concentrating the toilet habits to one spot inside the home to one spot outside the home. Finally, the papers are eliminated. We've never been crazy about this method, because for a period of time it encourages the animal to eliminate inside the home. In our experience, housebreaking usually takes longer when this method is used.

The second popular method of housebreaking involves using a crate or pen. The reasoning is that the animal is placed in a crate that is just large enough to be a bed. Dogs don't like to soil their beds, because they would be forced to lay in the mess. It works, and while in these confines most pups will control their bladder and bowels for a longer time than we might expect. Puppies at eight or nine weeks of age can often last for seven or eight hours without an accident, although we would *never* recommend leaving one unattended in a crate for that long.

Using too large a crate can often cause long-term problems. The puppy will go to one corner of the cage and urinate or defecate. After a while, it will run through the mess, tracking it all over the cage. If this is allowed to continue, the instincts about not soiling its bed or lying in the mess will be forgotten and the puppy will soon be messing every day when placed in the crate. Now a housebreaking method has turned into a behavioral problem, as the puppy's new hygiene habits become his way of life.

During housebreaking, whenever the puppy is inside the home but can't be watched, place it in the crate. This might be while you are cooking, reading to the children or away from home. The last thing you do before you put the puppy in the crate is take it outside to its favorite spot to eliminate. The first thing you do when you take the animal out of the crate is another trip outside. No food or water goes in the crate—just a blanket and maybe a chew toy to occupy its time. Overnight is definitely crate time. As your faith in the puppy grows, leave it out for longer and longer periods of time.

Most people do not recognize an important advantage of crate training. It does more than just stop the animal from messing in the house. It also teaches the puppy something very important: When the urge to urinate or defecate occurs, the pup can hold it. The pup learns that just because it feels like it needs to relieve itself doesn't mean it must do so immediately. This is thought to be the main reason why puppies that have gone through crate training have fewer housetraining mistakes later on.

This pen is too large to use for housebreaking with this puppy.

Divider panels allow you to change the size of the pen as the puppy grows.

Make sure you buy the right size pen. You want one that has just enough floor space for the puppy to lie down. But crates and pens are useful throughout a dog's life, and it would be nice if you didn't have to keep buying more as it grows. You don't. Simply purchase one that will be big enough for the dog as an adult, but choose a model that comes with or has a divider panel as an accessory. With these you can adjust the position of the panel so that the space inside the pen can grow as the dog does.

The last housetraining method involves no papers, pads or crates. Rather, you choose to spend all the time necessary with the puppy. This works very well for people who live and work in their homes, for retired persons or in situations where the owners are always with the animal. Whenever they see the puppy doing its "pre-potty pattern," they hustle it outside. It is important that the dog is watched at all times and that no mistakes are allowed to occur. This method has less room for error, as there is nothing like a crate to restrict the animal's urges, nor is there an acceptable place for it to relieve itself indoors, such as the papers or pad. For those with the time, this is a good method of housetraining. We still recommend having a crate available as a backup when you have to be away and during the night.

Whether you are using this method or the crate method, when the puppy is taken outside watch it closely and as soon as all goes as planned, it should be praised and then brought back inside immediately. You want the dog to understand that the purpose of going outside was to go to the bathroom. Don't start playing—make it a trip for one reason only. Verbal communication helps with this method, and we'll get into that in just a moment.

The feeding schedule you have the puppy on can help or hinder any method of housebreaking. You'll soon notice that puppies will need to go outside soon after they wake and also within 30 to 40 minutes after eating. Be consistent when you feed the animal, so you can predict when it will need to relieve itself. Plan your trips outside around these patterns.

Specific verbal communication will also help the two of you understand what's desired. It's an excellent idea to always use a word when it's time to head to the bathroom. We like "outside?" Remember that whenever you use a verbal command or signal, it's important that everybody in the family always uses the same word in the same way. Think of the word "outside" in this situation not only as a question you're asking the pup, but also as an indication that you want to go there.

Some dogs may get into the habit of going to the door when they want to go outside. This is great when it happens, but it isn't as common as some people believe. We've found that it is better to use verbal commands to initiate this sort of activity, rather than waiting for the puppy to learn this behavior on its own. Your consistent use of a word or phrase like "outside" will probably cause the puppy to come to you, rather than the door, when it needs to go outside. The pup more quickly sees you as part of the overall activity of getting it where it needs to go. We believe this is much better.

Once outside, encourage the dog to get on with the act in question. We use the phrase "do your numbers." This is probably a holdover from our own parenthood and hearing children use the phrases "number one" and "number two." You can use any phrase you like, as long as you consistently use the same one.

As soon as the dog eliminates, it is very important to praise with a "good dog," and then come back inside immediately. Again, make this trip—which started with the specific word "outside"—have a single purpose. If you are taking the pup out to play with a ball or go for a walk, don't use this word even if you know the dog will eliminate while you are outside.

All of this may seem simple, and it really is. The keys are that it will take time and you must be consistent. And of course, you must never lose your temper or even get excited.

SUMMING UP

Your new puppy is home and you've started the housebreaking process. This is just as much a part of training as the "come" and "stay" commands. However, mistakes that occur with housebreaking can cause more problems between you and your pet than those encountered with any other form of training. Be patient and stay calm.

A small dose of common sense will guide you through most of the care and training of your new puppy. Concentrate on making it feel secure and comfortable in its new home. Introduce the pup to other people, dogs and new situations so its confidence continues to build. Take your time, and do it slowly so that the puppy does not become overwhelmed or intimidated by what it encounters. You're on your way to having a great dog!

Chapter 5

THE FIRST SIX MONTHS— VETERINARY CARE AND COMMON MEDICAL PROBLEMS

As we mentioned in Chapter 4, your puppy probably needs additional vaccinations and other routine veterinary care after you bring it home. You also need to have your pup examined to ensure that it is in good overall health. Puppies less than six months of age can also be affected by a very wide range of medical problems. Canine pediatric books list thousands. For you to be told that your tiny puppy is suffering from any of these may seem horrible and unfair. However, most puppy maladies are easy to deal with once they are understood. In the last section of this chapter we will deal with the most common medical conditions your puppy is most likely to encounter.

It is important that your new puppy be seen by your veterinarian within the first few days that it is in your home. There is nothing worse than letting the entire family become attached to a new pup, only to find out that it has a serious medical condition.

Have your new puppy examined by a veterinarian within the first 48 hours.

Some abnormalities may never cause a serious problem, while others may limit a dog's life to a few weeks or months. When genetic conditions are found, it is the breeder's responsibility to either take the puppy back or in some way make some sort of compensation. It is very hard to take a puppy that you have become attached to back to the breeder and trade it in for another. This may be the right thing to do, but it is very hard to explain to children. An immediate medical exam prevents a bad situation from snowballing into a family crisis.

CHOOSING A VETERINARIAN

You need to find a veterinarian *before* you bring your puppy home. Every new puppy should be examined within the first 48 hours, and you should make that appointment as soon as you know when you're going to pick up the pup. If you don't already have a veterinarian, ask friends, the breeder or shelter employees for references. That's a good start, but remember that you have to be able to work with this person through good times and bad. Choosing the veterinarian that is right for both you and your dog isn't always easy. In some areas there may be only one that is available or close by. Regardless of your situation, the following may act as guidelines.

All veterinary clinics are different and may provide a wide range of services. Some also offer grooming and boarding, and these services may be important to you. Also find out if their regular office hours provide you with an opportunity to take your dog in for routine services without missing work.

Emergency service and its availability will sooner or later be of great importance to you and your dog. Find out if the clinic you're considering provides emergency service, or if you'll have to go somewhere else after hours. Today, many veterinarians have banded together to share their emergency calls so that each individual is not on call as often. Some metropolitan areas have specialized emergency hospitals where all local clinics refer their after-hours calls. This is fine, and may even provide you with better quality care, unless it means that you'll need to travel 50 miles farther after your dog has been hit by a car. You should know where you will need to go well in advance of an emergency. Also, ask other pet owners how easy it is to get in touch with the veterinarian or service when emergencies arise.

Which doctor will you see if there are several veterinarians associated with the same clinic? In most situations can you see the same individual, or will you just be handled by whoever happens to be free next? Obviously, this is a pet peeve of ours. You should develop a relationship of understanding with the veterinarian treating your animal. This is especially true when the dog has a prolonged illness in which rechecks or continued therapy are necessary. We believe your dog will usually do better in these situations if it is always seen by the same doctor.

The veterinarian's reputation can be checked by talking to other pet owners, breeders or shelter employees. There will always be cases where a particular person doesn't get along with a particular vet, but good veterinarians quickly develop a large following of pet owners who go back to them over and over again.

Costs for veterinary services are always an issue, but expect to pay a fair price for the services you and your dog receive. It will be very difficult to compare costs for anything except routine procedures. Our recommendation is not to get hung up on prices, because price comparisons are not practical in a critical situation. A dog is more than a financial investment; always choose quality care.

A PREVENTIVE MEDICINE PROGRAM FOR YOUR NEW DOG

The breeder or humane society probably started your new puppy on some sort of preventive medicine, and you need to continue. Today there are numerous diseases your dog needs to be protected from. For those who haven't had a dog in several years, you may be surprised to learn there are new diseases and also new ways of treating old ones.

During the first exam, while checking the overall health of your pet, the veterinarian will ask you about what, if any, vaccinations have already been given. Most breeders start vaccinating puppies at five or six weeks of age. Shelters usually inoculate all animals immediately upon their arrival. Make sure you have these dates with you, along with information about any worming medications that have been given, during your first appointment. The veterinarian will enter this information into his or her records and determine when the next immunizations are due. Today many owners inoculate their pets themselves, while others choose to have this done at clinics. Some states require a prescription from a veterinarian before you can buy the vaccine. Your veterinarian, and the place you buy vaccine from, will know if you need one.

Some bacterial and viral diseases are prevented through vaccinations. A series of shots, given every two to three weeks, continues through 16 weeks of age. These include familiar names like distemper, hepatitis, leptospirosis (usually not given to puppies under 12 weeks of age) and parainfluenza (also referred to as kennel cough). Additionally, for those that haven't had a dog in 15 or 20 years, there are new vaccines. Before the late 1970s, the few people who had heard of parvovirus or coronavirus did not realize they were also diseases of dogs. Both primarily cause severe intestinal disorders with diarrhea, loss of fluids, dehydration and sometimes death. Today, these are two of the most serious and life-threatening infectious diseases of dogs, especially puppies. Fortunately, there are excellent vaccinations to help protect against them.

A single combination immunization carries protection against all of the above diseases, making it easier on both you and the puppy. Most dogs are also vaccinated against Lyme disease before 16 weeks of age. A separate rabies inoculation is administered when the puppy is between 12 and 16 weeks of age.

Even though the puppy may have been previously wormed, you'll want to take a stool sample along for the veterinarian to examine for parasites. Just

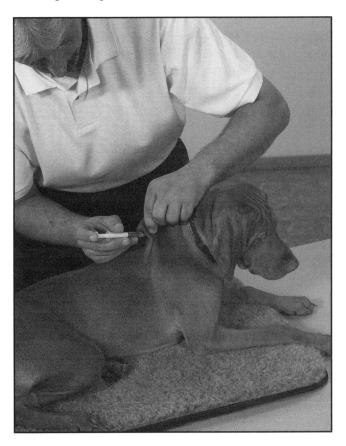

A single vaccination protects your puppy against seven different diseases.

because you don't see any worms in the stool, don't assume that all is okay. The common worms are roundworms, hookworms and whipworms. Most dogs with any of these infestations do not pass the large, two- to eight-inch-long adult worms in their stools. In most cases, all that leaves the body in the stool are the eggs, and they are microscopic. The clinic personnel will look for them under a microscope.

There are other common parasites that are not worms, but rather tiny single-celled organisms. Examples are coccidia and giardia. These are so small that even the adult forms can only be detected via microscopic examination. If evidence of any parasitic diseases are found, the veterinarian will dispense or recommend medications that can be used to eliminate them. This will usually require more than one treatment, each separated by 10 to 14 days.

Don't be overly concerned if you are told your dog is carrying one or more of these unwanted guests. More than 80 percent of the puppies that pass through our clinic doors on their initial visit are infested by at least one kind of parasite. Treatment is easy—just a liquid, granules or pills—and unlike the wormers of the past, they rarely make the puppy sick. Before you leave, ask the veterinarian if you need to bring another stool sample in after the treatment to be sure it was successful.

You'll find a more complete discussion of these parasites later in this chapter.

In most areas of the United States, heartworm disease is a serious problem. These parasites, five- to 12-inch worms, live in the large blood vessels of the heart and lungs of dogs, and occasionally cats. Over time, they slowly bring about heart failure due to the increased resistance they cause against the heart's pumping action. If the animal does not die, it is at least severely debilitated. The disease can be treated, but this is usually very expensive and the dog may have permanent damage to its circulatory system, greatly curtailing its physical abilities. That's why heartworm preventives are so important.

The disease is spread from infected animals to others by mosquitoes. We haven't devised a way to rid ourselves of mosquitoes, but we have learned how to prevent dogs from getting heartworm disease. This is accomplished by simply giving the animal a pill or a treated tidbit either once a day or once a month, depending on the type of medication chosen. Adult dogs should have their blood tested annually to make sure they are free of the disease before continuing on the preventive medication.

Today, because of ease of administration and its efficacy, almost everyone uses the monthly heartworm medication. Sometimes this is combined with general wormers or anti-flea preparations. Your veterinarian will recommend one of these preparations. In the last few years a lot of research has gone into the development of a heartworm vaccine, but as of yet we do not have an effective inoculation.

Fleas have always been a problem for pets. In the past, we assumed we were going to live with them and tried to find ways to either tolerate their existence or somehow limit the numbers that were on our animals. They feed on our dogs and cats, biting and sucking blood from them. They frequently feed on us, as well. We are fairly aggressive about controlling them, as their bites cause severe itching, resulting in scratching often to the point of self-mutilation. Some dogs develop allergies to flea bites and their entire bodies become and remain inflamed and itchy, even though they are only bitten once a month (see Chapter 11 for more on allergies). In extreme cases, fleas can take enough blood to cause severe anemia and even death.

To combat fleas, pet owners have used powders, sprays, shampoos, treated collars, dips, aerosol bombs, lawn sprays and other products. We covered our pets, homes and yards with all sorts of chemicals, natural and manufactured. Although these preparations often got a bad name and were blamed for all sorts of things, they very rarely caused a problem if they were used as directed. Most problems occurred, and still do, when people use the theory that if a little or only one product is good, then it must be better to use a lot or six or seven different medications on one animal and its environment at the same time. The cumulative effect of all these products was usually what caused problems. All of these products are still useful and do a very good job. However, they never completely got rid of the fleas.

Today we have better, safer and easier to use preparations for protecting our animals from fleas. Using the rationale that the easier something is to do and the less frequently we have to do it, the better the chance that we will succeed, pharmaceutical companies have formulated flea treatments that are very simple to administer.

These products attack fleas in two ways. The first group of products is directed at the adult fleas. The lives of these insects are divided up into several stages: egg, larva, pupa and adult. Fortunately for our pets, and us, the adult fleas are the only ones that bite. These preparations (insecticides) either kill fleas or repel them from our pets. Either way works, in that they keep the animals from being bitten.

The second group of products is the growth inhibitors. They are basically a birth control medication for fleas. They interrupt the flea reproductive cycle by preventing the egg and larval stages from developing. Eggs fail to hatch, or larvae do not grow into pupae. The end result is that the adult fleas are spending lots of their energy producing the next generation, but it fails to mature. Without continual recruitment from the younger classes, the number of feeding adults decreases.

To be really successful, most modern medications are a combination of insecticides and growth inhibitors. To make them easy to use, these products are used once a month in either tablet or pour-on form. These latter preparations involve pouring a small quantity of liquid on the skin on the

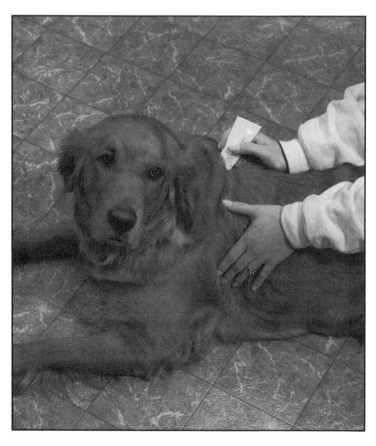

One pour-on application prevents fleas for a full month.

back or neck of the pet. In the next few years we believe that many new and even better flea treatments will be developed.

In some locations there may be additional or different preventive medicine your dog needs. Ask the veterinarian about these during the first visit. In fact, ask every question you can possibly think of. Unless the doctor has an emergency coming in the door, he or she should be willing to spend as much time as you need on this first visit. This probably isn't the right veterinarian for you if they aren't willing to take all the time necessary to make sure you start off knowing everything you need to know about the care of your new dog. Additionally, they are not a very smart businessperson. You are a customer, and if you like them, you'll be coming back through their doors for years to come!

The breed you've selected may have the option of future surgeries or treatment. An example would be ear cropping, which is typically done when the pup is between 12 and 20 weeks of age. The breeder probably informed you about these types of procedures. If you plan to have the animal spayed or neutered, the first visit is also a good time to find out at what age the veterinarian would recommend that procedure.

COMMON MEDICAL PROBLEMS IN YOUNG PUPPIES

In this section we are limiting our discussion to those conditions that are typically seen or first occur in puppies six months of age or younger. As we stated before, this age group can suffer from hundreds and hundreds of medical problems. However, of all the possibilities, only a dozen or so are commonly seen in most puppies. If you have a medical problem with your puppy in the first six months of its life, it's most likely to be among the ones listed here.

Hernia

A hernia is defined as the protrusion of an organ or other internal structure through an opening. In puppies, this usually involves abdominal tissue or organs protruding through an opening in the abdominal wall. The abdomen contains various organs, including the stomach, intestines, liver, spleen, kidneys and bladder, and all the blood vessels and interconnecting ducts and tubular structures that are associated with them. All of these are enclosed within the abdominal wall, which is made up of muscles and connective

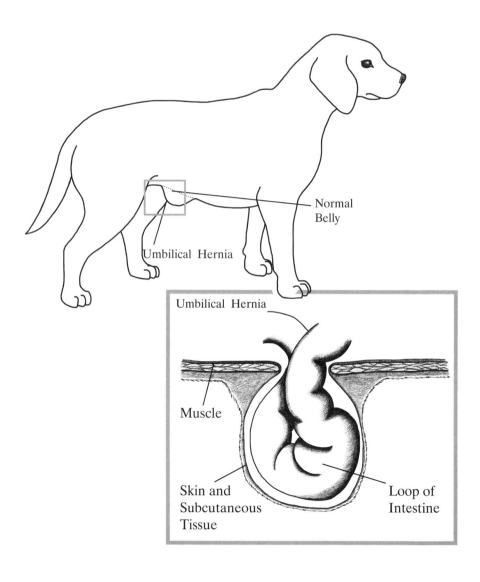

Normal
Belly

Umbilical Hernia

Umbilical Hernia

Muscle

Skin and
Subcutaneous
Tissue

Loop of
Intestine

tissue. When a hernia occurs in puppies, there is an opening in the muscular layer that allows the internal structures to pass out through it and lie directly under the skin.

Hernias are usually visible with the naked eye, appearing as a bulge under the skin. When this area is touched or probed, it is usually not painful to the puppy. It feels very similar to a plastic bag containing pieces of meat in a small quantity of water.

In puppies, hernias occur in two areas. Approximately 98 percent will be found on the midline of the abdomen, at the navel. While the puppy is within its mother's uterus, it receives all nutrients and oxygen necessary for life through the umbilical artery. Waste products and carbon dioxide are eliminated from the puppy's body through the umbilical vein. These two blood vessels are enclosed within the umbilical cord. Soon after birth the mother severs the cord, and over a few days the remnant attached to the puppy dries up and falls off. The opening in the abdominal wall that the cord passed through then slowly closes. The only remnant you will find of these structures on a normal puppy is a small scar, which we refer to as the belly button or navel.

In some puppies the umbilical opening in the muscular wall of the abdomen fails to close completely, or as rapidly as it should. If it is large enough, abdominal structures (most commonly fat or a loop of intestine) pass through and lie under the skin. They form a round, soft swelling that protrudes down from the pup's belly. It may vary in size from a garden pea to a tennis ball. Usually you can gently push on this bump through the skin and move it back up into the abdomen. After a few minutes however, it pops back out and the bulge reappears.

The remaining 2 percent of the abdominal hernias found in puppies are in the inguinal or groin areas, which are located on each side of the abdominal wall in the area where the inside of the rear legs attaches to the body. In male dogs, the testicles, their blood vessels and the related tubular structures are formed inside of the abdomen. Before birth, these pass through openings in the muscular wall of the abdomen. These openings are known as the inguinal rings. If these are too large, loops of intestines or the bladder commonly pass through them and lie between the muscular wall and skin. Typically, these hernias are much larger than the umbilical type.

In either of these hernias, the fact that this loop of intestine and fat are now lying between the muscular wall and skin by itself causes no serious

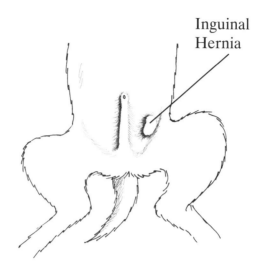

Inguinal
Hernia

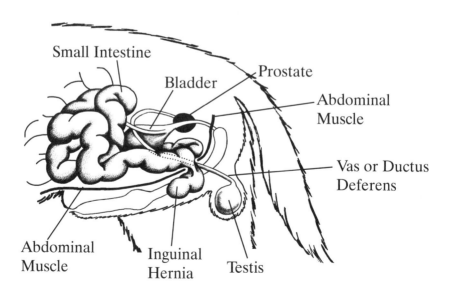

Small Intestine

Bladder

Prostate

Abdominal
Muscle

Vas or Ductus
Deferens

Abdominal
Muscle

Inguinal
Hernia

Testis

STRANGULATED HERNIA

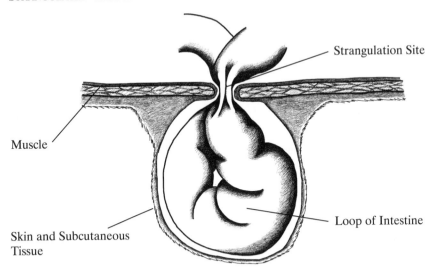

problem, though they probably aren't as well protected from injury and do distract from your puppy's sleek lines. Umbilical hernias are common, and some dogs have them for their entire lives without any problem. However, unless they are very small, they can be dangerous.

Commonly, the structures within a hernia can become strangulated. Strangulation means muscular tissue surrounding the opening in the abdominal wall becomes so tight around the organs and their blood vessels that neither food within the intestine nor blood can flow through them. This can occur either because the opening slowly closes down on the loop of intestine, or because the intestines and other structures swell to a size where they are too large for the opening. All of the structures that pass through a hernial opening have their own blood supply. As the muscular ring closes down on them, the blood is permanently shut off, resulting in the death of the structures. If this is not treated rapidly, the animal usually dies.

The intestines are part of a long, continuous tube through which food passes. If a loop of intestine has moved through the abdominal wall and is pinched off, food can no longer flow past this area. Whether the section of intestine actually dies or is merely obstructed, the consequences are the same. Untreated, the animal will die.

When your veterinarian finds a hernia on your puppy, they will suggest what should be done. They may choose to wait and see, or recommend surgery. Often, if the hernia is small the veterinarian will wait and repair it when they spay or neuter the dog—a procedure typically done at six to eight months of age. Inguinal hernias are always more dangerous, as they are usually larger and contain a larger mass of structures. They may need more immediate treatment.

If you just purchased the puppy and were not aware of the hernia, you may want to discuss this with the breeder. There will be extra expenses for correcting the hernia, even if it is done at the same time as the neutering. In addition, the predisposition for hernias, umbilical or inguinal, is inherited. These problems are transmitted from generation to generation genetically. That is why the breeder needs to know, and why, in an effort to eliminate harmful or unwanted characteristics in all dogs, it is recommended that these animals not be bred. Additionally, hernias are considered severe conformation faults, and a dog with one cannot participate in dog shows, even if the hernia has been surgically corrected.

If you purchased this puppy from a breeder or pet shop with this knowledge and paid less for it, then everything is okay. If you paid a premium or even normal price, you need to talk to the person you bought the dog from. If there is a question, your veterinarian will back you up with a letter stating his or her findings and recommendations. If the breeder wasn't aware of the problem, they will certainly want to know, as they will not want to repeat that breeding. Typically, these pups are sold as pet quality only and go with Limited Registration papers, so they cannot be used to produce more purebred puppies carrying the fault. (With Limited Registration papers, none of the dog's offspring can be registered as purebred.)

Cryptorchidism

This is a problem seen only in male dogs, in which one or both testicles fails to descend or drop into the scrotum. It is also referred to as retained or undescended testicles. In most mammals, sperm cells cannot survive at the normal body temperatures found within the abdominal cavity; they need to be several degrees cooler. The sac-like structure called the scrotum accommodates this need by holding the testicles away from the body. In most dogs, by seven weeks of age the testicles have descended or dropped into the scrotum.

During the initial examination, the veterinarian may inform you that one or both of your puppy's testicles have not descended. They remain up inside the abdomen, or under the skin somewhere in the inguinal area. In either

Normal Testicle

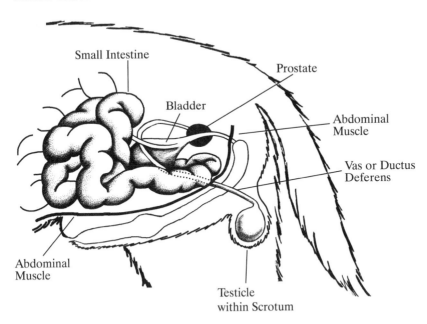

Small Intestine

Prostate

Bladder

Abdominal
Muscle

Vas or Ductus
Deferens

Abdominal
Muscle

Testicle
within Scrotum

Retained Testicle

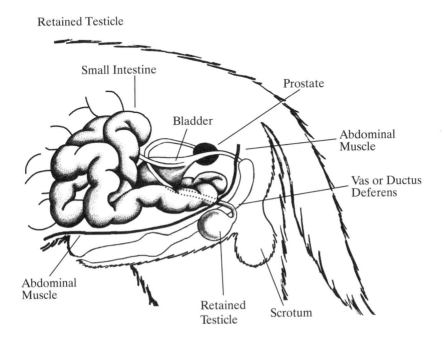

Small Intestine

Prostate

Bladder

Abdominal
Muscle

Vas or Ductus
Deferens

Abdominal
Muscle

Retained
Testicle

Scrotum

case, they are not in the scrotum where they are supposed to be. And if they aren't there by this age, they probably never will be.

As with hernias, this flaw is passed genetically from generation to generation. And, as with hernias, these dogs should never be bred and cannot be shown in dog shows. While the undescended testicle may be sterile, the normally positioned one will be fertile and the animal is probably quite capable of siring puppies. Therefore, all animals with this trait should be neutered.

If you bought the puppy from a breeder or pet shop and were unaware of the condition, you need to talk to the breeder. You may want to choose a different puppy (obviously not from the same litter, as its littermates probably also carry this trait in their genes), or request a refund. Once responsible breeders discover that a particular breeding has produced animals with this flaw, they will usually stop using the parents for breeding. They sell these puppies with neuter contracts as pet-quality only. Limited Registration papers are given, so the line cannot be continued.

At one time, it was believed a testicle that was retained in the abdominal cavity had a higher than normal incidence of cancer. Today this is not thought to be true, but we still recommend removing both testicles during the neutering. The retained testicle still produces the male hormones that are well documented to cause prostate disease, roaming and increased aggression. And, as we will discuss later, any dog that is not going to be bred should be sterilized for medical and behavioral reasons.

Parasites

Puppies have more problems than adult dogs with parasites, for two reasons. First, some parasites have evolved methods for ensuring the infestation of puppies; and second, parasites have a much more adverse effect on puppies than they do adults. (When an animal has a disease caused by bacteria or a virus, it is said to have an infection, but when the medical problem is caused by a parasite, it is referred to as an infestation.) Our goal in this chapter is to make you aware of the more common parasites and understand how they get into or onto your puppy, how you get rid of them and how you prevent them. (Fleas are discussed earlier in this chapter.)

Parasites are organisms that live in or on other animals, and in so doing cause harm to the other animals. The animal the parasites live on or in is referred to as the host. The harm the parasites do is usually, but not always, brought about by their search for food. They either eat a part of the host's body or steal its food. They might live on or in the host's body and suck its blood. Others live in the host's intestine, absorbing the digesting food. Parasites can be either internal or external. Internal ones live somewhere inside the host's body. External ones live on or attach themselves to the surface or skin of the host.

The common internal parasites that reside in our puppies are roundworms (or Ascarids), hookworms, whipworms, tapeworms, coccidia and giardia. All of these, as adults, live in the pup's intestinal tract. As adults, the worms are large enough to easily be seen by the naked eye, while coccidia and giardia are very small protozoans and can only be seen under a microscope. They all pass their eggs (which are only visible through a microscope) in the pup's feces to perpetuate their life cycle as more dogs become infested. Only tapeworms normally pass anything in the stool that we can easily see. They are segmented and cast off sections of their bodies, which look like grains of rice and may be seen crawling on the puppy's stools or on the hair near the anus.

Roundworms and hookworms are, by far, the most common parasites found in puppies. More than 70 percent of new pups coming into our clinic are carrying one or both of these. The adults of both worms live in the dog's small intestine. The roundworms are two to eight inches long and live off the food the puppy has eaten. The hookworms are usually one to two inches long and attach themselves to the wall of the intestines and suck blood from the small vessels found there. In large numbers, either parasite can cause significant harm. Roundworms can consume enough food to weaken the puppy, while the hookworms' blood-sucking can lead to severe, life-threatening anemia. In large numbers, either worm can block the intestines.

Roundworms and hookworms have developed an interesting method of perpetuating their species. These two parasites encyst in the mammary glands and uterus of a female dog. During pregnancy and while the pups are nursing, the worms cross over into the puppies' bodies, infesting them. The female puppies will then have larval hookworms and roundworms migrate through their bodies into their mammary glands and uteruses. Then, when these females have puppies years later, they will pass a new generation of parasites to their puppies. This is why most young dogs are found to have worm infestations when they are checked on their initial veterinary visit. These encysted parasites are very resistant to worming medications.

Roundworm and hookworm adults living in the dog's small intestine constantly produce eggs that are spread into the environment with the dog's feces. The roundworm eggs are very resistant to most environmental conditions, and will wait patiently until they are picked up and ingested by other dogs. The hookworm eggs hatch into tiny free-living worms that actually burrow through the skin and feet of other dogs. Once either hookworms or roundworms are in the new host's body, they pass into the stomach briefly, but before becoming adults they migrate along blood vessels into the lungs of this new host and reside there for awhile. They then are coughed up the dog's windpipe or trachea, swallowed, and enter the intestine, where they set up for the remainder of their adult life.

One of the main signs of roundworm and hookworm infestations in puppies is the cough that occurs when the worms migrate through the lungs. Puppies with heavy infestations will typically have less than expected weight gain and growth, potbellies, dry coats, poor appetites, vomiting and/or diarrhea.

Whipworms are similar to hookworms in that they also attach to intestinal walls and live off the blood and tissue of the host. They live at the junction of the small and large intestine and also in the cecum (a pouch at the beginning of the large intestine). They move from one dog to the next by passing their eggs in the stool of the infested dog. They do not cross from the mother to her pups, nor do they migrate through the host's body. Puppies infested with whipworms will have signs similar to those seen with roundworms and hookworms, except vomiting will be less frequent and the diarrhea will usually be intermittent.

Tapeworms are usually not as common in puppies as they are in adult dogs. This is because of the way they are transmitted from dog to dog. Tapeworms have an interesting life cycle in that they require an intermediate host, such as a flea, that must be eaten by the dog! If a dog has adult tapeworms in its body, segments of these parasites break off the worm and pass out in the stools. These sections can move on their own, and either look like rice grains or small white squares that move. These segments are often described as packets of eggs, and that is exactly what they are.

Once outside the dog's body, they soon break apart, spewing microscopic eggs through the environment. Fleas, rodents or rabbits then consume these eggs. These animals are the intermediate hosts. In them, the worm develops into the infective larval stage. Later, when a dog eats the flea, rodent or rabbit, the cycle is completed. The tapeworm attaches to the intestinal wall of the dog and matures into an egg-producing adult tapeworm. Tapeworms cannot pass directly from dog to dog. They need to go through an intermediate host. Because the dog needs to eat that host, we usually don't see signs of tapeworm infestation before the dog is three to four months of age.

Fecal exams are not as good for diagnosing tapeworms as they are for the other parasites, because only the packets or segments carry the eggs. If you see these worms crawling on your dog's stool or in its hair near the tail, tell your veterinarian. Additionally, don't forget that if your dog has tapeworms you may also have a flea problem you need to deal with.

Coccidiosis is a very common parasitic disease of puppies. They are not worms, but rather single-celled organisms like the paramecia and amoebas we all looked at in high school biology class. Their parasitic form lives in the cells that line the intestines of many different kinds of animals. Those that reside in dogs and puppies cause severe diarrhea, oftentimes with blood. The parasite's eggs (oocysts) are passed in the dog's stools and then must be ingested by another dog to continue the infective cycle. Puppies typically ingest eggs that were spread by their mother or other dogs living in close proximity to them. The oocysts are also very hardy, and can live in the environment for months.

Our biggest problem with coccidia is that we do not have a true cure. We can usually make the clinical signs go away, but not necessarily the parasite. The medications we use against this organism do not kill it, but only slow it down enough so that the animal can suppress the parasite's activity or decrease its numbers. Animals that are treated and seem to be cured may actually be asymptomatic carriers—that is, they have no signs but may still harbor coccidia and may occasionally pass its eggs in their stools. They are therefore a source of infestation to other animals. Kennels, pet shops or animal shelters that have this problem have a very difficult time totally ridding themselves of it.

Giardia is probably the most over-diagnosed parasitic disease in America. This is because of the symptoms it causes and the treatment used for it. Giardia is similar to coccidia in that it is a single-celled parasite that lives in the intestinal tracts of many different animals. It passes eggs in the host's feces, and these often contaminate water sources. Other dogs come along and drink the water or in some way ingest the eggs, thereby infesting themselves.

The most common sign of giardiasis is diarrhea, and in some cases it can be severe with blood. Diagnosis is a problem, however, because it is difficult to find the eggs in the stools of infested animals. Sometimes animals are treated for this disease just because of the signs and a lack of any particular diagnosis. The treatment is metronidazole (trade name Flagyl), and the nice thing about this medication is that it clears up many different diarrheal disorders. That's because it is also an antibiotic and is effective against many different gastrointestinal bacteria. The puppy can have any of a wide range of gastrointestinal bugs, we veterinarians diagnose Giardia, treat it with metronidazole, the animal is cured and we look great.

There are numerous medications to treat the various parasitic diseases listed above, but it isn't necessary to describe them in this book. Once a diagnosis is made, your veterinarian will either dispense or prescribe appropriate medication. Just make sure to ask about how to prevent a reoccurrence. The chances of reinfestation will be greatly reduced if you remove all stools from the yard and elsewhere in the dog's environment every day.

Ear Mites

In puppies, ear mites cause most ear problems. These infestations make the dog shake its head and scratch its ears. When you look into the ear canal, it may seem to be slightly inflamed and irritated, but what is obvious is the dark brown, granular discharge that looks like coffee grounds. The canals appear to be filled with this discharge, which is made up of dried blood and waste products from the mites. Both ears will usually be affected.

When a puppy has an ear mite infestation, it has been in close contact with another dog or cat that is carrying the parasites. Mites are arachnids—that is, they are related to spiders and don't fly. They move from one animal to the next by crawling. These are tiny, nearly microscopic animals and they do not take big steps. Therefore, when you discover that your puppy has ear mites, try to find the source. It could have been another dog or cat at the breeder's facility, pet shop or shelter. If not, it could be one of your or a friend's animals that your puppy has played with.

Ear mites are easy to treat, as long as you do all of your animals at the same time. Sometimes people discover that one of their pets has it and only treat that animal. The next week they are often treating a different one, and so on. Treat them all at once! Drops containing an insecticide in an oil base are usually used for 14 to 21 days. After you start the treatment, wait a few days to clean the debris out of the ear. Initially the ears will be painful as you clean them, but the medicine should reduce the inflammation and soften up the discharge, making it easier to remove.

Mange

This is a word that many use to denote any and all skin diseases. In fact, mange refers to a relatively few conditions, all of which are caused by mites living on or in the animal's skin. Mange is therefore a type of parasitic infestation. Although other forms are possible, there are three different types of mange that commonly affect puppies. Each of these is caused by a different kind of mite. One lives on the very surface of the animal's body, while the other two live within the deeper layers of the skin. We will deal with the less severe type first.

The most superficial form of mange affecting puppies is cheyletiella. Dogs infested with this mite are also said to have "walking dandruff," as the tiny mites can be seen with a magnifying glass working their way through the hair or across the surface of the skin. This mite commonly is a problem in pet shops, animal shelters or other facilities where there is a constant stream of new animals making their way through the doors. Once these areas are infested, it is much more difficult to eliminate the problem than it is in a kennel with a static population of dogs.

The mites may only cause severe flaking of the skin, but more typically they produce an itching sensation. The puppies then scratch or chew on themselves. It is common to see entire litters affected, and we have been involved with situations in which the mite infested every animal in a facility. In most cases the condition is easy to treat with weekly applications of mild pyrethrin and permethrin flea and tick products. In resistant cases, ivermectin injections will be used. These will be administered every 14 days.

The second most severe mite affecting puppies is Sarcoptic scabiei. This condition is also called sarcoptic mange, or scabies. This mite lives in the deeper layers of the skin and produces severe itching that causes the animal to scratch and chew on itself, often to the point of self-mutilation. This mite also affects people with the same symptoms.

One of our friends took his recently infested dog on a wilderness canoe trip that was to last for two weeks. They returned several days early, miserable and looking like someone had taken a steel wool pad to their skins. Animals and people with this disease can suffer terribly. Fortunately, with the advent of newer medications, the disease is now much easier to treat.

The scabies mite is isolated for diagnosis by scraping the dog's skin with an oil-covered scalpel blade, and then examining this material under a microscope. Of all the mites, this one is the hardest to isolate, and therefore a precise diagnosis is not always easy. It seems that a very few of these unwelcome guests can cause a lot of itching. In some cases, a veterinarian will initiate treatment even though the actual mite was not isolated. Considering how bad the animal is suffering and the potential for the owners to also become infested, this seems warranted. Flea and tick dips can and are used successfully, but many veterinarians now prefer ivermectin injections.

Remember that if your dog is diagnosed with sarcoptic mange, the disease can spread to people who are in contact with or close proximity to the dog.

Demodectic mange can be the most serious of all mite infestations affecting puppies. Some people refer to it as red or puppy mange. It is difficult to understand and has wide-ranging consequences for breeders, individual dog owners and veterinarians. Surprisingly, this is a mite that all—that's right, all—dogs have on their bodies. Those that develop the disease do so because their immune systems fail to function properly. A small percentage of dogs develop an incurable infestation, and for humane reasons are euthanized. This is a very complex and unique condition, and the final outcome for a particular dog may not be known for over a year.

All dogs have limited populations of the demodectic mites living on their bodies, but the organisms do no harm to the dog. They live in the hair follicles and openings of various oil glands within the skin. In this situation they are harmless commensals (that's an animal that lives on another, deriving benefit from the relationship without doing any harm to the other animal). These mites clean up wastes and excess secretions. Remember that these mites are on every dog you have ever seen in your life. It is believed that puppies are not born with these organisms, but get their own supply from their mother in their first two to three days of life. Mites crawl from her body onto the puppies and colonize their skin. As long as these are normal, healthy pups, no harm is done.

However, the disease arises when these mites invade the bodies of puppies that, for some reason, have less than adequate immune systems. It seems that on normal dogs, the canine's immune system suppresses or controls the actions of the demodectic mites so that they do not venture into the deeper layers of skin. Additionally, in these normal dogs, the overall number of mites remains relatively low. How the mite lives and what it affects is changed completely in young dogs with impaired or deficient immune systems. In these animals, the mite becomes a disease-causing organism. The condition is then referred to as demodectic mange, red mange or demodicosis.

Nothing is usually noticed until the pups are from three to six months of age. They act normally, grow and develop at rates identical to other members of their breed, and show no higher incidence of common infections. Then the owners start to notice dry, scaly patches with hair loss on the face and front legs. It is very common for the areas immediately around the eyes to be affected, making the pup look almost as if it is wearing glasses. This is referred to as the localized form. The puppy rarely scratches or shows any interest in these lesions, but scrapings of these areas show much higher numbers of mites than would be found in unaffected puppies.

Untreated, many of these dogs that have only a few mild lesions spontaneously recover at between eight and 16 months of age, never to have the problem recur in their lives. It seems that their immune systems finally function normally and the mites are suppressed into their normal commensal mode. The dog never eliminates them from its body, but the mites' numbers decrease and cause no further problems.

In a small percentage of dogs with demodicosis, the condition becomes much more severe as their immune systems are never able to control the mites. The disease enters what is referred to as the generalized form. Large areas of the skin become involved. Lesions often are found on all portions of the animal's skin. Hair falls out and the skin turns either light pink or it may become blackened by excessive quantities of pigment or because scar tissue has formed. In some cases, the lesions progress with large cracks forming in the dry, hairless skin. Secondary bacterial infections are common. This becomes a very challenging case for the owner and veterinarian.

As of today, we have no magic pill or shot to use against demodicosis. There are benzoyl peroxide shampoos that can keep some mild forms in complete remission, as long as they are used every week. There are amitraz dips that are very useful in controlling the mite, thereby providing relief. In either the localized or generalized form of the disease, ivermectin injections seem to provide some benefit. All of these products can be used together for a cumulative effect. Still, a cure is only possible if the animal's immune system functions normally. In dogs suffering from the generalized form of the disease, there will be a small percentage of cases in which this does not happen, with or without medical therapy. In those cases, because of the suffering and poor prognosis, the only humane alternative is to euthanize the animal.

We have learned in the last few years that the predisposition to developing demodicosis is inherited. Whether the animal develops the disease or not is at least partly determined by its genetics. Dogs that have shown lesions of this disease, even if they spontaneously cleared without treatment, should not be bred. This is a genetic defect that we must attempt to eliminate from dogs. If your puppy develops this condition, it is imperative that you contact the breeders of the animal. The news will not make them happy, because the standard recommendation today is that the affected puppy, its parents and littermates should not be used for breeding.

If your dog is diagnosed with demodectic mange, however, do not assume the worst. We have worked with hundreds and hundreds of these cases and can count on our fingers and toes the few that have not recovered from the condition on their own or with medical therapy. It is very important for you to stay in close communication with your veterinarian and make sure you understand the prognosis for your own dog.

Puppy Impetigo and Bacterial Skin Diseases

Puppies are often presented to a veterinarian with small pimples on the hairless area of their stomach. There may be from five to 30 pimples, looking like blisters that are an eighth to a quarter of an inch in diameter and filled with a thick, yellowish-white liquid. Most of us refer to this as impetigo. Although these pimples concern many owners, the lesions seem to be a part of growing up for many puppies and disappear without treatment. When the lesions remain for more than two weeks or increase in number, we usually recommend treating this condition with chlorhexidine or benzoyl peroxide shampoos and oral antibiotics. Some might not feel the antibiotics are necessary, but in our experience they have hastened recovery.

Dogs of all ages can have more serious bacterial skin diseases, but they are rare in puppies. Those that develop serious conditions at this early age often have impaired or faulty immune systems. These animals are similar to those that suffer from demodectic mange in that they may spontaneously recover if their immunity levels return to normal. In a few rare cases, if their immune systems do not become fully functional, the bacterial infections may occur repeatedly throughout the dog's life, or they may overpower the dog and lead to its death.

Tooth Problems

Puppies have all the same dental problems that our children do. They suffer from overbites, underbites and teeth that either fail to come in or fall out at an inappropriate time. And, as in human medicine, veterinary dental care has advanced to the point where many of these problems can be remedied.

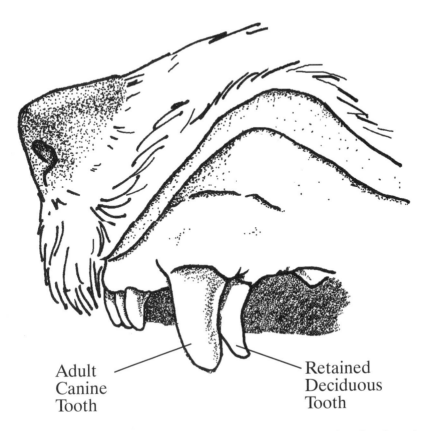

Adult Canine Tooth

Retained Deciduous Tooth

The simplest and probably most common dental problem involves the large canine teeth. Dogs, just like people, have two sets of teeth. The first set are the deciduous or baby teeth. This set comes in during the first few weeks of life and is gone before the animal reaches 10 months of age. These are replaced by the mature or adult teeth.

The large and exceedingly sharp deciduous canine teeth (the "fangs") are supposed to fall or be pushed out by six to seven months of age. In many pups this doesn't happen, and the baby teeth displace the mature teeth from their normal position. Watch these teeth closely, and if they are still present at six months of age, tell your veterinarian. He or she may decide to remove them. This is very simple and can be done when the dog is neutered.

Overbites and underbites are common and are even expected in certain breeds. This improper fit of the teeth does cause problems, however. Teeth that fit together nicely tend to keep each other clean. Those in the top jaw tend to scrape the tartar and plaque off those in the bottom jaw, and vice versa. This can't happen when the teeth in the two jaws are not in close proximity to each other. When the teeth aren't clean, tartar and plaque build up and it is common for this to lead to dental abscesses, loose teeth and gum disease.

With veterinary medicine today, owners have the opportunity to have these problems corrected, but this comes at a considerable cost. Before you start off on a course to straighten your puppy's teeth, we strongly recommend that you get a second and maybe even a third opinion. Many dogs live their entire lives with teeth that don't meet. Dental problems can usually be avoided if owners take it upon themselves to clean their dog's teeth at least once a week, if not more.

We strongly recommend starting to clean or brush your dog's teeth in puppyhood. They take it very well at this early age, and will then tolerate it better as adults.

Insect Bites

Your puppy is outside or down in the basement family room. You let it into the house or the puppy walks up the stairs. The puppy is acting and walking normally, but you happen to glance at its face and realize that its nose is swollen to twice its normal size. The puppy appeared fine just an hour ago, and now it looks like a canine Edsel! You may not have any idea what's wrong.

We get calls about puppies like this almost every day during the summer, and occasionally in the winter, too. This nasal swelling is a reaction to something, usually an insect bite. Outside it could be a bee, wasp, biting fly, spider or whatever. In the basement, it was probably a spider. Puppies are very curious and will try to sniff, bite or at least investigate every crawling and flying thing they encounter. When they get too close, they are frequently bitten or stung by these venomous critters.

In our practice, if the animal is breathing and acting normally, we'll have the owners give an antihistamine at home and closely watch the pup. We have never had one of these cases develop into a serious or life-threatening condition. If the owner seems concerned, we have them give the antihistamine and come into the clinic. It is easier on their mental health to sit in one of our examining rooms knowing we are right there with a pharmacy full of drugs if needed.

Diarrhea and Vomiting

If you get a puppy, sometime in the first few months, regardless of what you're feeding it, your dog will develop diarrhea or vomiting. Anything that puppies find is fair game to be eaten. This is especially true if it smells bad. They are also in the process of getting a complete new set of teeth, and this means they'll be chewing on and swallowing an amazing variety of things. With all this chewing and swallowing, you can expect softer stools and attempts to get rid of what they've eaten. Remember, there is no animal on the planet that can vomit more easily than a dog.

Confronted with messes like this, owners often wonder what they should do. Should you bring your dog to the vet every time it occurs? That's hardly necessary if the puppy is active and acting normally. Should you use special medications or force it to drink to prevent dehydration?

In most cases, veterinarians would recommend that you slow the system down. One of the few times a dog's instinctive behavior gets it in trouble is with gastrointestinal upsets, especially vomiting. Dogs that have an irritated stomach and are vomiting often want to drink water, sometimes in large quantities. This can perpetuate a vicious cycle. The stomach and its wall are irritated. The dog vomits and empties the organ. The animal then drinks a large quantity of water. This dilates the stomach, and that reflexively releases the digestive acids that further irritate the inflamed wall and its lining. This stimulates more vomiting, and so it continues.

Probably the best thing to do for an animal that has just vomited is to prevent it from drinking more. Withhold all fluids for at least two hours, and after that time permit it to drink only small quantities. Do the same with food. Withhold food for at least six hours, and then give the dog only small quantities of a bland diet. Do this for a couple of days. Intestinal protectants such as Pet Pectate or Pepto-Bismol will also help. Our favorite bland diet is boiled instant rice and cottage cheese in a 50–50 mixture. This same treatment is helpful for dogs with diarrhea.

Let us make it very clear that we're talking here about one-day bouts. Prolonged diarrhea and vomiting can signal a serious problem, and you should call your veterinarian if it persists for more than one day or if you see blood in the vomit or stool. And even on the first day, if the dog seems lethargic and ill, take it to your veterinarian. But if the animal is active, alert and willing to eat and drink, try conservative therapy at home.

Limping

Your puppy yipped out in pain and is now limping. How do you know if it needs to be seen by a veterinarian? We'll give you a clue on how to determine the degree of the injury without touching the dog. It will also help you decide if the animal needs to go to a clinic for a check-up.

When dogs injure their legs, they limp in one of two ways. Either they put some weight on the affected leg, or they carry it completely, not allowing the foot to touch the ground. In the first case, the 24-hour rule applies—wait 24 hours before you take the dog to the clinic. Dogs with broken bones or dislocated hips, however, will rarely put any weight on the leg at all, and need immediate veterinary attention. If the dog is letting the leg touch the ground, even a little, it is probably just a twist or sprain. But if the puppy is carrying it off the ground for more than a couple of hours, get it in for a check-up.

Don't give dogs that are suddenly limping on one of their legs any painkillers. For animals with a long-term or chronic condition, such as arthritis, that's probably good medicine. But for the acute, short-term injury, it is better for a dog to feel the pain. If you severely sprained your ankle, your doctor may give you something to kill the pain and tell you to stay off of it for a several days. You would do as you were told. If your puppy sprains its ankle and you give a painkiller like buffered aspirin, the pup will feel much better. Then, when a rabbit runs by, the dog may chase it and possibly cause additional damage. That's why we rarely use painkillers on puppies.

SUMMING UP

Use your veterinarian and stay in close contact whenever problems or questions arise. Unless it is their first week out of veterinary school, any question you might ask they will have heard many times before. Use this professional as an information source. We believe that is a part of their responsibility.

Reread the most common medical problems we've listed in this chapter. With most puppies, if problems are going to occur, they'll be on this list.

Chapter 6

A PHILOSOPHY OF TRAINING

There are hundreds of books and magazine articles written on training dogs. To make things even easier, entire courses are now presented on videotapes. There are also radio and television programs devoted to the subject. These various formats outline a wide range of methods and styles, hopefully all with the same goal: a well-disciplined, controllable dog—one that responds to your commands in an appropriate and timely fashion.

We have been very fortunate in that we have known and worked with some excellent dog trainers. These people have been our veterinary clients and friends. Often they have helped us with our own dogs and those belonging to the clients of our veterinary practice. We have read their books, attended their seminars and listened to their advice. Over the years, they have been a wealth of information for us. We readily admit that most of what we say in this book comes from their ideas and the thoughts they stimulated.

WHEN TO START TRAINING YOUR PUPPY

Some people believe that puppies younger than 16 weeks should not be exposed to any sort of a training program. They feel people should be using this time to simply expose the dog to its new home and family. They believe this should be a period, with few restrictions that allows the puppy to widen its experiences at its own pace. These ideas often stem from the concept that training will have a harmful effect on the socialization process, especially when discipline is used to define what is acceptable behavior and what is not. We disagree.

One reason we disagree is that the training methods we believe in do no harm. Don't expect to read anything about training in this book that will cause your pet mental or physical pain. We have no desire to frighten dogs, scold them into submission or use our hands or any tool to hurt them. It's not our style.

Remember, we're already training the puppy by housebreaking it. We are altering the animal's natural behavior patterns to ones that are appropriate for living inside our homes. This involves a lot of training, and if done correctly, no one would say that it hinders socialization. We take a dog's instinctive behavior and change it to one we approve of or want. The last sentence could be used to define either general training or the process of housebreaking. In this context, they are the same.

We think training, at least for housedogs, should start as soon as you bring a dog home. We see no reason to wait. As a matter of fact, we see reasons not to wait. Training is, as much as anything else, the formation of good habits. If you let your new puppy run wild for a long period of time, doing as it wants, bad habits will form. And when you're training your dog, you will find it is much easier and takes less time to form good habits from the start than to try to eliminate bad ones and replace them with the preferred behavior. This is one of the reasons we stress bringing your new puppy home at seven weeks of age. In addition to the effects on socialization, pups that make their grand entrance at 12 weeks or so are a much greater challenge to train because they have already formed many habits in a kennel situation that are not acceptable to living inside your home. As an example, they urinate or defecate wherever and whenever they desire, and sometimes they develop the behavior of tracking through these wastes.

We also like starting with puppies at seven weeks of age because they are so eager to please. They are very impressionable at this age. You are their new family, their home base. They, in their canine way, reach out to you for security and love. Believe us, they want this relationship to work just as much as you do. Assuming that your pup had a normal socialization process in its previous home, watch it carefully and you will note that after just two or three days it will probably come or respond to you whenever it is afraid or unsure of something new. It could be anything from a loud noise to meeting a new person or dog. The pup is seeing you as its protector, or at least someone it understands and accepts as part of its world. If, during this period, you can demonstrate in any way what you want, the puppy will attempt to please you. Be aware that licking your hand or face isn't done to soften up a potential piece of food, it is a sign of affection. Puppies like you and they want you to like them. When they understand what you want, they are eager to do it, if only because of the way you act when they succeed.

We need to take advantage of this behavior and start training when a dog is young. With some animals it may not do any harm to wait, but for most puppies it is much better to start right away.

How Do Dogs Act in the Real World?

If we are going to undertake to train a dog to be the companion we want it to be, it is important to understand what the animal is and what it wants to be. Remember that the domestication of dogs is a relatively recent event in the grand scheme of their existence. They have been around for millions of years, but have spent only a few thousand with us. They spent a long time forming a lifestyle that perpetuated their existence. In their world, before they teamed up with us, there were no food bowls sitting on the floor always filled with a balanced diet. No individuals, except other pack members, guarded them from injury and there was no large pharmaceutical industry to protect them from disease. Through natural selection, a canine model was formed that had the physical and mental abilities to continue their species. Their behavior patterns guided them through their day-to-day and year-to-year existence, helping them to make the right choices to protect themselves and their offspring. If this hadn't happened, dogs would be classified with the dinosaurs.

Their daily life was guided by the interactions that occurred between members of their group. Most wild dogs choose to live in packs. This is because hunting together does a better job of guaranteeing a near constant supply of food. Being carnivores, or at least high-level omnivores, wild dogs are usually predators. To kill an adequate amount of food at one time typically means bringing down a large animal. This is much easier for a pack of dogs to accomplish than it is for a single animal. Not only is it easier to find food if many different sets of eyes and noses are looking, but they can then cooperate in the chase and kill. There is also safety in numbers. Almost every animal has some enemy that is trying to eat it, and wild dogs are no exception. They are able to gain additional protection from these larger, or more efficient, predators by banding together in a pack, rather than trying to defend themselves alone.

Young pups are eager to please, and training can take advantage of that.

For dogs, being part of a group of dogs has provided them with many benefits. Much of their natural instinctive behavior revolves around learning how to deal with or interact with other members of their pack. Even as puppies, their play with their littermates is important. It teaches them hunting skills and how to interact with the other dogs. Young dogs jump up on each other or their parents in mock battles that imitate future hunts. In a controlled fashion, they snap and bite at each other just as they will at a prey animal.

To preserve some sort of order in the pack, a social hierarchy is established. To prevent constant and potentially harmful battles for who gets what or who is allowed to breed, the individual dogs each learn their relative position. Rather than have vicious battles every day, these pack positions are maintained through behavioral interactions. Dogs soon learn what submissive and dominant actions are and how to play the game. Specific postures and facial expressions are used as signals to maintain this order. Still, because of their instinctive will to survive and do what is best for themselves as an individual, most animals constantly try to improve their rank in the pack, and this can lead to brief skirmishes. This is their way of life, the best way for their species to survive.

Puppy games and skirmishes reflect some of the ways wild dogs establish a hierarchy in their pack.

Wild dogs do other things that help them to survive day to day. Dogs dig holes for protection. These may be either depressions to cool their bodies on hot days, or deeper dens in which to whelp and raise their litters. They bark at intruders to warn other pack members of a potential danger, or at other times to signal their own location. They use their stool and urine as territory-marking devices, to show that the space contained within certain boundaries is an area they control.

The things we've described here are behaviors that make a wild dog an effective being. They come quite naturally for the animal. However, most of this behavior we will try, through training, to eliminate. Most of the things a wild dog does in its day-to-day existence are unacceptable to us if they are going to be a part of our home and family. We don't want them digging up our yard, we don't want them to mark their territory inside our homes with urine or stool, we don't want them to bark excessively, we don't want them jumping on us, we don't want them to bite us, we don't want them to attempt to dominate us or any human members of the household, and so on. Regardless of how politically incorrect it may sound, we are not going to let the dog be itself. It has to change. We just have to remember that we have to make all these compromises worthwhile for the dog.

RULES TO UNDERSTAND BEFORE TRAINING BEGINS

Before we actually start training or even thinking about it, it is important that we get ourselves in the right frame of mind. If we do this and know where we are going, we will be much less likely to violate certain rules that may hinder or prevent us from attaining the goals we have for our dog. Additionally, we want to prevent ourselves from doing anything that may adversely affect the relationship we hope to develop with our puppy.

In the section on housebreaking in Chapter 4, we alluded to the fact that everything we do in training can affect either positively or negatively how our pup sees us. We start out with the idea of making our dog more like we want it to be, but if we are not careful our pet may end up seeing us as something it doesn't want us to be.

General Training Rule Number One is always be consistent. There should be no exceptions here if you want the training to go as rapidly and as easily as possible. Consistency involves your actions and words. From the very start you need to decide exactly what you are trying to teach or control and how you will do it. If you are going to use a certain word or phrase as part of a command, or in conjunction with a certain point you are trying to make, always say exactly the same thing.

Consistency is important for everyone in your household. Everyone who is involved in the training should know and use the same expression. As an example, let's think about the command "come." It obviously will not make things go faster if you use the word "come," your spouse uses the words "come here" and one of the children uses "yo, boy." All of this just confuses

Consistency is also important in what you will and will not allow. You can't
let your dog on the couch some of the time but not all of the time.

the dog. Remember, you are trying to train a dog using human language, and
you can't expect the puppy to be multilingual at eight weeks of age!

Every time you give a command or are working on a training point,
consistently carry it through to completion. Try to expect the same behavior
from the puppy each time. With "come," for example, don't tug on the leash
for the pup to come to you and then become distracted and forget what you
are doing. If you start pulling the dog in, but then stop when it's halfway to
you, it becomes confused. When you say "come," the puppy is supposed
to come all the way to you. If you don't make sure that happens, the pup
may think it's okay to only come in part way, or to completely ignore the
command.

If you use any form of praise or reward for a job well done, be consistent in how well the task must be completed before the praise or reward is forthcoming. If the puppy is supposed to sit, for example, don't offer praise if it only bends its back legs a little bit. People love to praise their dogs, and sometimes they are so eager to do this that the animal hears a string of "good boy, good boy" when it hasn't yet completed what it was supposed to. Over time this tells the puppy that it doesn't have to sit all the way down—a slight crouch will do. The puppy will come to believe that close is good enough.

When you start training the dog, think of it as classroom time. When children are in school, there is classroom time for learning and recess for playing. The same should be true with your puppy. When you start a training session, maintain a consistent training attitude for you and your puppy. Think training and not play. Work only on training issues and do them over and over. Stay in control, so that it doesn't become playtime for the puppy.

In the early stages of training, don't ever give a command unless you can control the puppy's actions. This is a part of consistency that many owners overlook. As an example, let's say you are currently in the process of teaching your puppy to come. The pup doesn't respond every time yet, but it is learning what the word "come" means. You are in the backyard together playing with the puppy and the children. It is recess, not classroom time. The dog is off its lead and suddenly takes off after a wild rabbit. Do not—we repeat, do *not*—even think about saying "come!" You know the puppy isn't going to respond because its mind is only on the rabbit. If you do scream "come," hopefully the dog will be so distracted that it won't hear you. Because if it does recognize the command but continues after the rabbit, the puppy has just learned that when you are not in control, it can get away with ignoring what you say.

During the training phase, if you are not in a position where you can control your puppy's actions, do not give it a command. Rather, move to the animal before you try to stop or prevent it from what it is doing. In the example of the puppy and the rabbit, you can either let it continue the chase or run and catch the puppy. Don't scream "come."

Along the way, you may occasionally modify your training method, finding that a certain style of training works better for your pup. That's okay, but do not keep switching back and forth, and remember to consistently use whatever method you have chosen. Just because one command is going slow, you shouldn't change from method to method hoping to find the magic formula that speeds up the process. This rarely happens, and in the interim the puppy may become hopelessly confused. We have found that regardless of the training method used, any individual pup may have trouble with a particular command, even if all the others go smoothly. This probably relates back to some experience in the animal's past.

General Training Rule Number Two is keep training sessions short. In many instances young children can become engrossed for several hours in a game, book or television show. Successful kindergarten teachers can make learning fun and productive, often for an hour or so. However, dogs, and especially puppies, do not have long attention spans. Young pups won't spend more than a few minutes chasing exciting, moving stimuli like a butterfly or bird. They simply lose interest and go on to the next thing. The same is true with training: They quickly become bored and shift their attention to something else. After they do, nothing further will be learned.

Puppies get bored pretty quickly, and once they are, they will not learn.

Generally speaking, most successful trainers limit training sessions to no more than 10 or 15 minutes, regardless of the age of the animal. This seems to be just enough for most dogs to enjoy, or at least tolerate. If sessions run longer, the learning process actually starts to go backwards. It is important that the puppy enjoy these sessions. If not, it may resent the entire training program. If you force a puppy to continue training after it has lost interest, distracted, resentful behavior may spill over into future sessions. Keep their minds occupied and keep it fun.

Set up a schedule and stick to it. It is much better to train for 10 minutes every day than 60 minutes once a week. Plan your training times around the pup's schedule. Don't expect the puppy to be a ball of energy and willing to learn if you try to train when it would normally be napping or eating. Plan your training sessions when distractions are at a minimum. If you have young children, it might go better if you trained the pup while they are at school or in some way occupied.

There are ways to get in additional training time, and the extra practice can be very important. If your pet is doing something that you are trying to train it to do anyway, use obvious opportunities to reinforce the command. A best-case scenario would be when you are getting ready to feed the puppy. You've learned that as soon as the animal hears you filling the bowl, it automatically comes running. As soon as it starts toward you, bend down with the bowl and say "come." It is a free, can't-fail training session!

Another example is when you are trying to train the puppy not to do something. Let's say you are trying to keep it from jumping on people. You've learned that every time you come home, the puppy rockets through the house and jumps up on your leg. You get home and you know exactly what it is going to do. Be prepared, and when it jumps up immediately put light pressure on its toes (we will discuss this method in Chapter 8). Then immediately bend down and greet the puppy just like you always do. Don't say anything about the jumping, as you two are happy to see each other. Whenever you can control the animal or know what it is going to do, it's a good idea to use these situations as a way to work on your training.

General Training Rule Number Three is stay calm and in control. This is where most people fail. Calm and in control refers to you, not the dog. In training situations you can never lose control or get excited, because when you do you may become mad, lose your temper and do something foolish. Training should be enjoyable for both you and the animal. If the puppy isn't having a good time, it won't learn anything. Likewise, if you are out of control or aren't enjoying yourself, you are not teaching anything.

During training there should not be any distractions for the puppy. You should guide it through the command so that the animal does what it should and is then praised for the successful completion of the task. If you are agitated, your puppy will pick up on this and not be thinking about the task in question. You have to be focused if you want your pet to be able to concentrate on the training. You will learn that your demeanor during training directly affects how much the puppy will learn. If you are up for this activity and enjoy it, the potential is there for the dog to make solid headway during each lesson. But if you are down, the pup's potential to learn will be too.

Carried to the extreme, if you get mad and lash out or treat the puppy harshly, you have destroyed any good that might have come out of this particular training session. You have also set back the animal's understanding of the command you were working on, and put a black cloud over the relationship between the two of you. When you do something to another

Interacting with your pet builds respect and trust.

person that you should be sorry for, you can sincerely express your regret and apologize. If they are of a forgiving nature, the act or unkind words are forgotten. Unfortunately, you cannot sit down with your puppy and explain that you are very sorry. What's done is done, and you must work long hours to regain the animal's trust. You will need to take time that could and should have been used for training just to become its friend again.

Some people do better if they do not talk to the dog during training. They teach the dog an action using just hand signals. We will go over this method later in this book, but if you tend to raise your voice when you sense that you are not in control (or are in the process of losing control), this may be a useful technique to try. Most people talk way too much during training, and for some this becomes a stepping stone to shouting and anger.

General Training Rule Number Four is do not over praise. In dog training, praise for doing something correctly can take a variety of forms. Some people prefer to give a treat, others may use the expression "good dog" and still others may give a gentle pat on the animal's shoulder. They all work, because they show the dog that you are pleased or approve of its actions. You said "come" and the puppy came. You said "sit" and it sat down. The animal did what it was supposed to, and received praise.

Where many owners err is in burying their animal in praise. Rather than say a single "good dog," they get down on one knee and let out a string of 40 "good dogs." Instead of a single stroke over the shoulder, they give the animal a full body massage. Instead of a single small piece of a biscuit or treat, the dog is given half a box. All of these overdoses do the same thing: They distract the dog from what it has just learned. Too much of a good thing and the animal forgets what the two of you are doing. The command and the dog's response are lost, and your praise is no longer reinforcing correct behavior.

Praise is important, but a dog needs only to recognize it as a thank you. You communicate to the dog that it did something correctly and you are happy it did. If your praise is always consistent in method and amount, the puppy will understand perfectly.

General Training Rule Number Five is always end on a positive note. Every training session should end with praise. The last thing you ask or command the puppy to do should be something it can do correctly. Especially when things are not going as well as you would prefer, for the last command choose something you know the pup absolutely can't fail at. When the puppy does it correctly, praise and move someplace else for some recess time or relaxation. Ending a session on a bad note may continue that failure into the next training period. You want the pup to finish one lesson and, because of the praise, to look forward to the next session. Always remember that to the dog, praise helps fulfill its desire to please you.

General Training Rule Number Six is forget discipline. Now, before you overreact, understand what we mean. To some trainers and most dog owners, discipline means punishing the animal for something it has done. To these people, punishment usually means to hurt the animal in some way. In our minds this just isn't necessary. If discipline means punishment or causes pain, forget it.

Let's look at the most common reason people discipline their dogs: It's for something the animal did. Notice we didn't say "something the animal was doing." We used the past tense. People punish their dog for something it did in the past. Examples would be finding a stool in the house during the housebreaking process. You didn't catch the animal doing it—you only discovered it later. The pup is picked up, scolded and put in its crate. A second example would be if someone's dog runs away from home. Two or three hours later it returns, and to make it see the error of its ways, the owner punishes it. They use a rolled-up newspaper to give it a spanking. Neither of these animals has any idea what behavior is being punished. They didn't sit there thinking, "Gosh, I wonder what I did lately that deserved punishment?" Dogs don't reason. Just because they got punished, they don't assume they did something wrong. All they know is that their owners were mad. Their anxiety about this can lead to even more unwanted behavior.

Often, punishment that occurs as part of training is brought about because the owner is impatient with the pace the dog is progressing. The owner is trying to push the animal through training too fast, assuming the dog should already know a certain command. Be patient, and remember that with most training you are altering the natural instinctive behavior of the animal. In training, the best punishment for an incorrect behavior is a lack of reward. If the animal does it right it is praised, if it makes a mistake it receives no praise. If praise from you is important, the lack of it will send a message. Repeat the exercise until the pup gets it right, and then offer praise. Praise is positive reinforcement; punishment is a distraction.

Still, there have to be good ways to communicate to the animal when it is caught in the act of misbehaving. And there are, but they aren't going to hurt anybody. In some cases a stern "no" is all that is required. You catch the animal urinating in the house, you say "no," pick the puppy up and carry it outside. Dogs understand a change in the tone of your voice much better than they do most kinds of punishment.

In human behavioral medicine today, "time out" is believed to be an excellent way to get across to children that they are acting in an unacceptable fashion. When they act up or do something wrong, they are isolated for a "time out" period. This is a new way of saying "go to your room" or "stand in the corner." The same technique can be used with dogs. If they are out of control, barking excessively or jumping on the furniture, they are given some "time out" by being placed in a cage or crate. A stern "no" may also be part of the message.

In place of punishment, we can also simply choose to ignore a misbehaving dog. When children act in a way that is solely to gain attention, ignoring them usually discourages the behavior. In some cases this also works for dogs. A dog might bark just to get a treat or to go outside. If you want it to have neither, consistently ignoring the barking will probably break the behavior pattern. There's no reason for the dog to continue barking if the behavior doesn't get it what it wants.

Most things we want to punish our dogs for really indicate a lack of training. Rather than punishing the dog for doing something you don't want, train it to do what you would prefer. Until that can be accomplished, a firm "no," and being placed in a crate or ignored will bring an end to most unacceptable behavior.

BE HONEST—CAN YOU TRAIN?

Be honest with yourself. Not everybody can train their dog. Many people say they don't have the time, but if they cannot spare 10 minutes a day then do they really have the time to have a dog? Maybe the issue is that they do not enjoy training. This is understandable. Training is not for everybody. Some do not have the patience for it, some cannot control their temper and some simply do not enjoy it. If you think any of these describe you, then you probably shouldn't try to train your dog. However, you can't live with an untrained dog. It might be smarter to use a professional dog trainer. Your dog won't care. In fact, it would probably prefer it. A good professional trainer will only help a dog, while an owner who loses control may cripple the dog's personality and self confidence. If you think you honestly cannot handle the job, use a trainer.

SUMMING UP

When you start training your new puppy is up to you, but from our experience, you are better off starting as soon as it comes home. Through interacting with your pet, you will build respect and trust.

Training, done correctly, should always provide the animal with praise. More than anything, puppies want to please you, and this praise tells them they are.

Understand your dog and what it is. Training is a way we alter dogs so they can move from their world into ours. We have described "owning a dog" as a relationship between two individuals—you and the dog. However, when training is successful, the dog changes.

For this process to occur with as little stress as possible to either of you, it is important that you understand certain basic training guidelines outlined here. Think about each one of them and how they relate to teaching the basic commands and correcting behavioral problems, which we'll discuss in the next chapter.

Chapter 7

TRAINING YOUR PUPPY

There are numerous training methods for dogs. Trainers and authors have developed many styles that use different training philosophies. Most of these methods, if followed consistently, are successful. The end product usually portrays to some extent the style of the training used. If the training is overly harsh and restrictive, the dog can develop into a robot-like creature. If the method is without consistency or structure, the dog may grow into one that never truly learns or develops any definite skills. Puppies trained in this fashion will often respond to or obey their humans only if a command appears to be the most enjoyable of all possible choices available to the animal at that moment.

We believe training should produce a dog that always responds to your commands, but that does not cause it to lose any of its individuality in the process. The dog should understand what is right and wrong while in your home or in the presence of other people, but this should not decrease the enjoyment it derives from being with you or your family and friends. We don't want a dog that knows every command in the book but in our presence fears the thought of our next demand. We believe you should be your dog's best friend, not because you feed it every day or take it outside, but because it likes you and enjoys being with you. The training process should encourage friendship, not discourage it.

In our minds, one of the most important features of any method used to train any kind of animal is that it must allow you to be in control. We don't mean simply to be in control of the animal, but rather, to **be in control of yourself!** More problems arise during or because of training when the human loses their composure, causing the animal to suffer in some way.

To harm the animal or cause a setback to the training process does not just mean physically hurting the dog. Losing your temper, screaming or yanking harshly on the leash in a way that frightens or distracts an animal will wipe out any good that might have been done during that training session. Sessions on the following days will probably also be affected. If it's severe enough, losing control of yourself during training can have a deleterious effect on the long-term relationship between you and your dog. The bond that exists between an owner and a dog should be thought of as sacred, and nothing in training should disrupt or endanger it.

The training style that we prefer is very low key. We see no reason to get mad, raise our voices or even become excited. As a matter of fact, we like to go as long as possible without even talking to the dog! Training should be an enjoyable experience for you. You will be spending time with a friend—your dog—in what should be a relaxed mood. And just as with one of your children, seeing the puppy learn and successfully respond or perform a task is a rewarding experience.

At the same time, we want the dog to enjoy the training process. We can't let the puppy get bored, be intimidated or in any way feel any pain. Our actions cannot be allowed to distract it from learning. We want our dog to look forward to these sessions. The training process should be fun for the puppy, as it is spending time with one of its best friends—you. As it completes a task, it will be praised and this will fulfill that natural canine desire to please. The sessions will always end on a positive note, leaving the pup happy and looking forward to the next one.

Remember that dogs, and especially puppies, have short attention spans. We don't want them to get bored. Keep your training sessions short. It is better to train for 10 minutes once a day than an hour on Saturday. Don't work on the same command over and over through an entire training session. Rather, try to intermix two or three different ones to help fight boredom in both you and your puppy.

We want the training process to be simple. There is no reason to make it complicated. We can gain what we want through repetition and praise. We want the method we use to be foolproof. As you carry out the training, the dog's reactions will be controlled so that it can only learn to do something correctly, rather than being asked to decide what is right from a group of choices.

Controlling Your Dog's Response

Training is always a two-step process: Motivation is followed by praise. First you get the dog to do something, and then you reinforce the action by praising it. For example, if you are teaching the "come" command, you somehow need a way to get the dog to come to you so that you can praise it. The lesson is repeated over and over, and as the dog is continually reinforced with praise, it learns the correct response to the command. The praise is the easy part; a consistent method of motivation requires some thought. Different training styles use different methods to get the response you want to the command you are trying to train. These motivators are rewards, gestures or verbal coaxing and contact.

The reward method is popular and works for many people. Let's say you want to train the puppy to lie down on command. Using this method, you sit the puppy beside you. You let it sniff some good-smelling treat like a morsel of cheese, freeze-dried liver or meat that is inside your closed hand. Then, you put that hand in front of the animal's nose and slowly sweep it down and forward, allowing the pup to follow it down. Most trainers using this method would also use a verbal command, such as "down." If necessary, as the dog's body nears the floor, you push down on the animal's back with the other hand and gently press it to the floor. Once the dog is down, you give it the treat. After a few repetitions the puppy learns that as soon as it is lying down it gets the treat, along with some praise. The treat therefore becomes the motivator that gets the puppy to do what you want.

The second method uses coaxing. This can be verbal or through gestures, or both. Teaching the "come" command, you kneel down and clap your hands. To a puppy this is a friendly gesture and it runs to you. As soon as it starts in your direction, you say "come." As the pup arrives it is praised. This is repeated over and over. The goal is to have the puppy associate the word "come" with going to you and being praised. After a while, you will not need to kneel down and clap your hands; the command will be enough. Here the motivator that gets the animal to come to you is kneeling down and clapping your hands. Eventually, the command "come" will be the motivator.

The final method of motivating the action you want is direct contact with the animal. This can be done by touching the animal yourself, or using a collar and leash. To teach the "come" command this way, you put a collar and leash on the puppy and gently pull it to you. This is our preferred method of motivating action during training. We like it because the puppy cannot fail. You control the dog's actions and they are therefore the same every time to a given command. We believe the puppy learns best when this is so.

The direct contact method almost becomes a separate language between you and the dog. It soon learns that your gentle tug on the collar or hand pressing on its back is part of a command. The dog recognizes that you are trying to tell it something. This can make it easier to teach other commands, as well.

Many trainers use a combination of different motivating techniques. We do, but we always consider direct contact to be the primary one and use it to get the response we want.

FORMS OF PRAISE

During training, once the puppy has successfully completed an action, it needs positive reinforcement and needs it immediately. This will come in the form of praise, which encourages the pup to do the same thing again. It also makes training more fun, and this is just as important. There are three common ways of rewarding animals during training: treats, verbal praise and direct contact.

Treats are a very common form of reward. The animal wants them, and if it establishes a connection between correct behavior and getting something good to eat, it will try its best to do what you want. The best treats both taste and smell good, and can be eaten in a single bite. You want the treats to have an enticing smell so they can be concealed in your hand yet still attract the dog's attention. Good taste makes the treat a true reward. Bite size is important so the dog doesn't fill up, plus the puppy can eat it quickly so valuable training time isn't wasted. And you don't want any mess on the floor, as the crumbs will distract the puppy. As we said, cheese, freeze-dried meats or bits of cooked meat, such as hot dogs or cold cuts, all work fine.

However, we don't like to use treats when we train, because we think they can be more of a problem than they are worth. Relying on them means you can't train as well if the pup isn't hungry. It may tire of the treat you are using, and you've got a real problem if you ever spill a few extra ones or the entire bag. Try working on the "come" command after you have spilled 20 pieces of cheese on the floor! The training session is basically over.

Additionally, if you rely on treats as a training reward, when you don't have any treats it may be hard to train. It's important to have set training times and work on a schedule, but there will be times when it's possible to work on a command because of what's going on or what your puppy happens to be doing. We discussed this a little bit in Chapter 6. For example, when you first get home from work, you know the pup will run to greet you. It's great to say "come" as soon as the dog starts running your way. The problem is that if you've just arrived home from work, you probably do not have any tasty dog morsels in your pocket or briefcase.

Verbal praise can also work as a reward, and it's something you can offer in any situation. Use a calm, soft, soothing tone that says it all to your dog. It will recognize this as praise every time. Remember, what you say isn't important—it's how you say it. The puppy doesn't know English any more than it knows Swahili. You could just as well praise your puppy with "old shoe" or "fish heads" as "good dog," and it will still work perfectly. Once you pick a word or phrase, use the same one every time. Try to get everyone in the house to use it too. As in all aspects of dog training, consistency is important.

The tone you use is also very important. Harsh, stern tones don't come off as praise. Maybe they sound more like a growl to the pup. Remember when your mother lowered the tone of her voice and said your entire name—even the middle name? You knew you were in trouble. If you want to praise your dog verbally, don't raise your voice or sound gruff. Don't get excited either, use gentle tones.

Finally, keep it brief. Just as with treats or any form of praise, don't overdo it! When you praise a dog, it doesn't do any good to repeat "good dog, good dog, good dog, good dog, good dog, good dog." One, at most two, is all that's needed.

Praise can be an excellent reward, but our favorite form of reward during training sessions is simple contact with the dog. We use a stroking motion, gently directing our hand backward over the shoulder. We call this the shoulder stroke. It was taught to us by the trainer Delmar Smith, and we think it works perfectly.

While to you this may not seem like much of a reward, your dog will enjoy it. It feels good, and probably simulates a common dog-to-dog behavior. We are sure you have seen two friendly dogs rub their shoulders against each other while walking. We aren't talking about one dominant dog trying to push another around, but rather a behavior in which both dogs are of equal status and signal this with an "I'm okay, you're okay" shoulder-to-shoulder rub.

The shoulder stroke. Your hand starts in front of the shoulder and moves backward.

We like this method of reward because it can be done anytime, anywhere and you don't need to carry around treats. You don't have to worry about saying the same thing every time you praise the dog. Also, the shoulder stroke is consistent—the same every time. It therefore cannot confuse the puppy in any way. It can also be used with any command.

We don't stand there and pet a dog over and over; once is plenty. You are sending a message through physical contact, not giving a massage. Also, don't stroke the dog so hard that you push its body around. This can be distracting and confusing. The dog may even think you are trying to teach it a new command.

You can say "good dog," give a piece of cheese *and* stroke the shoulder, but it isn't necessary. In fact it is probably a bad idea, as it can confuse the animal. As we said, too much praise is confusing to the puppy, and getting two or three rewards at the same time is probably even worse than too much of a single one. Choose the form of reward you want to use and stick to it. The puppy will recognize it immediately as an indication that it did something right. Keep making use of the dog's inherent desire to please you, and training will always go faster and with fewer problems.

Nonverbal Training

When we use the contact method to motivate the puppy to initiate and complete the action of a command and the shoulder stroke to praise it, there is no need to talk. We prefer to go through a training exercise many times before a word is ever used to indicate a command. We want the animal to be able to learn the command easily without any distractions.

We think silence during this initial stage of training any command is much less confusing for the animal and better for the trainer. The dog is going to learn several commands, and will be motivated by us having some form of contact with it. This could be pulling the leash or placing our hands on the dog to gently push it into the sit or down position. The dog will learn to respond to the physical contact first, and when we are sure of its response, we will add the verbal command. We promise you that if you use this method, training will go much faster because the dog will clearly understand what is wanted.

The second nice thing about not talking at this point in the training process is that it helps you concentrate on what you're doing. Humans are naturally verbal communicators, and we have to concentrate very, very hard not to say a word. If you concentrate on not talking, you'll be amazed how much easier it is for you to control yourself and remain calm, and that is one of the keys to a successful training program. During training it is always better to worry more about what you might do wrong than about what the dog is doing right. Anything the trainer does wrong will cause many more problems than anything the animal does at all.

So for now, not a peep. Don't worry, once we know the dog has learned a command and can consistently carry it out, we will put a word with it.

PREPARING THE DOG FOR COLLARS AND LEASHES

During training we want to attach a leash to the puppy's collar and use this to control its actions. Unfortunately, the animal has probably never worn a collar and won't know how to react to it, especially if the collar is used with a leash. You cannot bring your seven-week-old puppy home on a Saturday and start using a collar and leash on Sunday. It won't work, because your pup isn't prepared for these tools. You need to get the puppy accustomed to the collar, and you also need to choose a type of collar.

Different types of collars can be used during dog training. The most common type seen on dogs is the simple leather or nylon kind that is fastened around the animal's neck with a metal or plastic buckle. These can be left on the dog all of the time.

Two styles of leather collar and some nylon collars; the top two have quick-clip buckles, and the bottom one has a standard buckle.

Choke-style collars are made of chain, leather or nylon. These loop around the dog's neck and have a metal ring on each end. One ring is for attaching the leash and the other forms the loop. When you pull on the leash, these collars constrict down around the animal's neck—hence, their name. Choke-style collars should not be left on an unattended animal. By themselves, they won't choke the animal, but they can slide off its head or get caught on something.

The last type of collar is the prong or pinch style. When the leash is pulled, these grab the dog's neck and either pinch the skin or poke into the animal's neck. They also should not be left on the dog when you are not present.

During training, when we are using a leash or a long line, we prefer the standard leather or nylon collars with their traditional buckles. (The terms lead or leash usually refer to those that are four to six feet long, while a long line or check cord is much longer, often 12 to 30 feet.) Many people prefer leather collars because they will slide around the dog's neck easier than nylon. Whichever of these you prefer, make sure the collar is tight enough during training. It must remain at the top of the neck, against the head. You should just be able to slide two fingers between the collar and the animal's neck.

This collar is too far down on the dog's neck for effective training. In this position the dog will instinctively pull against you, as the collar basically rests against its chest.

This collar is in the correct position for training exercises.

If the collar is too loose it will either slide off over the head or back down the neck against the dog's shoulders. It's obvious what the problem is if the collar slips off the dog's head: The animal escapes and you are no longer in control. If a collar slides down the neck it is no longer very useful for training, because it does not control the animal's head. During training, it is important that you control the dog's head. That is the only way you can control which way the animal moves.

Regardless of the collar style you are going to use in training, the puppy needs to get used to the sensation of wearing a collar. For this we prefer the simple nylon ones with the quick-clip buckles. They are easily adjustable for a wide range of sizes and can be enlarged as your puppy grows.

When you first put a collar on a puppy, it will scratch at the new attire with its hind legs or try to bite it. This goes on for only a few days, and then the collar is forgotten. Once a pup is accustomed to wearing a collar, it should have one on for its entire life. The only exception is when the dog is being bathed. Collars are great when you need to quickly grab your dog to gain control, plus they are a great place to hang one of those life-saving name tags.

LEASH TRAINING

Once your puppy is accustomed to a collar, it's still not ready to begin training. We will want to attach a leash as well, and then give the pup some time to adjust to that. It needs to get used to the sensation of being pulled or directed with a check cord or leash. You could start by attaching the leash to the collar and trying to walk the dog, but we wouldn't recommend it. When your dog is getting accustomed to new things, let any initial fear or dislike be directed at the object and not at you. You don't want a new experience to result in distrust or apprehension of you.

If you attach a leash to the puppy's collar and immediately start pulling, the pup will spin round and round, possibly up on its hind legs or even fall to the ground, and through all of this it will be biting at the leash. This can go on until the pup is exhausted. This is not productive for your training program. It is better to put the leash on and simply allow the puppy to drag it around. You should be nearby, but do not hold on to the leash. The puppy will occasionally get caught and briefly react, but you won't be the one doing this terrible thing. The goal is to get the puppy used to resistance from the other end of the leash.

Some breeders will tie a short rope around each puppy's neck when the litter is five to six weeks of age. This forms a collar with an 18- to 24-inch trailing piece. The litter is then placed outside to play—but of course, with careful supervision. Each trailing piece of rope tempts the other puppies to grab and pull on it. All of the puppies are soon pulling on each other's rope leads. This game is allowed to continue for 20 to 30 minutes, and quickly exposes the puppies to collars and the pull that is felt when a leash is used. A few sessions like this and the pups go to their new homes leash and collar trained.

Whether the puppy comes to your home accustomed to the leash or you first let the animal teach itself, you still need to work with the puppy on a leash before you think about using it for training. For this initial work, use no more than a four- to six-foot nylon or leather leash. We want to remain close to the dog so we can control its actions. Take short walks where there are no children or other tempting distractions. During these first few introductions to the leash, don't apply very much pressure on the pup's neck. Let the animal lead you, but occasionally try to gently turn its head one way or the other. It will help if you turn your body before you tug on the leash, so that the puppy is following you as much as you are directing it with the leash. A few short 10- to 15-minute walks will usually be all that is needed for a good introduction to the leash.

Your next goal is to be able to walk with the dog on a leash without it attempting to rip your arms out of their sockets. Some trainers successfully

Left to right, a cotton web lead, nylon check cord, rope check cord and leather leash.

use choke or prong collars to restrain or eliminate this behavior. These can be useful when trying to leash train large adult dogs. For puppies, however, they are not necessary. We prefer to use the same simple leather or nylon buckle collars we use throughout our training. At this age, we have little problem controlling dogs with these conventional collars. Additionally, by using the same one we use for general training, we can easily work on some of the commands while walking our dog.

A leash-trained dog is one that will walk calmly with us without tugging on the collar. As we introduce the puppy to the leash, it may try to go faster than we do or move off to the side. Either of these actions can be quickly corrected with a quick snap of the leash. When the dog tugs against us, we will snap the lead back quickly just four to six inches. This is done as needed, but this rarely means more than one to three times. These leash-training walks should be no longer than 15 to 20 minutes. Start out in uncongested areas with few distractions. Slowly work your way into areas with children and other dogs. Whenever the dog strains against you, snap the leash and its head back quickly. Unless you get carried away, this will not hurt the puppy but will quickly correct its behavior.

We don't talk to or try to verbally correct the puppy with leash training. There is no reason to teach a verbal command you will never use after the animal is trained! It may even distract the pup from the snapping motion, which is the only communication we need.

Teaching "Come"

Of all the people we see in our clinics, probably only 30 percent of their animals know the "come" command. In other words, if the dog is off its leash and the owner says "come," the dog will not reliably respond. This is sad, as this is the most important command a dog should know. Sooner or later it may prevent a dog from getting hurt. Additionally, most people would enjoy their animal much more if the dog would only respond to this one command. People feel frustrated with dogs that run away or that they have to chase down to control.

This certainly isn't a difficult command to teach. Unfortunately, most owners either make a halfhearted attempt or never carry the training through to completion. Earlier in the book, we explained how problems with housebreaking could cause long-term problems between owner and dog. The same is true with teaching "come." With this command, you are trying to get the animal to come to you. If you ever lose control of your emotions and scare or hurt the dog, you cannot expect to be successful at teaching this command. If the dog is afraid or intimidated by you, why would it want to come to you?

Teaching "come" needs to be done slowly and consistently. Don't try to rush it, and this is no place for discipline of any kind. While teaching "come," it is either praise or nothing at all, depending on the dog's performance.

The method we prefer for teaching this command uses only a collar and a check cord and is very simple to do. It uses a lot of the puppy's natural instincts and only a little of your own force. The animal will want to please you, but more than anything, if you act and position yourself correctly it will actually want to come to you.

In most situations, if you squat down a young puppy will usually run to you, as it sees this action as an inviting welcome. You should use this to your advantage when training "come," even though the pup is on a leash or check cord. The animal's compliance will be reinforced with a reward when it arrives, and the rope is only used to ensure that the pup makes it all the way. If the puppy starts fighting the gentle pull of the check cord, it probably isn't ready yet to work on the "come" command. Back up and work on leash training until it is used to responding to the sensation.

Crouching down stimulates the puppy to come to you. The check cord
only controls its response and guides it in.

The training sequence goes like this: While the puppy is at least 20 feet from us and wearing a collar attached to a check cord, we crouch down facing the puppy. As we stated, the puppy will probably run to us without any coaxing, but if necessary we will gently pull it to us using the check cord. Once the pup starts to come, make it come all the way to you, using the cord if necessary.

We won't say anything to the pup during these first few exercises. No use confusing the puppy with sounds it doesn't understand. (Remember, they are not words to the dog, only sounds. The word "come" means nothing in canine vocabulary.) When the puppy reaches us, we will reward it with one or two shoulder strokes. It would be best if the puppy remains standing on all four feet, so try to keep it from lying down. At this point, don't worry about where the puppy is standing in relation to you. In the next step we will position it where we want.

Remain there together for 10 seconds or so, and then get up and walk away from the pup. If it follows directly on your heels, stop and wait for it to go off on its own to another spot to investigate something. When the dog isn't looking, drop down and repeat the above process. If it doesn't look at you immediately, give a gentle tug on the check cord so that its head turns and it can see you crouching. Let the puppy's natural reactions take over—it should start toward you. If the dog doesn't, gently pull it in as needed. This will put a slight amount of tension on the cord, guiding the puppy to you. Be to keep the check cord off the ground so the puppy doesn't trip on it. During a single training session, repeat this exercise 10 or 15 times without ever saying anything. This should take about 10 minutes.

After a few 10-minute sessions, when you see the puppy is consistently responding and coming in, start pulling in while standing, but with your back bent slightly forward. You may need a little more pressure initially on the check cord, as this is not quite as an appealing posture for the pup as the crouch.

Working on "come" from the standing position.

At this stage of training, when the animal reaches you, guide it around to your side so that it stops right beside your knee with its head looking forward. (Place the pup on the same side you will train the dog to heel on.) Don't praise until it is in this position. Prevent it from going behind you. Don't say anything yet; just reach down and give one or two shoulder strokes. We want the pup to learn the command before a spoken word is ever associated with it.

While your puppy is standing beside you, do not let it lean into you. If it does, use your knee to push it away. This can be a first and natural attempt at the dominance game. Dogs will crowd against each other to establish their position in the pack hierarchy. Don't let your dog start this behavior. With some animals it will develop into a more serious problem later on.

Every time you bring the puppy to you, make sure it comes all the way. Don't let it stop short of you or be distracted and go somewhere else. We want to prevent an unwanted behavior from developing. If the animal can get away with not coming all the way to you now, it will definitely do this later when it is off the lead and would rather be doing something else than responding to your command. Bring it in all the way every time.

After two weeks or so, when the puppy is consistently coming to you, it will be time to start talking. You'll know you are ready to add the verbal command when the animal demonstrates it has learned the action. As soon as you give the first tug on the check cord the puppy will start moving and come all the way to you. The puppy knows what it is supposed to do!

This same pattern will be seen when we teach any command with the nonverbal method. The dog completes the task consistently in response to the contact, made either through the collar–check cord combination (as with the "come" command) or directly with your hand (as with the "sit" and "down" commands). Your praise has then reinforced its actions. When your puppy shows you it knows the right action, you know it's time to add the verbal command.

When you do start talking, keep it very simple. Just say "come" or "here Spot," or whatever word or short phrase you prefer. The animal is still on the check cord, so it can't fail. Just repeat the same process as before. As you start the verbal phase, however, do it from the standing position. The instant you make that first tug on the check cord, say the command word. Say it once and only once. You want the command to be very plain and very simple. A string of "come, come, come, come, come" will only confuse the dog. It will also be inconsistent, because if you say the command once or twice or five times, depending on the situation and how frustrated you are, the dog will hear each group of words as a single command and not understand which one really means "come." Say "come" and pull the dog gently to you, keep it moving so its head ends up by your knee, and then give a shoulder stroke. Repeat this exercise over and over during your training sessions, but intermix it with other commands as your dog is learning them.

After a few more training sessions, try to place a time gap between when you first say the word "come" and when you pull on the check cord. Wait just a second to start with, but slowly increase the interval over several tries. After a while, you will notice that the animal is responding to the word and you can stop pulling on the cord. Slowly it's happening—the dog is learning the verbal command.

Many people make a huge mistake at this point and give up the check cord too soon and rely on their voice alone. Quickly they will see the animal

The dog is guided in to your side as it reaches you.

If the pup leans into you while sitting or standing at
your side, gently push it away with your knee.

test them and either not come back all the way or simply take off in a different direction. During these early stages of training never use the verbal command when the dog isn't on the check cord. It can easily disobey you and develop bad habits.

Once you are totally satisfied that your puppy knows a command and obeys it consistently while it is under your control, you may choose to give up that control (in this case the check cord) and try using the verbal cue alone. These first few tests off the check cord should be done in small areas without distractions. You want to be able to quickly get to the animal so that it cannot ignore the command or escape. Take it slow; this is a critical time. You do not want the animal to fail. Slowly increase the distance between you, and use the command in areas with more and more distractions. Praise the dog just as you did before. Positive reinforcement is very important at this stage.

When you notice the animal is not responding, as will happen, go back to the check cord. Notice we said "when" and not "if." Every animal will slip in its discipline to some degree. Whether the breakdown occurs in two days or two years, go back to the check cord. Whenever an animal fails to respond, always go back to the previous training step and "re-tune." Do it immediately. The sooner you do it after the dog disobeys, the less chance a bad habit will form.

TEACHING "SIT"

In training this command, we use the same philosophy as we do with "come." We use the collar and leash or check cord, along with our hands, to help us motivate the puppy to accomplish the command, and we use the shoulder stroke to praise it. Again, no words are spoken until we know the puppy understands and will do the command.

This is a relatively easy command to teach. Begin with the dog standing beside you, probably right after the dog has come to you in response to "come." Gently put upward and backward pressure on the check cord. This elevates and moves the dog's head slightly back. Keeping the hand that is on the check cord in this position, use the other hand to gently push down on the animal's rump.

These two actions force the dog to sit. Give it a shoulder stroke or two. If it tries to rise, resume the pressure over its back with your hand. Keep the

Start the "sit" command by pulling up on the leash, and then gently push
down on the puppy's back above the hips.

animal in this position for at least five to 10 seconds. When you want it to
move, lightly snap or twitch the collar with the check cord, take a step forward
and the puppy will get up and follow you. This twitch is used to indicate that
the puppy can get up from the sit position. Don't let the pup move until
you've signaled it can. Later, you will release it with a verbal command.

As we said, training "sit" should be interspersed during a session with
training other commands. Mixing up the commands keeps the puppy (and
you) from becoming bored.

While teaching "sit," you will notice that after a few sessions the pup will
automatically sit down just from the action of pulling up on its neck with the
check cord. Placing pressure on its back with your hand will not be necessary.
When this happens, you can start using the verbal command "sit" as you pull
up on the cord. Don't rush this step. It is probably best to go through several
sessions with the dog performing perfectly before adding the verbal cue.
Follow the same sequence as you did with "come." At first say "sit," and
immediately pull up on the rope. Later, start slowly separating the two actions,
with the spoken word coming first. Remember to praise every time.

Now it's time to add another verbal command. Remember, before we
started talking we kept the dog sitting until we twitched the check cord. Now
let's use the word "OK" to signify it is all right to move. This is called a
release word, because it releases the dog from the command.

When only the spoken word is needed, you will soon be able to work with the dog off the leash. The final step is when you can give the "sit" command and, even though the dog is a considerable distance from you, it responds correctly. Remember, whenever the animal starts to disobey the command, always go back to the previous training step and reinforce the correct action.

TEACHING "DOWN"

By the time we get to this command, most dogs are off leash for "sit" and have pretty well mastered it, but are still working on and reinforcing the "come" command. With the dog in the "sit" position, put just enough pressure on its back directly over the shoulders to force it to lie down. Note that we are putting the contact pressure in a different spot than we did with "sit." This is important, as it means we are telling the dog to do something different. With some dogs, during the first few tries it is necessary to sweep their front legs forward as well. Do this gently, and don't try to knock the animal down. Once down, give the dog a shoulder stroke.

Some people believe that going from one command to another in this fashion is confusing to the puppy, but we have not found that to be the case. We actually prefer to build one command on top of another.

"Down" becomes a command you can easily work, whether you are in a formal training session or not. As long as you take the command through to completion in circumstances where you can control the animal's actions, this training can be done anywhere. Work on it as you watch television, read at your desk or sit at the dinner table.

With "down" as with "sit," don't let the dog get up until you give the release word. Before you get to the verbal part of training, release the dog by twitching the collar with the check cord. If the dog is not on a lead, you can simply tap its collar with your hand. After you are talking with this command, use the same "OK" to release the dog from the "down" position as you did with "sit." Always use the same release word because it always means the same thing—the command is over.

You will know when to start saying "down." When you notice the dog dropping into position as soon as pressure is placed on its back over the shoulders, you will soon be able to add the verbal command. As with the other commands, don't rush it. See a consistent pattern before you assume the dog is ready to go to this next step.

TEACHING "STAY"

This command is added onto the "sit" or "down." Start with the dog in either of these positions a foot or so from you. You need to be close. The pup may or may not be on the check cord. Make sure the pup is looking at you, then raise your right hand with the palm open and say "stay." That's right, say something! This is the only command we prefer to start off with a word. Remember, the dog already knows "sit," "come" and "down," and has been working with the words associated with those exercises. We are just adding onto those commands, and so we can add the word "stay." If the puppy starts to move, go to it immediately, put it back where it was and repeat the word "stay." Don't get angry; this will be a little confusing to the dog. If it stays, walk to it and give it a shoulder stroke, then walk a step or two away. Do this several times, but stay very close to the dog.

As the dog learns the command, start using "OK" to release it. Usually it will understand and come to you. If it does, praise it. However, if you say "OK" and the dog doesn't move, don't say "come." Use "OK" again and pull lightly on the leash at the same time.

Patience and repetition will quickly teach the "stay" command. As your puppy gets better at it, slowly move farther away from the dog and into areas with more distractions. This is a great command to teach your dog. Someday it might be near a moving car, and for its own safety you want it to stay right where it is.

TEACHING "HEEL"

Everyone would like to have their dog walk in a disciplined, mannerly way by their side without the use of a leash. You turn and the dog turns, you stop and it stops. This is actually very easy if you work at it consistently.

Start with the dog at your side using a leash or check cord. Its shoulder should be even with your knee. We like to have the dog's body about three to four inches from our leg, with its head somewhat in front of us so it can see what we are seeing. This is the correct "heel" position.

You can choose whichever side you want, but after you have decided and start training, always work with the animal on the same side. No switching back and forth. Keep a very short length of leash available to the animal. If it is on your right side, have only a short amount of leash or cord between the collar and your right hand. Any excess should be held across your body and coiled in your left hand.

Now walk forward, keeping the dog right beside you. At first do not do any fancy turns, just slow, gradual ones. Whenever the animal tries to stray out of the correct position, snap or twitch your right hand three or four inches. The dog will quickly learn that to prevent this uncomfortable snapping, it must stay in position. Work on "heel" for brief three- to five-minute walks once a day for 10 days or so. At the end of this period, you will be amazed how little pressure, if any, you need to put on the leash to maintain the dog in the "heel" position.

Praise is given intermittently during training, but only when you have stopped and the dog is at your side. As you stop and the dog stops, even if you had to snap the leash slightly to restrain it, once the pup is in the right position reach down and give a good shoulder stroke.

Whether standing still or walking, your dog should
always be in this position during "heel."

After the animal is responding correctly, add the verbal command "heel" as you walk off, keeping the dog at your side. While the animal is still on the leash you can also say "heel" and bring it to your side with the leash. Give a shoulder stroke as soon as it gets there, and then start walking, again keeping it at your side with the leash. As you develop confidence in your dog and pressure is not needed to maintain the correct "heel" position, start short exercises without the leash. As soon as the dog fails to respond correctly, return to using the leash.

USING OTHER WORDS OR PHRASES

Very few owners can have a dog and not use the expression "good dog." It can and should be a form of praise for a command properly executed. It's all right to use this phrase, but try to restrain yourself until the dog knows the command very, very well. Adding new words during training is confusing and always slows down the dog's learning process.

One of the reasons we like nonverbal training is that it keeps us in control of ourselves. But dogs also learn faster in the simpler environment of a non-talking trainer. The use of "good dog" doesn't make things go better or faster for the dog; it mostly makes you feel better. Often what happens is the owner starts saying this tiny two-word phrase over and over, getting the dog more and more excited. In this state the dog can't concentrate or absorb anything.

The simple shoulder stroke works just fine for praise. Stick with it alone for as long as you can. Once the dog really understands all the commands you want to teach it, then start with "good dog."

You will also need the expression "no," but we don't use it as part of basic training. It's used when and only when an animal is in the midst of unacceptable behavior away from the training environment. We never use "no" while we are teaching commands! It's all right to use when you catch the dog urinating on the floor, nipping at your child or barking at the neighbor. It is then used in a stern, low tone and said only once. It's all right to use the command in combination with the dog's name (as in "Spot, no!"), but not to say, "Spot, no, no, don't do that you messy thing!" After its name and the first "no," the dog just hears a confusing jumble. We've often wondered how many dogs think their name is "no, no, bad dog."

We mentioned the use of a few other words and phrases in the section on housebreaking in Chapter 5. For a puppy up to six months of age, those plus the commands in this chapter seem like more than enough.

SUMMING UP

Training of the basic commands, if done in the way we've outlined in this chapter, should go fairly easily for you and your puppy. Remember to stay calm and in control of yourself, and to keep training as simple and rewarding as possible for the puppy. If you can do this, we promise your pet will learn rapidly and the training process will bring the two of you closer together.

Chapter 8

BEHAVIOR PROBLEMS OF PUPPYHOOD

Every puppy, like every child, will get into trouble once in a while. This could be for eating your best pair of shoes, running into the neighbor's yard and pulling the laundry off their clothesline, knocking over a lamp, spilling the water dish, or any of a wide range of one-time disasters. We can talk to and reason with children about these misadventures, but for puppies it's harder. They do most of these things once and only once, and it isn't worth trying to figure out a way to discipline them for it. If you catch them at it, a stern "no" would be appropriate. But for most incidents, discovered after the fact, it's difficult to discipline the pup in any way that it would understand.

There are, however, much more troublesome behaviors that can develop into ongoing problems. These will cause you much more grief than the loss of a pair of shoes or a lamp.

JUMPING ON PEOPLE

Dogs often jump up on people. They stand on their back legs with their front paws on the person. This is normal behavior for a young dog. Puppies in a wild pack do it all the time. They jump up on each other and on their parents. Puppies of our domestic dogs do the same. It serves as play, and also to teach them how to act as a predator or how to challenge other pack members in the dominance hierarchy.

In some homes, puppies are encouraged to jump up on their owners. Obviously, this is a mistake. While it may be seen as cute or as a sign of affection when the puppy is small, it can be terrifying when done by a 100-pound Rottweiler.

Many owners complain about their dogs jumping up. They shout "no" or "no, get down" or any one of a wide range of phrases that make perfect sense to them but that are not understood by the dog. They scream and punish the animals, but not much seems to help. Some of these corrective actions may excite the dog even more, and when this happens nothing is learned.

In all honesty, this behavior can be eliminated completely in a week or less; and, as usual, we don't think you need to say anything. You need to communicate to the dog that this isn't acceptable behavior, and you shouldn't waste words about it.

Corrective training is very simple and can be done by anyone of any size to any dog of any size. It can be done one of two ways. When the animal jumps up on you, either lift your knee so it hits the animal's chest, or lightly step on the toes of one of its back feet. Neither will hurt the dog. All you want to do is make something that's been fun suddenly uncomfortable. Say nothing. No words are needed. Done consistently, either of these actions will eliminate jumping behavior.

Lift your knee gently into the chest of a jumping dog to discourage it.

Stepping lightly on the toes of the back foot also works.

These same actions can be used to discourage young dogs that sexually mount a person's leg. Young dogs do this as part of their education about how to mate and as a form of dominance behavior. Unfortunately, this is often directed at our children or us. If you do not stop them, this mounting behavior can go on for years.

Of the two methods we've described, we prefer stepping on the dog's toes. It is easier and can be done on dogs of all sizes. It's nearly impossible to bring your knee into the right position if you have a very small dog. Some trainers recommend using their shoe or foot in place of the knee, but it is much more difficult and less effective.

Remember that you are not going to step down on the toes or kick the chest and make the dog yip in pain. That much force is not necessary. We have never encountered a situation in which this behavior could not be eliminated in a week or so with gentle, consistent correction.

PUPPY NIPS

Puppies like to bite and chew on almost anything that enters their world. Just as with jumping, nipping between littermates is their style of play. This also teaches puppies how to use their main hunting tool—their mouth with all those teeth—later in life. Unfortunately, this behavior often carries over into their interactions with the people in their new home. All the people, including the children, are brought into the game. Puppies have very sharp teeth and their nips and bites can hurt and be terrifying to small children.

The simplest method we have found for handling this behavior is to very, very quickly grab the dog's mouth and hold it shut, while simultaneously saying a single, stern "no" in a low tone. This is usually done by putting your thumb over the top of the nose and your fingers below the bottom of the jaw. We hold the mouth closed for a few seconds. The dog will whine, as this is uncomfortable. There is no need to firmly squeeze the upper and lower jaws together. Don't try to cause any pain. Wait four to five seconds and then let go. Don't make any further fuss, but go on with whatever you were doing.

This will take a few sessions, but the animal will soon put together the connection that the bite instantly causes its mouth to be held shut. We don't like to see children brought into this form of discipline. Sometimes it looks like fun to do this to the pup, and they may instigate the bite so they can hold the jaw. Additionally, they may either get hurt or hurt the puppy.

Hold the mouth shut briefly after the puppy playfully nips to discourage the behavior.

STOOL EATING

Young dogs, especially in the winter, will often eat their own or another dog's stools. It is believed that this is a holdover from an instinctive behavior of wild dogs. In the winter, food is often limited for young canines. Many starve to death. In an attempt to get more energy, they eat their own stools or those of other dogs. We know that domestic dogs put on some low-calorie diets or not fed enough food will sometimes eat their stools simply out of hunger.

This isn't a pretty habit, and few owners want their dogs to do it. It can also be a potential source of bacterial, viral and parasitic diseases. Two of the most serious infectious diseases affecting dogs today are parvovirus and coronavirus. These are transmitted by dogs ingesting feces or fecally contaminated materials that carry the virus particles. Most parasite eggs are also consumed by ingesting feces.

Many owners believe this is a sign that their dog, regardless of its age, is deficient in some specific nutrient or vitamin. This probably isn't the case. Today's commercially prepared dog foods have an excellent spectrum of nutrients, along with various vitamins and minerals. Additional supplementation rarely cures this problem. Most nutritionists see stool eating as a behavior problem.

Today, this problem is dealt with by feeding special medications to dogs with the habit. Most of these products contain large, indigestible vegetable proteins that pass through the dog's digestive tract and go out in its stool. The passage through the body affects these proteins so that they give a bad taste to the stool. Two of the commonly marketed products are sold under the trade names Distaste and Forbid. They work for the vast majority of dogs.

If a dog is eating the stools of another dog, the product must be used with the second dog so that its stool becomes distasteful.

SUBMISSIVE OR EXCITED URINATION

When excited, young dogs often spontaneously urinate. They have no control over this and sometimes do not even realize they have done it. Others will urinate as a sign of submission in the presence of another animal (or person) that they consider dominant. These animals may also not be able to control their actions. Submissive urination is sometimes seen in puppies or young dogs that have been abused. However, many puppies that are perfectly normal and from good backgrounds may also develop a pattern of involuntary urination. These problems seem to be caused either by a lack of neuromuscular control over the bladder or by previous treatment that frightened or intimidated the puppy.

Training procedures and even medications have been used on puppies that urinate involuntarily. The training can work in some cases when done by experienced individuals, but most people only make the problem worse. Sedatives have been tried, but they only seem to be useful while the animal is on them, and have no lasting benefits.

There is little to be gained by trying to figure out why your puppy urinates involuntarily. Instead, try to determine what actions or events cause it to occur. For some this will be easy. Excitement or sudden movement toward the puppy may cause it to urinate. For others, it might be something as simple as direct eye contact. Whatever the cause, do your best to eliminate these situations or actions. It will help when greeting the puppy to bend your knees and get down on its level, rather than standing over the pup and bending forward. Looming over it that way can be intimidating to a young dog. Most puppies will outgrow this behavior by six months of age, especially if we let them mature through this stage of their life in a gentle and calm environment.

Be patient. When an accident occurs, don't make a fuss. Remember the puppy can't help itself. Clean it up and forget it.

Chapter 9

ADOLESCENCE— SIX MONTHS TO TWO YEARS

You've lived through the first six months of your dog's life. It's housebroken and most of the basic commands, such as "come," "sit" and "heel," are coming along nicely. The dog is having a significant effect on your life. For some, the home seems to revolve around the puppy, because it has become such an important member of the family. For a few, the puppy has become a burden. The newness has worn off, and what was once fun may have become a chore.

The dog's next stage, adolescence, will probably strengthen and solidify your feelings toward your pet. For those that enjoy and love their dog, these feelings will increase as the dog becomes an adult. Every day they will see that the dog requires less care but provides more companionship and enjoyment. For those who are starting to wonder if having a dog is right for them, adolescence may be the straw that breaks the camel's back. Training has failed to produce a dog they enjoy being with—either because of their lack of consistency or because not enough time was invested—and the animal has reached an age where it regularly tests them and the limits they try to put on it. Such people may have already lost control of their dog. If not, they surely will in the months to come.

The adolescent period is one of great change for any dog. In a few months it changes from a cute little puppy into an adult. Its behavior also changes, from dependence and acceptance to independence and testing. For dog lovers, this is a great time. They no longer need to make so many concessions or compromises because of the dog's age. They see their puppy mature and develop mentally and physically into the dog they wanted from the start.

MORE TRAINING

As the dog begins to mature, its training needs to continue. Even when the dog is able to perform all the basic commands consistently, it is important to routinely practice and reinforce them. Dogs will frequently develop bad habits over time, or at least be less precise in how they carry out a command. By occasionally going over the basics, you will become aware of developing problems and what points need extra work. Do not change your style or method of training because of the dog's age. What we explained in earlier chapters works for a nine-week-old puppy, and will work even better for an 18-month-old dog.

If you are starting to struggle with your young dog, seek assistance. There are numerous obedience courses in most communities. Don't be ashamed to seek a group class or a private trainer. We said that training isn't for everyone. Whatever your occupation is, probably very few of the rest of us could do it. If you still want to try training the dog yourself, start right from the beginning and work up. Don't try to make a disciplined dog by building onto bad habits. We guarantee it will not work.

ADOLESCENT BEHAVIOR PROBLEMS

Most dogs that end up relegated to the back yard or given up for adoption meet this unhappy fate between the ages of six months and two years. People discover they really don't enjoy having a dog, the children have lost interest, the owners cannot control it, it has become too expensive, it has been found to have some medical condition that is not easy to deal with—the list goes on and on. Some reasons are understandable; most are not.

Dogs in this age group often develop serious behavioral problems that their owners don't know how, or don't want, to deal with. With a little knowledge, the average dog owner can handle most of these problems, although the more difficult ones may also require some professional help. Let's take a look at the common problems seen in a canine adolescent.

Destructive Dog Syndrome/Separation Anxiety

You are gone for several hours or a major portion of the day. You come home to be greeted by your best friend, only to find it has destroyed half your home. Your clothing and furniture have been chewed on, the rug is a mess of frayed and ragged bits, waste baskets are knocked over, and the towels from the bathroom are scattered everywhere. Some people call this destructive dog syndrome, while others refer to it as separation anxiety. In our minds, it is a dog, bored to death and left alone, having the time of its life.

A lot of dog owners claim their dog is destructive out of spite. But it's hard for us to believe the dog acts like this to punish you for leaving it alone. Some do suffer from true anxiety when left alone, but most are afraid of nothing in this situation. They are just filling their time alone with whatever activities they find available. We have had owners leave video cameras on to record the pet's day. In most of these cases of household destruction, it appears on these home videos that the dog was simply enjoying itself.

This is a difficult problem to deal with or correct, because you aren't there to discipline the dog when its behavior warrants it. In fact, by the time you get home the demolition derby is over and your dog is ready to be a wonderful, pleasant, loving pet. And by then, a correction would be meaningless. In fact, don't waste your time on one—your dog will have no idea what the correction is for.

When you understand the problem is an expression of boredom, you can try to provide the dog with things to keep it occupied. Appropriate items to chew and play with will help divert attention from the inappropriate ones. Pick up the rawhide and other toys while you are home, so the dog doesn't get used to having them. That way, they'll seem more special when the dog is alone. When you leave, put a few out—hopefully finding ones the dog enjoys. We always like the toys that allow you to hide a treat inside them. Current ones are the Buster Cube or the Kong rubber toys. Some dogs will spend long hours trying to get the food inside.

Try to put the dog in a dog-proof environment where it will not be tempted by so many forbidden things. What dogs may call toys, you may refer to as a new pair of shoes. It often helps to leave a radio or television on. Some canine behaviorists say it's better to set the radio for stations that play classical or predominately instrumental music. We have no idea if this makes a significant difference.

It helps if you can have a friend or relative drop by occasionally and take the dog out for a walk. In some cases you may want to simply drop your dog off someplace where it can be with people throughout the day. There are doggy day care centers, and they should be listed in your local Yellow Pages.

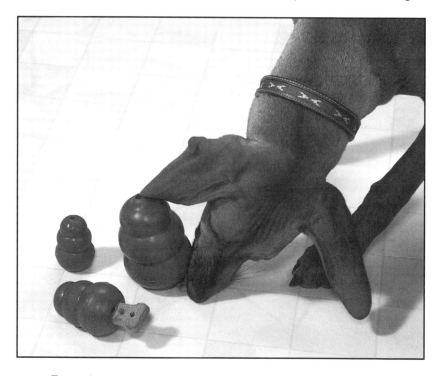

Toys with treats inside, such as these Kongs, will help keep your dog busy while you're away.

In really serious cases where nothing else seems to work, a destructive dog may need to be in a crate or pen when left alone. Put a toy or a large rawhide bone in with it, so the dog will have something to do.

Some dogs continue this behavior even in their crate. They bark incessantly and often drool to the point of soaking themselves and the crate. These dogs are not bored, and probably do suffer from what could be a true anxiety condition. When the problem is this severe and the owners have no other option, we will prescribe tranquilizers. We do not want or expect these dogs to remain on these medications for long periods of time. We usually start out at an average dose that we know will calm the dog, and then over a few weeks we slowly decrease the dose. Often this solves the problem and the dogs adjust to being alone.

Fear Biting

Dogs with this problem are fearful of strange situations or people. When they are afraid, their natural reaction is to expose their teeth, growl and bite. These dogs are usually timid in nature, and the problem may have developed because of poor socialization as a pup, from a single traumatic event, as the result of prolonged abuse or as an inherited trait. If you own a puppy that is starting to exhibit fear aggression, you must make every attempt at an early age to carefully expose the dog to a wide range of situations and people under calm and controlled conditions. This behavioral problem is much easier to prevent than it is to cure.

Once you realize you have a true fear biter, you must make some difficult decisions. First, you must realize that having such a dog is a great legal liability. Admitting that you have a problem dog further exposes you to potential lawsuits. There are treatments for these dogs, including medications and special training programs, but they certainly are not guaranteed. We recommend that owners with this kind of problem dog work with a professional trainer or behaviorist.

Under the guidance of experienced behaviorists, a fearful dog usually goes through a four- to six-month program. The first phase is a form of behavior modification. The dog is made to sit or lie quietly around individuals it trusts. During these exercises, these individuals carry on mock conversations with nonexistent people. This can concern a fear biter, because it suggests that an unknown person is near. To calm the dog, treats are given.

The dog is then encouraged to stay in this position while its human friends move out of sight but remain within earshot. The pretend conversations are continued. The dog is again encouraged to remain calm with additional treats. Over a period of time, the dog is placed in new environments and situations and the same exercise is repeated. The purpose of this therapy is to accustom the dog to the possibility that new or strange people are right around the corner. With patience and repeated sessions, there is usually some improvement.

After the dog has shown that it can tolerate these actions without any anxiety, it is slowly introduced to situations that in the past caused its aggression. Treats are constantly used to calm or relax the dog. Anti-anxiety medications are sometimes used during the later stages of therapy.

This is a long process involving hundreds of hours over a four- to six-month period. We have only briefly outlined the process here. To finally correct the problem and eliminate the behavior requires patience and a tremendous commitment. And there is no guarantee that these efforts will be successful.

We are sure that this level of professional treatment is out of the reach of many dog owners. However, a professional dog trainer may be able to help your dog, or teach you how to train your dog, to overcome this problem in less than six months. If you choose to work with a trainer, make sure they have experience working with fear biters.

You can also try to correct a fear biter on your own. You must use common sense and be very patient. These dogs need to overcome both their fear and their aggression, and this is not easy. You must slowly introduce these dogs to various individuals and new situations in a controlled manner. You must constantly reassure the dog so that it does not feel intimidated. Treats and rewards are very useful.

One last point of ours may seem offensive, but we must be honest. Every day in America thousands of healthy, loving dogs without this problem are euthanized in veterinary clinics and dog shelters. If you must have a dog, think about the child who could be severely injured by the dog you now own. Maybe the dog you have is a liability to you and all around you. Possibly, it would be better to exchange your problem dog for one who will never have a chance to live in a loving home or even be alive next week.

Aggressive Dogs

Some male dogs that display aggression will behave a lot better after they've been neutered. Their behavior is believed to be caused, to some degree, by the male hormone testosterone, which is produced in the testicles. When these structures are removed, it will take several months for the residual levels of testosterone to be eliminated from the body. After that, you may see some improvement—you also may not.

Aggression is typically a failure of socialization and discipline. It is easier to prevent aggressive behavior than it is to correct it. Your best bet is to work with a professional trainer, who will show you how to make yourself top dog in your dog's pack. Please also read the last paragraph under fear biters. We offer it as food for thought. A normal dog should never bite anyone out of aggression—not even once. Not even under extraordinary conditions.

Unwanted Barking

We can divide unwanted barking into two parts: barking when you are home, and when you're not. It is never easy to cure either of these problems. When you are with the dog, try to use our typical training technique: contact with the dog. For problems that occur in your absence, we suggest some of the newer technology.

To eliminate excessive barking in your presence you need to recognize what stimulates this activity. It might occur when the dog is crated or when it sees people outside. Maybe there is someone at the door, or the dog is responding to the sounds of cars or a siren. To start with, never encourage a dog of any age to bark unless it has a specific purpose. What starts out as a game often becomes unwanted and uncontrollable behavior.

Try to learn when the dog will bark and anticipate its actions. Move toward the dog but stay out of its sight. As it starts to bark, say "no, don't bark!" in a low but stern voice. At the same time, wrap your hand around its mouth with your thumb over the nose and fingers below the lower jaw. Hold its mouth shut for four or five seconds. The dog won't like this. It may whine, but remain firm, calm and in control. And remember, the idea is to correct the dog, not to hurt it.

As we said, tackling this problem is never easy. You are trying to override what may have become a programmed behavior for your dog. It automatically reacts whenever the same stimuli are there, and it will take time to change this automatic reaction.

For excessive barking when you're not home, we rely on the newer anti-bark collars. These work by delivering a negative experience when the dog barks—either a noise that is supposed to distract the dog, a spray of citronella or a mild electrical shock. We have had mixed results, at best, with the collars that use sound, but have had good results with the other two.

Citronella is harmless in this form, and is sprayed in front of the dog's face to distract it from barking. The electronic collars give a very low-level electric shock if they are used correctly. It is actually less than you feel when you walk across a carpet wearing socks and then touch a light switch. Nevertheless, it is uncomfortable and gets the dog's attention. The vibrations produced in the dog's throat as it barks activate both of these collars. They are powered by small batteries and can be left on the dog while you are away.

An anti-bark collar can be a useful tool.

Many people misunderstand how these collars are used. Used correctly, they are excellent tools and have saved the lives of thousands of dogs that would have otherwise been destroyed due to excessive barking in urban communities. Remember, in many areas laws require you to prevent your dog from barking.

It's important to understand that excessive barking when you're not home is often caused by sheer boredom. Try to leave the dog toys to play with and things to do. And make sure it gets plenty of attention and exercise when you are home.

Carsickness

Dogs usually do not have true motion sickness the way we do. Most problems they suffer in a car are simple anxiety. For some reason they have developed a true fear of car rides. They shake, drool and may even vomit or urinate. Many of these dogs will go through this entire spectrum before the car is even started. Just being in the car sets them off. Dogs can develop this reaction any time during their life, but most do before they reach two years of age. Exposing young puppies to frequent short car rides often prevents this problem from developing.

Once a problem has developed, you can overcome it with training or medication. Training involves reintroducing the dog to cars slowly over one or two months. We want the dog to be comfortable in cars, so we need to make being in a car a good experience. For this we will start by using treats. During the first stage of training, do nothing more than go out in the driveway, put the dog in the car and give it a treat. Don't even close the door. Try this

Crating a dog in a car can help make it feel safe and keep it calm.

once a day for several days. Don't give the dog a treat at any other time of the day during this training. Getting in the car means a treat.

In the next stage, get in the car with the dog, shut the door, give it a treat and then immediately get out. You can do this for a week or so.

Don't move on to the next step until the dog has become totally comfortable at each stage of this training. When your dog is ready for the next step, start the car while the dog is eating the treat, and then shut it off after just a few seconds and get out of the car. In the next stage, back the car up a few feet, turn it off and get out.

Gradually make these trips longer, until you are driving around the block. Slowly expose the dog to longer rides in areas with more and more noises and distractions. And every step of the way, every time the dog gets in the car, it gets a treat.

This may seem like a lot of time to spend for a simple problem, but it really isn't. You'll spend less time reconditioning your dog to car rides than it may take you to teach the "come" command.

For dogs that get sick during car rides, we can also use nonprescription sedatives and prescription tranquilizers. Neither of these is going to knock the dog out. They just take the edge off the dog's nervousness and calm it down. Nonprescription sedatives are sold under the trade names Serene-um or Pet Calm, while the prescription products often contain acepromazine as the active ingredient. Any of these usually take about an hour to work, and last for four to eight hours. Always experiment with these medications before an actual trip, so you will have an idea of their effectiveness on your dog and when they may need to be administered again.

MEDICAL CHOICES YOU MUST MAKE

Your dog is maturing mentally and physically. At less than 12 months of age, most dogs are able to breed. Males under six months of age have been known to successfully mate with females. Most female dogs have their first heat cycle between seven and nine months of age, and this is almost always fertile. Your dog, whether it's a male or female, is ready to breed! You need to decide whether or not you want to breed your dog, and what you need to do in either case.

There are lots of myths about heat cycles and breeding in dogs. Some say that it is necessary for a female to either have one litter or to at least be allowed to go through a heat cycle before spaying. These theories suggest that it helps the dog to develop correctly. Without it she may not reach normal size or mentally mature. According to every veterinary text written today, none of this is true. In fact, in most cases leaving a dog intact actually increases the incidence of certain medical problems.

Today, we know that female dogs that have gone through heat cycles have a higher incidence of breast cancer. It is believed that the hormone estrogen, which is produced in high levels during heat cycles and pregnancies, stimulates breast cancer cell formation in dogs. Bitches that never cycled have a much lower chance of developing this life-threatening disease.

The idea of a young female dog (under 24 months of age) having a litter of puppies also goes against everything we know today. Before this age, it is difficult for us to predict very much about the dog in question. We have little idea of how her abilities, temperament or potential for medical problems will develop. In Chapter 3 we went over some of these points, but they are worth revisiting.

Most veterinarians and breeders want dogs that are to be used for breeding to be examined and shown to be free of any serious medical conditions. An often-used example is hip dysplasia. We cannot certify dogs free of this condition until they are past their second birthday. Individuals that use dogs for specific tasks, such as hunting or guard work, want to be sure the dogs they are breeding are able to carry out these activities. Remember, you are breeding this dog to produce more dogs for the same purpose. If the female in question can't do the tasks required of her breed, why produce more dogs with these substandard abilities? And every litter of puppies contributes to the worldwide problem of pet overpopulation.

If a female dog does not *need* to cycle or have a litter of puppies, what should we do? The questions you really face are do you ever want to breed your dog, and are there any advantages or disadvantages in doing so? There are people that would prefer we stopped all breeding of dogs. This would, of course, eventually mean there would be no pet dogs for anyone, and this is their ultimate goal. We assume if you're reading this book, that idea is neither logical nor acceptable. Most of us look forward to living with dogs throughout our lives, and therefore some have to be bred. Today, you have every legal right to breed your dog, and you may choose do it for a wide range of reasons.

However, we have reached a point in America where we need to be very selective about which dogs are bred. Unless you can honestly say your dog is special and will add significantly to the overall quality of its breed, don't breed it! There are thousands of dogs in every city that are euthanized only because they cannot find a home. There are others that have serious medical problems that are genetically transmitted from generation to generation. Still others have behavioral problems that make them ill suited to fit into our society. We have too many dogs today, and many of these have problems that are the product of poorly planned breedings. Leave breeding to the people who are knowledgeable about dogs and their problems, and who try with every litter to improve the overall quality of their breed.

If you decide not to breed your dog, male or female, what should you do? Should it be spayed (if it's a female) or neutered (if it's a male)? Regardless of how simple a procedure is, surgery always carries some risk. There is also the expense. Is there a way to weigh all the possible advantages and disadvantages of these sterilization procedures?

Let's look at female dogs first. A spay is an ovariohysterectomy—complete removal of the ovaries, oviducts, uterus and associated blood vessels. It is usually recommended that this be done when the dog is five to eight months of age, which is typically before the first heat cycle. We spay our own pet dogs at six months of age. For the surgery, we use general anesthesia. The dogs feel little discomfort, and usually go home the same or the following day. Humane shelters often spay or neuter their dogs at five months old to make sure the procedure is done. We have no problem with this.

The ovaries are where some female hormones, including estrogen, are produced, and removing them has some significant effects on the dog. A spay done before the dog's first heat just about eliminates the possibility of developing breast cancer. This is important, because this is the most common malignant tumor found in female dogs. Additionally, spaying eliminates future heat cycles and the mess and problems associated with them. There are also numerous diseases that may arise in the uterus and ovaries. These can be forms of cancer or life-threatening infections. Some are fairly common. The surgery eliminates all of them—forever. In a practice such as ours, we can easily say female dogs that are spayed early in life live longer, with fewer problems and at less expense to their owners than those left intact.

The only problem we see in spayed dogs is a slight increase in urinary incontinence. All older female dogs can develop this condition, in which they are unable to control their urine. While they are sleeping or relaxing, a small amount of urine may trickle from their bladder, soiling themselves or their beds. Fortunately, this can be easily controlled with medications. It is thought the reason spayed females have a higher incidence of incontinence is that they have lost estrogen, which adds strength to the muscular sphincter at the opening of the bladder. This topic is discussed in more detail in Chapter 12.

For a male dog, neutering means castration—removal of the testicles. This is usually done when the dogs are between five and 12 months. As with the females, we neuter our male dogs when they are six months of age. And, as with females, there are several benefits to the surgery.

There are several different forms of cancer that can arise within the testicles, and neutering eliminates the possibility of these occurring. The testicles are where the male hormone testosterone is produced. This hormone affects the behavior of male dogs. Male dogs that are not neutered are attracted to females in heat via airborne chemicals called pheromones. Dogs can travel miles searching out these potential mates. Dogs that are neutered at an early age are no longer attracted by pheromones and are less likely to stray from their homes. Neutered dogs are also usually less aggressive toward other dogs and toward people. This is thought to be the result of the loss of testosterone.

Testosterone also has effects on other parts of the dog's body. The prostate gland is dependent on this hormone. If the dog is neutered, the prostate shrinks to a fraction of its normal size. This is important, because more than 70 percent of unneutered dogs over the age of eight years have enlarged, infected or cancerous prostate glands. These are exceptionally painful conditions. Neutered dogs rarely, if ever, have these problems.

Testosterone also affects the muscles and glands found directly below the tail. Over time, this hormone causes these muscles to weaken, and hernias may develop. The perianal gland found in this same area can become cancerous due to the lifelong stimulation of testosterone on the tissue. Neutering the dog greatly reduces the incidence of both of these conditions.

Neutering male dogs is sometimes credited with things it will not do. Some people believe male dogs will not lift their rear legs to urinate if they are neutered. This is not true. A neutered male may be less interested in marking his territory, but he will still usually lift his leg. Neither will neutering alter the chemical makeup of the urine so that it does not kill or burn grass. The high levels of nitrogen found in urine do kill plants, and neutering does not change this. Neutering will not make the aggressive biter a nice house pet. Neither will it affect the hunting or performance abilities of a dog.

There are no known medical or behavioral disadvantages of neutering male dogs. Some may have a potential to gain weight, but this can be controlled by diet and exercise.

Now, we hope you can understand why veterinarians recommend that male and female dogs that are not going to be used for breeding be spayed or neutered. They will typically have fewer behavioral problems and live longer, healthier lives with less expense to their owners.

The Most Common Medical Problems of Adolescents

Many of the medical problems found in this age group are related to the dog's rapid growth. This growth causes significant changes and stresses on various parts of the body. Some of these problems are inherited, and some are congenital problems (abnormalities the dog is born with that may not be caused by its genetic makeup) that manifest themselves as the dog gets bigger. Some simply are more common in this age group because they are affected by the natural physical development or behavior of the dog.

There are several common abnormalities affecting the eyes and their surrounding structures. Two extremely common ones are defects in the size and shape of the eyelids. Any of these eye problems found in dogs six months to two years of age may require surgical correction.

Ectropion

This is a condition in which the lower eyelid turns out and sags downward, exposing the underlying pink tissue called the conjunctiva. Basically, the lower lid is too large for the size of the dog. The condition usually affects both eyes.

Ectropion may cause little problem in some dogs, but the open pocket formed by the lid often collects dust and debris, leading to repeated irritations, often with bacterial infections. Dogs with this condition will often tear excessively, with this moisture spilling out onto the hair below the lid.

When infections arise, or the tissues surrounding the eye are irritated, they are treated with anti-inflammatory salves that contain antibiotics. If the degree of ectropion is severe or if there are repeated infections, it can be corrected by surgically removing a small wedge of tissue from the eyelid. This decreases its size and brings the lid into normal contact with the eye.

Everyone has seen dogs with mild ectropion. It is commonly seen on the Saint Bernard, Basset Hound, American Cocker Spaniel, Bloodhound and the various Mastiff breeds. It can also be found on mixed breeds. Dogs with ectropion should not be used for breeding.

Ectropion affecting the lower eyelid.

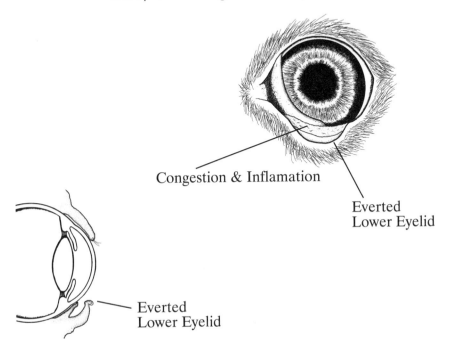

Congestion & Inflamation

Everted
Lower Eyelid

Everted
Lower Eyelid

Entropion

Entropion is basically the opposite of ectropion. In this condition, the outer surface of the eyelid, usually the lower lid, turns inward and rests against the eyeball. This is a more serious problem, because the outer surface of the eyelid is covered with hair, which is very irritating where it comes in contact with the eyeball. Irritation can lead to ulceration and severe damage to the cornea (the clear surface of the eye). The eyes of dogs with entropion usually tear excessively, and many animals will paw at the eye in an attempt to relieve the irritation. One or both eyes may be affected.

Many dogs tolerate ectropion, but this is not the case with entropion. Left uncorrected, the cornea will be seriously damaged. Surgery is the only long-term treatment for entropion. Surgery is not difficult and involves either increasing the length of the eyelid or eliminating its inverted posture. Either technique works very well. If the condition is diagnosed before the dog's

Entropion affecting the lower eyelid.

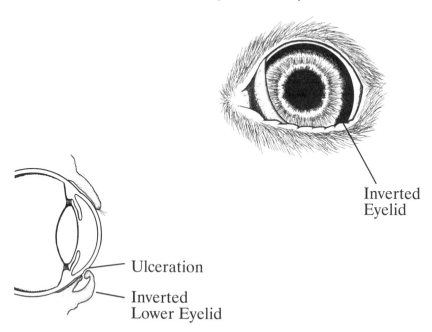

Inverted
Eyelid

Ulceration

Inverted
Lower Eyelid

head has grown to its full size, it is sometimes difficult to determine how much surgical correction is needed. While the dog continues to grow, temporary relief may be given with medication or a temporary surgery called eyelid tacking.

Entropion is found in a wide range of breeds. Dogs with this condition should not be used for breeding.

Cherry Eye

This term is often used to describe two different conditions of the third eyelid (also called the nictitating membrane), which is the pink flap of tissue in the inside corner of the eye. For veterinarians, the term *cherry eye* usually refers to a prolapse of the third eyelid (prolapse is when an organ falls or slips out of place). But many breeders call both a prolapse and an eversion (turning out) of the third eyelid cherry eye. In either case, the condition appears as a small, pink ball lying against the inside corner of the eye.

Most dogs with cherry eye show no outward signs of irritation. But long term, it can damage the eye and interfere with the normal drainage of tears. Either form of cherry eye can be corrected by a simple surgical procedure.

Everted cherry eye.

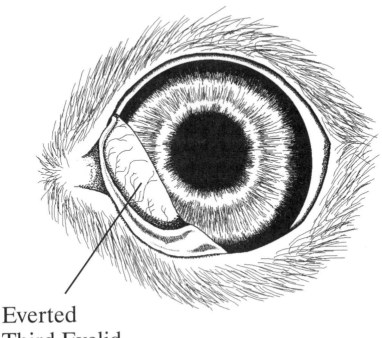

Everted
Third Eyelid

Hip Dysplasia

There are several conditions that affect the skeleton and its development in adolescent dogs. As the dog gets bigger, these conditions become more apparent and affected dogs limp or show pain, or both.

Hip dysplasia is a very, very common degenerative condition affecting the hip joints. Veterinarians in busy practices deal with the condition almost daily. The hip joint is made up of the femur (the long upper bone of the rear leg) and the pelvic bone. A ball-and-socket joint is formed where the head of the femur (the ball) fits into the acetabulum (the socket) in the pelvis. In normal dogs, the ball is smooth and round, and fits tightly into the socket.

In dysplastic dogs, the bones forming the joint do not fit together tightly. Instead, a small space separates the two bones. This is called joint laxity, and is believed to allow excessive movement between the bones. Sometimes surfaces rub against each other that are not designed for this kind of contact. Over time this stimulates abnormal bone formation, and the ball-and-socket

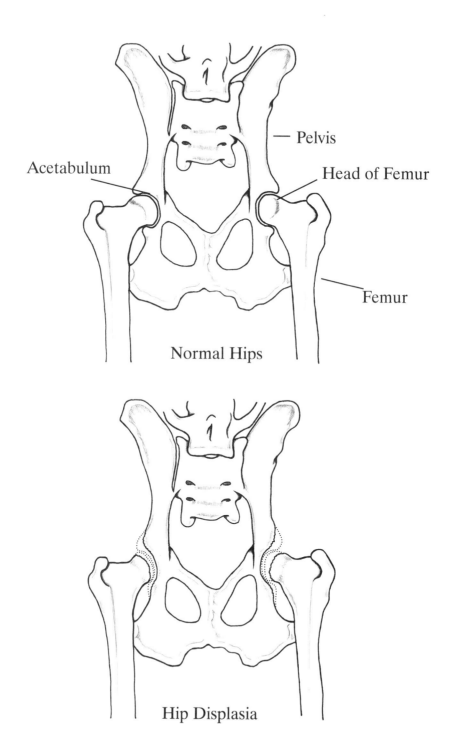

Pelvis

Acetabulum

Head of Femur

Femur

Normal Hips

Hip Displasia

part of the joint are remodeled. This abnormal bone formation typically progresses into severe, painful arthritis.

Hip dysplasia is a genetically transmitted disease affecting most breeds of dogs, although it is more common in the larger breeds. It is also found in mixed breed dogs. Both hips are usually affected. Young dogs usually do not show any outward signs of the disease until they are five to 10 months of age. The problem will first be noticed as difficulty or pain when trying to get up after lying down. Mildly dysplastic dogs may also exercise vigorously and show no clinical signs until the following day.

Without treatment, most of these dogs reduce their activities on their own, due to the pain and discomfort. This leads to muscle atrophy and loss of strength in the hind legs. As the dog ages, this becomes a vicious circle: The less it exercises, the weaker it becomes; and the weaker it becomes, the less it is able to do. In the final stages of hip dysplasia, some dogs are unable to rise or move about without assistance and are euthanized for humane reasons. Regular exercise helps prevent this loss of strength, but the pain must be controlled or the dog won't be able to exercise.

A small portion of dogs with hip dysplasia, even though their lesions are severe, never show any outward signs of the disease at any time in their lives. It is believed these dogs somehow alter their posture or gait to minimize the pain associated with using their rear legs.

Diagnosis is made through physical exam and X-rays. On palpation, your veterinarian may note a laxity in the hip joint. In some cases there's an abnormal click as the ball and socket come together. The best way to make a definitive diagnosis is with X-rays. This can be done as early as eight weeks of age with some of the newer techniques, such as the PennHip method developed at the University of Pennsylvania. In most cases, however, significant and obvious lesions from the disease are not seen on the X-ray films until the dog reaches six to nine weeks of age.

Hip dysplasia can be treated either surgically or with various medications that attempt to control pain and slow the progression of the disease. Surgery does not cure or eliminate the disease, but there are techniques that remove the arthritic surfaces completely. None of surgeries are inexpensive and the medications must be given for the rest of the dog's life. It is important that dysplastic dogs, and all dogs suffering from arthritis, not be allowed to gain any excess weight, as this exacerbates all the existing problems.

Medications include a wide range of products that either attempt to alter the arthritic surfaces or manage the dog's pain. Some of the newer treatments include nutritional products such as glucosamine, chondroitin sulfate, vitamin C and related compounds. While the mechanism of action of these compounds is not completely understood, there can be little question that they improve mobility and reduce pain for many dogs. These same products are used successfully in human medicine. They are sold under numerous trade names, including Joint Care, Gluco-C and Gylco-Flex. These nutritional supplements can be used for the life of the dog and are frequently recommended by veterinarians.

Pain medications are also frequently used, especially in the period before surgery. The most commonly used products include buffered aspirin, glucocorticoids (steroids) and ibuprofen compounds formulated especially for dogs. With any of these medicines, it must be understood that the dog will need to stay on them consistently for the rest of its life, unless surgery is done. In some cases they may even be continued after surgery.

Surgical corrections are usually aimed at either eliminating the bony components of the joint or decreasing the force of interaction between the two bones. It is not uncommon to totally replace dysplastic hips with artificial ones. This is an excellent procedure, but is obviously very expensive.

Many other dogs have the ball of the ball-and-socket-joint surgically removed, with nothing put back in its place! It seems impossible that we would take out half of this supporting structure and then send the dog off to fend for itself. But it works, and done correctly, it usually works very well. The muscles in the area strengthen and firmly hold the rear leg in place. This shouldn't surprise us, as the bones of the dog's front legs do not attach to the rest of the skeleton, except by muscles. In addition, dogs support 65 percent of their weight on their front legs and only 35 percent on their rear legs.

There are other excellent procedures somewhere in between these two. A triple pelvic osteotomy leaves both portions of the ball-and-socket joint within the dog, but moves the socket to a different position. This attempts to allow the two bones of the joint to remain closer together, hopefully preventing degenerative arthritic changes.

All these surgeries are done directly on the bones of the hip joint. Another procedure, pectinomyotomy, cuts a small muscle that runs between the hip joint and the lower femur. It is thought that this procedure decreases the pressure between the two arthritic bones and thereby relieves much of the dog's pain.

Obviously, there are new medications and surgical procedures being developed all the time. Hopefully, by the time you read this a more economical and curative treatment will be available for hip dysplasia.

Dogs with hip dysplasia should still have daily exercise to prevent muscle atrophy, but keep it moderate. This maintains their strength, so they are better able to deal with the disease in their later years.

Still, it would much better if we didn't have to deal with the problem. Hip dysplasia *can* be eliminated. While many variables affect its incidence, genetic factors seem to be the main cause. Dogs should never be bred until they are 24 months of age and certified free of this disease by a more traditional x-ray examination. While some carrier dogs will still slip through the screening, if every dog were properly screened we would be able to eliminate or greatly reduce the incidence of hip dysplasia over just a few generations of dogs.

While some people believe feeding various nutritional supplements or maintaining young puppies on different ground surfaces may prevent hip dysplasia, there is no evidence to substantiate this. Hip dysplasia is determined genetically, and only careful breeding can prevent it.

Osteochondritis Dissecans

This condition, known as OCD, affects several joints within the dog's body. In any joint, two bones come together and movement is allowed between them. Where the two bones meet, an exceptionally smooth area of cartilage covers their surfaces. This acts as a cushion and protects the underlying bones. If anything disrupts or disfigures this cartilage, movement in the joint is painful. In a dog with OCD, this cartilage becomes damaged or grows abnormally. Instead of being firmly attached to the bone it covers, it separates or cracks, causing great pain. In some cases, small pieces of cartilage break off and float free in the joint. They do not die, but rather continue to grow and increase in size. These are known as *joint mice*. The cause of this disease is unknown, and may be brought on by a wide range of nutritional and/or genetic factors.

In dogs, OCD lesions are most commonly found in the shoulder. This is the joint formed between the humerus (the long bone of the upper front leg) and the scapula (the shoulder blade). The disease is typically found in large, rapidly growing dogs between the ages of six and 12 months. It is five times more common in male dogs than in females, although we don't know why.

Once there is a lesion, affected dogs will limp on the affected front leg. In severe cases they will carry it, not letting it touch the ground. Untreated, this joint may become arthritic and will never be able to be used correctly.

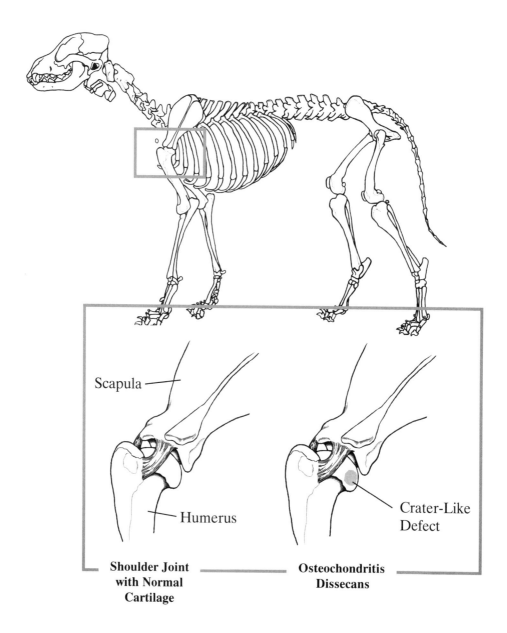

Scapula

Humerus

Crater-Like
Defect

**Shoulder Joint
with Normal
Cartilage**

**Osteochondritis
Dissecans**

With early diagnosis, treatment usually consists of nothing more than restricted activity. Dogs with an OCD lesion can be walked briefly on a leash, but are definitely not allowed to run and play, especially with children and other dogs. Crate rest will typically be required for at least four to six weeks. In some severe cases we have restricted these dogs for 12 weeks, to ensure the lesion healed.

Some dogs do not respond to rest, and surgery is therefore indicated. This is a fairly simple procedure. The joint is opened and the defective cartilage and/or joint mice are removed. The dog is rested for two more weeks following surgery as a new layer of cartilage grows back over the bone. It is then slowly brought back to full activity level over an additional two weeks. Recovery after surgery is almost always complete.

Panosteitis

Panosteitis is an inflammation of the long leg bones. It is most common in German Shepherds, but occurs in most large breeds, more often in male dogs. The condition comes on spontaneously without any known cause, and usually disappears just as mysteriously.

Typically, owners see their dog starting to limp between six and 12 months of age. The dog may limp on one leg for a while and then switch to a different one. Many of these dogs will have fevers off and on, but certainly not consistently. When the fever is present, the dog may act lethargic and not eat well. Affected dogs often show pain if pressure is applied over the middle sections of the long leg bones. The signs usually go on for two to five months, and then disappear. There are no known long-term or residual problems associated with this disease.

Panosteitis can only be definitively diagnosed through x-rays. The center sections of the affected bones have an abnormal, mottled appearance. Usually no medical treatment is required unless the dog is in significant pain. If it is, the dog is given buffered aspirin. Occasionally, steroids such as prednisone or prednisolone are also used.

Gastrointestinal Foreign Bodies

A dog can swallow something dangerous at any time in its life, but this is more common during adolescence because it is chewing more as its adult teeth come in. All dogs of all ages chew on things, but dogs between six and 24 months of age are known to swallow a large range of things that may cause significant problems. Some items are vomited back up, some move on through the intestinal tract and are passed with the stool, and some get stuck somewhere in the digestive system and have to be surgically removed. Obviously, the only items that pose problems are the ones that require surgery.

In our practice, a partial list of items we've surgically removed from dogs include meat bones, wedding rings, engagement rings, earrings, paper clips, car keys, house keys, money (bills and change), knives, arrow heads, rocks, ping pong balls, golf balls, tennis balls, sponges, peach pits, sticks, nails, safety pins, string, netting from a roast, meat wrappers, spoons, fish hooks, fishing lures, shotgun shells, sea shells, dog collars and the remnants of a six-pack of beer—cans, cardboard and all. We're sure we've forgotten a few. While we are often asked, it may interest you to know that we have never removed a piece of rawhide from a dog, or had reason to.

When these items become lodged in the gastrointestinal tract they can cause many different problems, depending on where they stop and what, if anything, they poke through. It will also make a difference if they cause a complete obstruction, or only a partial one.

When dogs eat some indigestible item that either lodges someplace or moves very slowly through their system, a consistent group of signs will be noted, making it easier to deduce the problem. The dog will vomit and have diarrhea, and usually stops eating. It may still try to drink, but some if not all of this will be regurgitated. All of these actions are attempts to rid itself of this unwanted, unneeded item. There usually is no fever, unless the foreign body has punctured the stomach or intestine. If the dog is unsuccessful in expelling the foreign body, it usually dies.

Every veterinarian has at one time or another diagnosed liver or kidney failure in a dog when the actual problem was an intestinal obstruction. The dog stopped eating and drinking and the liver and kidney systems shut down due to dehydration. When blood work is done, the results indicate liver or kidney failure. The actual diagnosis is only found through exploratory surgery or a post-mortem exam. Whether you think your dog has eaten something or not, if it's sick enough that it will no longer eat or drink, a veterinarian should see it immediately. An x-ray may be the quickest way to check if there is a foreign body involved.

Car Accidents

Young dogs that have not yet learned the safe boundaries of their home range or do not respond to verbal commands have a greater chance of getting hit by a car than those of any other age group. The records of our clinic prove it. Getting hit by a car is so common that it actually has an abbreviation in veterinary literature—HBC. During the summer it is our most common after-hours emergency.

The idea of a dog getting hit by a 4,000- or 5,000-pound mass of steel seems like a no-win situation for the dog. One would assume few live through the experience. After all, everyone has seen the bodies on the highway of dogs that lost this battle.

This may surprise you, but most dogs that are hit by a car do not even break a bone. In saying this, we are not restricting ourselves to the ones that get tapped while the car is still in the driveway. No, we are including the dogs that come into clinics with tire marks going right over their bodies. Dogs are amazingly tough animals! They never cease to amaze us.

One day, while traveling an interstate highway through the Midwest, one of us saw a dog run onto the highway and get hit by a truck. The impact sent it careening into the next lane, where it rolled and bounced under a car. The car itself bounced up as its tire went over the dog. As the dog cleared the rear bumper, it was thrown into a ditch, where it got to its feet and set off without a limp for the nearest farmhouse. In disbelief we took an off-ramp that was nearby and swung back to the house. We had a quick talk with the farmer, who allowed us to go to the garage where the dog was lying on its bed. We examined it; there were cuts and bruises, but the dog was hardly at death's door. There were no broken bones and the dog wasn't even in shock. The farmer chose not to take the dog to be checked by a veterinarian (a course of action we *do not* recommend). Two weeks later we drove to the farm and saw the dog standing under a tree staring at the highway.

If your dog is hit by a car, no matter how good or bad things look, don't panic, just get the dog to a veterinary clinic immediately. While it may look fine, there could be internal injuries. If the dog cannot move, slide its body onto a board or blanket. If it is in pain and is apt to bite, wrap several thick blankets around the body and head to make it safer to pick up and transport.

When you arrive at the hospital, if the dog appears to need it the staff will administer intravenous fluids and special medicines to prevent shock. If there is a potential for infection, antibiotics may also be used. It may surprise you, but unless something else is indicated, that may be all they do for the next hour or so. They want to stabilize the dog. The pain of moving it around for x-rays may push the dog into shock. No anesthetic procedure is recommended unless there is a life-or-death reason to do it. Remember, no matter how bad things look, there is about a 98 percent chance your dog will be fine and home in a week. In the past 20 years, of the dogs that got to our clinic alive, less than 2 percent lost their lives.

The same is true for any instance of severe trauma to your dog. Don't panic—it always looks much worse than it is. A little blood looks like a lot of blood. Cuts heal from side to side and not end to end (in other words, a 12-inch gash heals as fast as a one-inch cut does). The bones in most dogs heal quickly. Stay calm and get the dog to your veterinarian as quickly and as safely as you can. Give the dog a chance to survive and it probably will.

Congenital Defects

There are numerous conditions that fall into this category. Individually, each is rare. However, grouped together they are not that uncommon. They are also among the sadder conditions that we must deal with. As dogs reach their adult size and weight at six to 16 months of age, congenital defects of the major organ systems become apparent. Dogs are sometimes born with defective heart, liver or kidney systems. The dogs often do fine until they reach their full size or weight. With the added workload of increased size, the system starts to fail. Suddenly, after the entire family has become deeply attached to the dog, they are presented with the fact that its life is limited to the next few weeks or months.

At this point, and understandably so, owners often put themselves and their veterinarian in impossible situations. They cannot believe what is happening and are not willing to accept the diagnosis. They often demand what cannot be done. They may hold the veterinarian responsible for the diagnosis or for being unable to save their young dog.

Emotions can run wild at a time like this, and sometimes it helps everyone concerned to get a second opinion from a different veterinarian associated with a different clinic. Once dogs with congenital defects start showing signs of illness, their condition should be easy to diagnose. Hearing the same diagnosis from a second source may not make it more acceptable, but at least it makes things understandable. And if the first veterinarian was wrong in their diagnosis, thank goodness you sought out a second opinion!

SUMMING UP

You and your dog have made it through puppyhood, and now it's on to the challenges of adolescence. Continue your training sessions with your dog. It is too early to stop training, even though your dog seems to understand most of the commands. Dogs will test you during their adolescence, more than in any other stage of their lives. Remaining consistent with the training will prevent bad habits from forming. If you run into serious problems or if you find training just isn't for you, enroll yourself and your dog in obedience or training classes, or get a professional trainer to help you.

Be aware of the common medical problems that occur during this period. We've outlined the ones you are most likely to encounter. Learn to recognize some of their signs and seek veterinary assistance if you suspect a problem. Remember, even with emergencies, most are treatable conditions and you and your dog will make it through them.

Chapter 10

STARTING OUT WITH AN ADULT DOG

When people bring a puppy into their lives, they usually plan to acquire it. They are looking for something they want, something that fulfills their needs. Hopefully, when they find the dog they want, it satisfies their desires—it's the right breed, the right temperament, the right coat and the perfect size. They immediately see it as something that they love. These people usually go on to be excellent owners because they have put considerable thought into exactly what dog they want.

When people bring an adult dog into their lives, they may go through the same selective process as those getting a puppy. They know they want a dog, they just prefer to start with an adult one. They may or may not have a specific breed in mind. They select their new pet from a breeder, a breed rescue group, a humane society or a private individual. They follow the same guidelines outlined in Chapter 3 for where to get a dog. They usually go on to be excellent owners, because they put a lot of thought and effort into getting exactly the dog they want.

A few people aren't looking for a dog, but end up with one anyway. They see a dog that they believe is either abused or neglected, and they decide to adopt it. They had not thought about getting this particular type of dog, or probably any dog at all. We would never recommend this as a way of acquiring a pet. However, in our experience as veterinarians we have worked with many such people who ended up with dogs out of sympathy, and they usually turned out to be excellent and responsible owners. With time their feelings of sympathy are replaced by love for the dog.

Selecting the adult dog that is right for you can be both fun and rewarding.

Whether you found a dog on the street, brought one home from the pound, took in your relative's dog or decided on breed rescue, it is important to understand that beginning with an adult dog is not the same as beginning with a seven-week-old puppy. There are more differences than size. Sometimes an adult dog comes into someone's home and bonds immediately, is housebroken, behaves perfectly and knows all the basic commands. We hope that is your experience, because then you hardly have to change your day-to-day lifestyle. But sometimes it's not that easy.

When a puppy comes into your home, it usually is outgoing and eager to be with you. It may see you as a quick replacement for the security its mother provided. In most cases it has had no bad experiences with people—at worst it has simply had no experiences with people. If you kneel down and clap your hands, it will automatically run to you seeking what we humans would describe as friendship. Children that are five times its size can pick it up or pet it, and the puppy will not be intimidated. It will enjoy the attention and affection and probably lick the youngsters' faces. Puppies seek you out; they want to be with you and all members of your family.

Adult dogs, especially those over 24 months of age, that suddenly find themselves in a new home are sometimes filled with apprehension. Regardless of their personality—be it timid, outgoing or aggressive—they may be withdrawn at first and show little desire to form any bond with the new people. For some of these dogs, this house seems like just another temporary stop in a long sequence of confusing events. They never got used to the last place, and they have no idea where they are now. For others, they have been with abusive humans before, and they are frightened. For yet another group, they were ignored and their personalities developed without any interactions with members of their own or our species. They were isolated. For most of these dogs, the last thing they want is to be grabbed by a child. If they are, they are not likely to lick the child's face. If you kneel down and clap your hands in front of these dogs, instead of running to you, the reaction is more like, "so what?" Or worse, they will cower or retreat in fear.

When you bring an adult dog into your home that shows more reserved or apprehensive behavior, whether you got it from a breeder, a friend or the pound, it needs to be given time and space. Do not go to the dog to praise or pet it. It will be better if you are patient and let the dog come to you. Let it be by itself. In most cases it will find a spot out of the way where it can lie down and watch you and what you are doing. It needs to make its own decisions about you; you cannot force yourself on an adult dog as you would a puppy.

Children need to be cautioned about the new family member. It is natural for youngsters to run over and hug or start petting the dog. With a reserved dog this has to wait, for both the safety of the children and the mental well-being of the dog. We may not know how the animal will react, and the dog may already dislike any human shorter than four and a half feet tall. The dog needs to be the one to make friends with the children, not vice versa. That's true for the adults, too.

Most adult dogs that are new to your home would be intimidated by the impatient play of children.

When the animal first comes into your home, plan on spending as much time as possible with it. You do not want it to feel alone. The noises you make during the normal activities of your day will be better than silence. If you must be away from the home, a radio left on will help a lot. For the first week, don't have any friends over.

For an adult dog that seems more reserved than you would expect, you must use what you know it wants and needs as points of interaction. If a dog is having a hard time coming out of its shell, let food help break down the barrier. Feed it small quantities frequently during the day, and talk to it as the food dish is placed on the floor. Say the same things in the same tone of voice each time, so your words indicate that it's mealtime. Stick with dry foods at regular feedings, but a few treats each day may also help. If the animal is leash trained, go for long walks in isolated areas with few distractions. You probably don't know how the dog reacts to loud sounds or large moving objects, so avoid lots of traffic or places with many children.

Don't rush into a training program. Learn what the animal can and cannot do, and build on that. If it doesn't know the "come" command, that's unfortunate but it has to become your friend, or at least not fear you, before you can put it on a check cord and expect it to come to you. While training may not start for a while, do not let the dog develop any bad habits. You can't let it run uncontrolled through the neighborhood for two or three weeks, and then suddenly expect it to stay home when you want it to.

The Veterinary Examination

Even if the dog looks and acts healthy, it still needs to be checked by your veterinarian. There is always the possibility it has a problem that may not be obvious to you, but that might need some sort of medical care. Sometimes animals are dropped off at an animal shelter with conditions unknown to the employees that are expensive to impossible to correct. You want to know about these before the entire family gets attached to the animal.

Take any information that might have been given to you about the dog's history. This should include any vaccinations, wormings and heartworm preventives given. If the animal is on any medications or has had any significant health-related event in the past, the veterinarian should put this into the dog's records. All of this information will also help the veterinarian determine if the animal is due for any vaccinations or other treatments.

HOUSEBREAKING AN ADULT DOG

Most adult dogs will already be housebroken. Even so, watch your dog very carefully the first few days. It won't know how or may not be willing to indicate to you that it needs to go outside. You need to take the initiative and take it out regularly. Talk to the dog, as we suggested for puppies in Chapter 4. Praise the dog when it urinates or defecates, and immediately take it back inside. Even though it is supposed to be housebroken, if the dog is going to be left alone you should probably place it in a crate at first. It would be better to plan on spending lots of time at home for the first week or so, but this may not always be possible. Try to be gone briefly at first, and then over time slowly extend the length of your absences.

If the dog is not housebroken, you need to treat it just like a puppy and use the same methods outlined in Chapter 4. Typically, housebreaking adults goes rapidly, because adults are much better able to control themselves physically than puppies are. An exception to this is unneutered males that may start lifting their rear leg and marking their territory in their new home. Even if you were to neuter the dog immediately, the testosterone that controls this behavior would remain in the body for months, and marking behavior would continue for most of this time. These dogs will need to be confined with a kennel or crate. When they are out of their crate you need to be with them and watch them carefully at all times. If you actually catch them eliminating in the home, it's all right to scold them. If you do not catch them in the act, it would be wrong to scold or punish them in any way, and the behavior will be even more difficult to eliminate.

GENERAL TRAINING

You will want to teach the same commands to an adult dog that you would to a puppy. It's even more important that your older and larger animal be trained, because it is much more difficult to control simply because of its size. If a 40-pound mixed breed dog jumps on your grandmother, she could be seriously injured. If your small child is walking the new 70-pound Labrador Retriever on a leash and the dog decides to run across the street, the results can be disastrous.

Puppies are easier to train than adult dogs, simply because they are so much more willing to please you and are easier to control. They rush to you when you crouch down. They rarely have had experiences in their past that will make them fight or resist commands.

Just as with the puppy, before you start training the dog has to be accustomed to being walked on a leash. This and all the other commands are the same as we outlined earlier for puppies. Please read both Chapter 6 and Chapter 7. If you are a first-time dog owner starting with an adult dog, it may be better to go to formal obedience classes. There you will be able to work together with an experienced trainer.

SUMMING UP

For whatever reason you start out with an adult dog, just remember how it is different from a puppy. There are many advantages to starting with an adult, but you do have to go a little slower and not expect immediate, unquestioning trust. When your dog does learn to love you, it will be all the sweeter.

Chapter 11

THE ADULT YEARS—BEHAVIOR AND BASIC CARE

Your dog has grown. It's somewhere between two and eight or 10 years old. The point where an adult dog becomes an old dog varies somewhat with the size of the animal. A small breed like a Chihuahua will typically live to 15 or 16, while a giant breed like a Great Dane may be very old at 10. Each dog is different in how it matures and ages. Still, for our discussion of adulthood we are looking at those animals that are through their adolescence but are not yet senior citizens.

For most dog owners this is the age they planned for. When they selected the breed or type of dog they felt was perfect for them, they were judging how it would look and act or what abilities it would develop, based on what they saw in adult dogs. Even though they looked at Lhasa Apso puppies that were cute and impossible not to like, somewhere in their minds they were picturing these animals as adults, standing eight inches at the shoulder and with long, silky coats. If they wanted a Pointer, maybe in their mind's eye they saw the dog rock-solid on point with its tail held straight up. And if it was a dog destined to be a day-to-day companion, they longed for it to get through its puppyhood and relax with them as they read a book or walked slowly down a forest path.

We should enjoy every stage of our dog's life, but their years as an adult will make up the majority of the time they spend with us. That's why we should plan mostly for this period.

157

If you envisioned your dog as a hunting companion, now is the time to enjoy and appreciate its skills.

ONGOING TRAINING

Even if you started training the basic commands, "come," "sit," "stay," "down" and "heel," when your dog was a young puppy, and continued that work through its adolescence, you still need to continue some training. You should be using the commands every day in your day-to-day interactions with the dog, and this will reinforce them, but an occasional re-tuning or touch-up on the points the animal sometimes fails to do correctly is probably necessary from time to time.

Problems often develop with commands the dog has already been taught because people allow their dog to get away with not responding as it should.

The dog picks up on this quickly and develops a relaxed attitude about compliance with what you ask.

A lack of consistency in how the commands are executed can also create problems. Perhaps other people enter the picture and use different terms or never allow the animal to really complete a command. For example, your child may say "come." The dog starts toward the child, but the child gets distracted and moves away and it's either impossible or unnecessary for the dog to complete the action of the command. In their own way, animals are very smart; they learn something from every experience they have. In this example, the dog quickly learns that coming part way or just a bit closer to you is good enough when you say "come." If you want the dog to react consistently to each command, you must be consistent in what you expect. A dog should come all the way to your side every time you call it, and everyone who gives the dog that command must expect the same results.

Training should be an ongoing process.

For dogs that have not been adequately trained so far, don't believe the old adage, "You can't teach an old dog new tricks." You certainly can! Age is not a factor in what an animal can be trained to do. Very old dogs, over 10 years of age, can easily be taught any of the basic commands if you use the same simple methods we outlined earlier in this book. The problem most people encounter with adult or older animals is that they do not start with the basics. As we have said before, you cannot start in the middle of a training program. Collar and leash training comes first, and then build on this using motivation and praise. The dog needs to understand how the system works and what's in it for dogs. If it does things right it will be praised and will enjoy the attention, but just as important, this will be satisfying the animal's natural desire to please you. Dogs have that desire at every age.

Just remember that you can't skip the obvious steps. Teaching a dog to retrieve a thrown ball will go easier if the animal knows "come." After all, once it gets the ball in its mouth, it is supposed to bring it to you. It will help if the animal knows "come" so you can direct it to return to you after it has the ball.

ROUTINE CARE

Many owners give up routine care when their dog becomes an adult. They think the animal is able to take care of itself, and assume that the veterinarian will do whatever else might be necessary. They put down food and water, and take the dog for walks, but that's all they do. Speaking as veterinarians, the more you are involved in the routine care of your pet at home, the less time and money you will need to give us. People who take more than a casual interest in their animals prevent some problems and catch others before they become serious and expensive to cure.

Take the time to give your dog a good once-over at least once a week. We don't expect you to do a complete physical, but simply be observant while you are petting or sitting with your dog. A checklist to go over should include the animal's coat, teeth, ears, eyes, feet and toenails, and look for lumps or bumps anywhere on the skin. Running your hand over these parts is easy and the dog will probably enjoy the attention.

Coat

The coat is right in front of you, and you probably touch it every day. Still, many problems start there and grow into major ordeals because no one was paying attention. When people bring their pets to our clinic it is our responsibility to give the animal a good physical examination. We do it whether they are in for routine vaccinations or to have a potential problem checked. Many times we and the owners are very surprised at what we discover on our routine once-overs. We may find the animal is carrying several hundred fleas, ticks or even maggots within its coat. We all know that these unwanted guests didn't just happen to hop on for a ride a few hours ago.

We recommend that at least once a week, especially in the warmer months, you look at the deeper layers of your pet's coat. You can't look too deeply into the coat of a Rottweiler or a Doberman Pinscher, but you still need to get down with them and, in a good light, examine their coat. With this kind of careful examination, you're much more likely to find the first one or two fleas or ticks (or signs of these) that have moved onto your dog and thus be able to start treatment before the animal becomes totally infested. Other things to look for are areas of the coat that are soiled with stool or urine. Flies often lay their eggs in these areas, and the resulting maggots crawling against and irritating your pet's skin make for one of the most disgusting sights in veterinary medicine. And please don't think this is uncommon, especially in longhaired dogs.

In addition to looking for small crawling critters, look at the hair and skin. Especially during the winter months, these may dry out because of the lower humidity in our homes. The coat may seem to lose its shine or luster and a fine white dander may be seen coming off the skin. This is common and is easily handled—we'll tell you how a bit later. Make sure the animal's coat isn't getting thin or the hair more brittle. Look for patches of hair loss. If you find any patterns of hair loss or obvious skin lesions, have them checked by your veterinarian.

Dog owners often worry about bathing their animals. They are afraid the shampoos will either injure the hair or destroy the natural oils produced by various glands found within the dog's skin. Any dog that is dirty can be bathed, and any dog can be bathed every two to three weeks without harming the coat or skin. In fact, most animals do better if the excess oils, normal debris and dead skin cells and hair are removed regularly. Much of this material is an abundant food supply for the bacteria that are usually found on our skin. By keeping the skin and coat clean, the numbers of these organisms are kept low and the more harmful, disease-causing ones are often prevented from colonizing our pets.

Whether you do it in conjunction with a bath or not, regularly brushing your dog's coat will do wonders for its overall health. It cleans the coat and skin, removes matts before they become a problem, stimulates new hair growth, increases the skin's oil production and provides you with an excellent opportunity to find any six- or eight- legged critters (fleas, ticks, mites or lice) that shouldn't be there. Additionally, most dogs love brushing.

Brushing will do wonders for your dog's coat, and most pets love it.

Ears

One of the more common problems seen in dogs is ear infections, and we will devote some space to these in the next chapter. To prevent them, during your weekly once-overs you need to check both ears. Examine the canals to make sure they are clean. Wax and debris can build up and are great media for promoting bacterial growth. Any build-up needs to be cleaned out.

Keeping your animal's ears clean will prevent most infections. There are many ear cleaners on the market that quickly dissolve and break down this material so that it can be wiped out with a cotton swab or ball. Some examples are Ear Clens or Pet Otic. Don't use rubbing alcohol. It does a great job of dissolving the wax and other debris, but it burns if there is any irritation on the ear under this material. Don't use hydrogen peroxide either. It does a good job of cleaning, but its foaming action often forces material down the canal against the eardrum. Additionally, many dogs don't like the fizzing and heat produced by the hydrogen peroxide reaction.

People are often afraid to stick a swab or their finger down into the ear canal for fear of puncturing the eardrum. It is almost impossible to even get close to this structure, because the canal bends before it reaches the drum. As long as you are gentle, you can clean as deeply as necessary.

The canine ear.

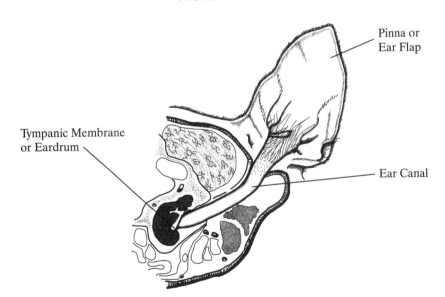

Pinna or
Ear Flap

Tympanic Membrane
or Eardrum

Ear Canal

Once you've cleaned out the ear canals, it is important to wipe away any excess moisture left behind from the cleaning products. Dogs' ears need to be dry to prevent infections. In fact, many infections start soon after a bath or swimming if the ears are not dried. Use absorbent cotton balls to soak up any liquid, and then apply an ear powder. This can be left in and will quickly absorb any residual moisture from the cleaning and also keep the ears dry for several days.

Eyes

Without touching them directly, examine the eyes. Look for excess material or tears that are building up or staining the hair and skin below the inside corner of the eye. Tears are suppose to flow across the surface of the eye and out though a tiny opening to a canal that interconnects with the nose. In some dogs, because of the shape of their faces or the conformation of their eyelids, this fluid spills out over the lower eyelid at the inside corner of the eye. It usually starts out as a brownish discoloration of the hair, and eventually becomes thick, dark-colored material that builds up and cakes in the hair. The skin under this area is constantly wet and often becomes irritated. In many animals, the hair in this area will slough off, leaving a red and bloody sore. As soon as you see any stains, keep the area clean and remove from the hair any stain that occurs. Do not wait for more problems to develop. Products made just for this are sold under names such as Show Eyes and Diamond Eye. These preparations are not to be put directly into the eye, but only on the hair and the skin below it.

Quickly examine the eyeball itself. Check to make sure the whites of the eye really are white, rather than appearing bloodshot or red. If you see any red, it means the blood vessels in this area have increased in size or number, usually because of some sort of infection or inflammation. Hunters will commonly see the eyes of their dogs become bloodshot after running through dry, dusty grass. Solutions are made just for flushing out and cleaning the eyes of dogs. Opticlear is one excellent over-the-counter product. If an infection is present, antibiotic ointments or drops are used. These will be prescribed by your veterinarian.

Look in the actual eyes and make sure they look the same. The pupils of the two eyes should be the same size. The cornea, the clear membrane that our own contact lenses rest against, should be perfectly clear. If you see any problems or abnormalities of the eyeball itself, your veterinarian should see the animal immediately.

Teeth

We will discuss this in greater detail in Chapter 12, but do frequently check your dog's teeth and the other structures inside its mouth. The mouth can be the site of numerous problems for dogs and their owners. Most can be prevented by cleaning the teeth at least once or twice a week. This may seem kind of unusual, and we'll admit that most dog owners don't do it, but those that take the time to clean their dogs' teeth eliminate many problems for their pets and usually save themselves a considerable sum of money over the animal's life. Dental problems are always less common in dogs that eat only dry food, but as most animals age, some problems usually arise.

Check your dog's teeth regularly. Dental problems should be caught early.

The mouths of dogs are filled with all kinds of bacteria, all of which are only too happy to dine on any food that is left behind on the teeth and gums. Dental plaque is nothing more than a soft, thin film made up of food, mucus and bacteria. Over time it hardens into calculus or tartar, which slowly works its way between the teeth and gums or underlying bones. In an average veterinary clinic, several dogs parade into the dental area every day to either have their teeth cleaned or abscessed teeth removed. All of this can be reduced or eliminated if you clean your pet's teeth once or twice a week.

How do you brush a dog's teeth? You can use a liquid dental cleanser with a toothbrush, dental sponges or pieces of cloth. There are also toothpastes made just for dogs that are used exactly as we would our own toothpaste. (Do not use human toothpaste on dogs! Our toothpaste is made to foam and then rinse. But the foaming action is not good for dogs, and they can't rinse and spit the way we do.) We promise you that you will spend much less money in your vet's clinic if you take a few minutes each week to clean your dog's teeth.

Nails and Feet

At least once a week check your dog's toenails and feet. Dogs that are active and outside much of the time will naturally keep their nails worn down. However, most house dogs need theirs trimmed once every two or three weeks. The nails on dogs grow constantly. If they are not cut back they either grow back into the foot or are broken when the animal catches them on anything from carpeting to door thresholds. Either of these is very painful.

Many pet owners are afraid to trim their dog's nails for fear of hurting the dog if the nails are cut too short. Their nails are just like ours—dogs feel nothing if only the nail part is cut, but it is painful and the nail may bleed if the quick is cut. Light-colored dogs have clear nails and it is easy to see the division between the living pink tissue section that contains the blood vessels and the white portion that is trimmed. There is no question about where to cut. On dogs with black nails, use the flat surface of the bottom of the toe pad as your guide. Extend the line of the pad forward through the nail, and never cut any shorter than that point. If you do cut a nail and it bleeds (as we all have done occasionally), use styptic powder and it will stop immediately. Even without this powder, in normal dogs the blood will clot quickly without any significant loss.

REGULAR MEDICAL CARE

Every dog should be seen at least once a year by a veterinarian. We aren't saying this to get more business—it simply makes good sense. Dogs go through their entire lives in 10 to 15 years. What may take years to happen in us will develop much more quickly in them. A year in their lives has been likened to seven in ours. This may not be exactly true for every breed, but for the sake of our discussion it's pretty close. Do you honestly think it would make good sense for you to wait more than seven years to have an examination by your physician? That is what you are doing if you wait more than a year for your dog to see its doctor.

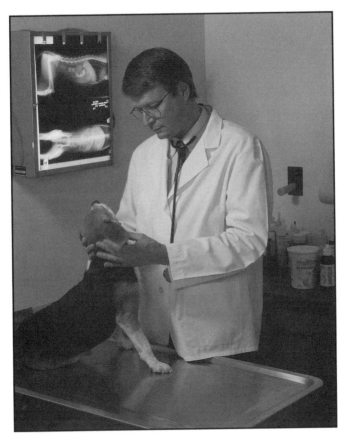

Every dog should visit the veterinarian at least once a year.

Routine yearly exams allow us to discover medical problems early in their course. Whenever we have to treat any serious medical problem, we wish we could always start in the early stages of the condition. This is true for all medical problems: It is always easier on the animal and less expensive for the owner if treatment is started in the acute phase, rather than the chronic phase. With some conditions, the more serious problems occur because the less serious ones have gone untreated. If an animal injures its knee or has a kneecap that won't stay in place (called luxating patella), it is usually easy to correct. However, when the condition has been allowed to go untreated for a long time, secondary arthritis develops within the joint and there may be no effective treatment for that.

Keep in mind, too, that your pet cannot tell you when it doesn't feel well. It can take time before the signs of some diseases become obvious. Meanwhile, your dog may have been feeling poorly for awhile. Frequent visits allow the veterinarian an opportunity to discover a problem that the owner may not even be aware of. As an example, most cases of bladder stones that are treated in our clinic are diagnosed during routine physical exams while the animals are in for their vaccinations. These are not tiny stones—we have palpated the abdomen of animals that act normal, to find stones the size of tennis balls—yet the dog has not indicated their presence by symptoms or clinical signs. Bladder stones of this size take at least several months to form.

There are also routine preventives that need to be taken care of annually, whether they are done by a veterinarian, a vaccine clinic or by the dog's owner. All dogs need to receive yearly vaccinations for diseases such as distemper, hepatitis, parainfluenza, parvovirus and coronavirus. Rabies vaccine needs to be given every one to three years, depending on local laws and regulations. In most areas of North America, Lyme disease vaccinations are needed yearly. Dogs that are frequently boarded, participate in dog shows or field trials or for some other reason are frequently exposed to many other dogs, should be protected against the canine cough complex (kennel cough). These are all necessary regardless of the animal's age.

Unless the dog is routinely wormed, a fecal check should be done by a veterinarinan once a year to check for intestinal parasites. Most dogs do not show any significant signs of infestation. The parasites place a certain strain on the animal, but this may not be apparent in dogs that are otherwise healthy and receive adequate nutrition.

In most areas of the United States, dogs need to be on a heartworm preventive. Usually this is a once-a-month pill or treat containing the drug that protects the animal from this life-threatening disease. Before an adult dog initially goes on heartworm medication, it needs a blood test to make sure it does not already have the disease. If it does, immediate treatment is required or the dog will probably die. Most veterinarians recommend that all adult dogs have their blood tested once every year or two, even if they are on preventive medication. This is done to ensure that these products are working correctly.

As we explained earlier, flea and tick medications have greatly improved in the 1990s. Now most problems with these parasites can be prevented by a single monthly treatment. These liquids are poured on to the dog's back. They remain there or are absorbed into the animal's skin. They are available in prescription or over-the-counter forms. It is believed that by the year 2000, 75 percent of the dogs in America will be on one of these products.

SUMMING UP

Your dog is now an adult, and should be able to participate with you in most of the things you do. These are the best years; enjoy them, for they will pass too quickly. The strong, active animal you now have will soon be slowed by its senior years.

Chapter 12

THE ADULT YEARS— VETERINARY CARE AND COMMON MEDICAL PROBLEMS

Dogs between two and 10 years of age can be affected by thousands and thousands of different medical problems and diseases. Some are very rare and some are very common. In this chapter we've outlined the ones your adult pet is most likely to encounter. This list would be altered somewhat if we were only talking about a specific breed. Still, in the history of our practice, 90 percent or so of the dogs we've treated were affected by this same destructive dozen. Other chapters of the book cover conditions such as hip dysplasia, epilepsy, parasites, mange and additional problems. Please look through the index for specific problems that concern you.

DENTAL PROBLEMS

This is actually a group of several different but interrelated problems. However, every day, no matter how slow our veterinary clinic might be, we will see adult or older dogs that have dental problems. Most could have been prevented with better home dental care. We talked about cleaning your dog's teeth in Chapter 11.

The dental problems that plague dogs are the same ones that affect us. They can have cavities, gum disease, plaque, tartar, dental abscesses, tooth loss and even mouth cancers. We all know what cavities are, and are probably familiar with the rest of this list, too. Plaque is that thin, soft, moist film on the surface of teeth that haven't been brushed recently. It is composed of bacteria, remnants of food and mucus. Tartar is also known as dental calculus. It is the hard, limestone-like material that forms on the surfaces of teeth. Tartar is actually nothing more than calcified plaque.

The most common dental problems in dogs are a result of poor oral hygiene. This really does start with the type of food they're eating. Regardless of what food manufacturers might try to tell you, dogs need to be on dry food exclusively—and it is important that it be fed dry. The abrasive action of eating dry food routinely helps to scrape plaque off the teeth and massage the gums. It is all the "brushing action" some dogs get. Dogs that are on softer, commercially prepared dog foods such as canned foods or semi-moist ones are notorious for their dental problems. Table scraps have the same result.

Dogs with poor occlusion (the fit between the upper and lower teeth) will also have more dental problems. And, just as with people, some dogs seem to have a genetic predisposition to these conditions.

Regardless of the food, the sequence of dental disease in dogs goes as follows. The teeth develop a film of plaque over some of their surfaces. Over time, this calcifies into tartar. The tartar increases in size and thickness, working its way between the teeth and gums. Slowly the gums recede and lose contact with the teeth. Bacteria then spread below the gum line and into the lower structures responsible for holding the teeth in place. The roots of the teeth separate from the bony jaw, and bacteria in these areas cause numerous abscesses. The affected teeth loosen and start falling out.

This process can have significant effects on the rest of the body. As the bacteria multiply, so does the probability that they will cross over into any of the numerous blood vessels of the mouth. Bacteria are then carried throughout the body by the circulatory system. This results in infections and abscesses at many sites. The most commonly affected are the heart valves, liver, kidneys and lungs. It is very possible for severe dental problems to lead to endocarditis (a bacterial infection of the heart valves), liver or kidney disease, or pneumonia.

The veterinarian's first objective is to clean up the dog's mouth. The dog is usually given a general anesthetic. Any teeth that must be removed are extracted, and then the surfaces of the teeth and the areas below the gum lines are cleaned with an ultrasonic device similar to the one used in a human dental clinic. The dog is then placed on antibiotics for at least seven to 14 days, depending on the severity of the case. The owner is usually counseled on how to clean the dog's teeth regularly. If they are able to do this, they will probably never need to have their pet's teeth cleaned again by a veterinarian.

EAR INFECTIONS

Also referred to as otitis externa, or outer ear infection, this is the most common infection that will bring you and your dog into the vet's office. In our children, ear infections are also very common. However, children have inner ear infections, which means they affect the deeper structures inside the eardrum. While these are also possible in dogs, they are relatively rare. The common infections for dogs stay within the outer ear canal, outside of the eardrum. Usually these infections do not directly affect the dog's hearing. This is because the eardrum is not affected, and sound waves can still travel down the ear canal.

Dogs with outer ear infections will scratch at their ears and shake their heads. They have the sensation that there is fluid in their ears. In some cases this is, in fact, the case. The ears may be very painful and the dogs whine or snap at you when they are examined. Often owners first realize there is a problem simply because of the odor. Looking down into the canals, the surfaces are usually red and inflamed. There will generally be a dark mixture of wax and debris in the ear canal.

One or both ears may be involved. This may depend on exactly what is causing the infection. In younger dogs, especially puppies, most cases are caused by ear mites. These usually affect both ears. In adult dogs, however, bacteria is usually the culprit. Many bacterial ear infections will only affect one ear. Yeast and other organisms may also be involved, especially in chronic cases.

All breeds can be affected, but those with ears that droop or hang down—Cocker Spaniels, Golden Retrievers, Poodles, Labrador Retrievers and Irish Setters, for example—have a higher incidence of infection. It is likely the flap restricts airflow in and out of the canal, making the ear a moist haven for bacteria.

While it would seem to be just a case of bad luck if your pet gets an ear infection, there are some predisposing factors. Ears that are never cleaned and have a substantial amount of wax in them along with a build-up of other debris, are, of course, likely to become infected. The wax and other material are excellent food for disease-causing organisms. Ear canals that have moisture in them are also much more likely to become infected. This can happen after the dog swims or is bathed and the ears are not properly dried. Other diseases, especially allergies, also increase the chance of a dog getting an outer ear infection. Allergies cause the glands of the ears to produce much more wax and, as would be expected, bacteria colonize the ear canals. We shall see later in this chapter that some breeds have a higher incidence of allergies, and therefore a higher incidence of ear infections.

When a dog comes to a veterinarian with otitis externa, the treatment will depend on the type and severity of the infection. Mild forms are usually treated with an antibiotic ointment or liquid. If the tissue lining the ear canals is inflamed or painful, a product containing both an antibiotic and an anti-inflammatory agent, such as a steroid, may be prescribed. These are applied on the surface of the skin or ear canal.

There are probably more than 100 topical products on the market today made to treat ear infections in dogs. They contain a wide range of different antibacterial and anti-inflammatory combinations. Some also include medicines directed at yeast or fungus. At home, the owner places the medication into the affected ear once or twice a day for seven to 14 days. In most cases this eliminates the problem. Our rule of thumb is that the dogs must be treated until everything looks, acts and smells normal, and then for another seven days!

If the ear canals are filled with wax and other debris, the veterinarian will clean them out before treatment is started. If the dog is in pain, it may be necessary to sedate or even anesthetize it for this to be done. The dog is then sent home with a topical medicine. Usually we prefer not to have the owners attempt to clean the ears at home for two to four days. This gives the medications a chance to decrease the inflammation and pain. After a few days, excess medicine and any debris should be removed daily before more medicine is applied.

If the infection is severe, the dog may also need oral antibiotics. Now, not only is the medication being placed topically on the surface of the ear canal, it is also being distributed in the deeper layers of the skin by the circulatory system.

Some infections do not respond to the antibiotic-steroid preparations. Usually this is because the bacteria are resistant to or not affected by that particular antibiotic. In these cases, a different medication can be chosen, perhaps with the help of a *culture and sensitivity test*. This test isolates the organism causing the infection and then tests several different antibacterial agents against it. To do this correctly, the dog is taken off all medications for four days. The veterinarian then runs a sterile swab over the infected area. The swab is rubbed across the surface of a culture plate and the bacteria are allowed to grow. Later, a sample of these organisms is transferred to a second culture plate. Small pieces of paper containing various antibiotics are arranged across this second plate. In two to three days, it will be seen which antibiotics have killed the bacteria. A new ear preparation is then chosen that contains one of the antibiotics that have been shown to be successful in the test.

This process usually works very well. The only problem is that the bacteria's sensitivity or resistance to a particular antibiotic may change over time. In these cases, the dog responds to the new medication at first, but after a while the signs associated with the infection return. The culture and sensitivity test may have to be redone to determine which antibiotic should be used next.

Some dogs have ear infections over and over throughout their lives. These chronic cases can be managed with repeated culture and sensitivity tests. In a small percentage, the prolonged irritation to the ear canals causes them to close down or almost grow shut. Hearing is then affected, plus it is almost impossible to get medications to the site of the infection. For these dogs, the only answer is to surgically remove a portion of the external ear canal. In an average 40-pound dog, the length of the ear canal is shortened from about three inches to less than half an inch. The eardrum is not affected, so the dog still hears and the infections are much easier to treat. This is an excellent procedure, but it does not necessarily mean the dog will never have another infection. They may be less frequent and easier to treat, but may still occur.

As with so many medical conditions, ear infections are easier to prevent than they are to treat. Make it a habit to routinely clean your dog's ears. After this is done, place a small quantity of ear powder in the canals to keep them dry. Always wipe out and dry the ears after the dog swims. Try not to get any water in them while bathing the dog, and dry them afterwards just to be sure. At the first sign of a problem, always have your dog checked by your veterinarian.

ALLERGIES

Allergies constitute the most common skin disease in dogs. There is no close second. They affect many different dogs, purebreds and mixed. Certain breeds have a higher incidence of allergies. Many, many dogs suffer from allergies, and the things they are allergic to make a long list, and include pollen grains from grasses, trees or weeds, all kinds of foods, insect bites (especially fleas), carpet fibers, tobacco smoke, plastics, medications and detergents. The possibilities probably include everything a dog might encounter throughout its life.

We divide allergies into four categories: inhalant allergies (such as pollen and smoke), contact allergies (such as plastics and carpet fibers), food allergies (individual grains or meats, preservatives and so on) and flea bite allergies (it is believed these dogs are allergic to a specific protein found within flea saliva).

Regardless of what the dog is allergic to, the reaction is the same. When your dog is allergic to anything, the problem will appear as a skin disease. The actual thing the dog is allergic to, and this may be a single molecule, is called the *allergen*. Once it is on or inside the dog's body, the allergen stimulates the release of the substance *histamine* from a wide variety of body cells. The cells most affected, however, are within the skin. This causes a local inflammation where those cells are, causing the dog's skin to itch. The dog then scratches and chews on itself, sometimes to the point of self-mutilation. The areas most commonly involved are the feet, the sides of the body and the ears.

Some dogs may suffer for only a brief period during the year. This is a seasonal allergy, and it flares up when the thing the dog is allergic to is present in the environment. Other dogs might be allergic to the carpet fibers throughout the home, and therefore their allergic reactions would be present 12 months a year. As with people, many dogs start out being allergic to a single substance, but over time develop sensitivities to additional things.

Often when owners are told their dog has developed an allergy, they wonder what is new in the dog's environment. That isn't how it works. To be allergic to something, the body must become sensitized to it over time. It is very unlikely that a dog would be allergic to something on its first contact with a substance. The cells of its body must develop a reaction to it. For this reason, very few dogs show signs of allergies in their first year of life. Their bodies have not had the opportunity to develop the allergen sensitivity. Most dogs do not show clinical signs of allergies until they are two to three years old. If severe signs are seen in dogs before this age, the prognosis is not good, as the allergies will typically get worse and the dog will react to more and more things as it matures.

While allergies can be severe and difficult to treat or control, they are not life threatening. These dogs may suffer throughout their lives, but the allergies will not kill them. However, they often develop secondary problems with bacterial infections of the skin or ear canals that can be more serious for their overall health.

The clinical signs of allergies are seen on the skin, which may become pink or reddened in the areas between the toes, on the sides of the body and within the ear canals. With flea bite allergies, the area on the back just over the base of the tail will be affected. Other changes or irritations to the skin are often caused by the dog's scratching and chewing. Many dogs that are untreated will scratch and chew on themselves most of their waking hours. In a small percentage of food allergies, there may also be vomiting and diarrhea.

In the past, treatment dealt little with diagnosis or non-medical therapies. Most dogs with allergies, regardless of what caused the problem, were simply placed on steroids. The ones most commonly used were prednisone, prednisolone or derivatives of these, administered through injections, tablets or topically. This was usually fine for dogs that had only brief seasonal allergies. For dogs that had year-round allergies, however, this meant prolonged steroid use. Sometimes the steroids caused more severe problems than the allergies. The long-term therapy constantly bombarded the internal organs with these medications. Over the life of the dog, conditions such as Cushing's disease (which affects the adrenal glands), diabetes and liver and kidney abnormalities were noted.

The side effects of prolonged, daily steroid use are better understood today. For a two- to three-week seasonal allergy, most veterinarians still prescribe short-acting steroids. But for allergies that last longer, or for sensitivity to many substances, we try to choose a therapy that either decreases or eliminates the need for steroids.

Two non-steroid therapies are commonly used for allergies in dogs. The first can be used to either eliminate or decrease the quantity of steroids required, and consists of nutritional supplements and antihistamines. The omega-3 and omega-6 fatty acids are known to decrease the body's response to allergens, and are combined with other substances in the nutritional supplements. They are sold under trade names such as Vitacaps and Derm

Caps. Along with these preparations, many veterinarians and breeders recommend high levels of the B vitamin, biotin. This substance is thought to lessen the severity of allergic skin reactions. The last part of this therapeutic regime is an antihistamine such as Benadryl. This works within the skin to tie up or prevent the release of histamine, which actually causes the itching.

Hyposensitization is the other non-steroidal way of treating allergies. Skin or blood tests are used to determine exactly what the dog is allergic to. Then, the dog is given small injections of that substance that, over time, lessen its sensitivity to the specific allergen. This process is called *hyposensitization*. This treatment can be very successful for eliminating an allergy. The problem is that tests and hyposensitization products have not been formulated for all allergens. Additionally, the things dogs are allergic to may change over time. Usually, the dog reacts to more and more things as it matures. The testing and hyposensitization process must therefore sometimes be done two or three times over the life of the dog.

In some severe cases there is no effective alternative to steroid therapy. Fortunately, we have learned how to use these products in such a way that they cause fewer side effects. Once the signs of the allergies are eliminated, the dosage is slowly lowered until either prednisone or prednisolone is administered orally, in the lowest dose possible, only once every other day. Using this regime, dogs with severe allergies can be maintained for years without significant problems. Veterinarians should do regular blood tests to ensure that the internal organs and glands of the body are not being affected. Remember that this long-term use is only recommended for dogs with severe year-round allergies.

Dogs with food allergies must be diagnosed using food elimination trials that isolate exactly what the animal is allergic to. Once determined, these foods must be eliminated from the dog's diet. (Although they are much discussed, food allergies are not common in dogs.)

Dogs with severe allergies should not be bred, because this trait can be passed on genetically. Certain lines in some breeds are well known for their allergy problems.

Hot Spots

Also known as *acute moist dermatitis,* this is usually a disease of the longhaired breeds and those with dense undercoats. It is often a local allergic reaction to a specific allergen. Insect bites, especially from fleas, are often found to be the cause. Hot spots are circular lesions, usually found on the head, over the hip and along the side of the chest. They will be moist, raw, inflamed and hairless, and can be quite painful. These sores can change dramatically in size in a very brief period of time. What was the size of a quarter may easily be eight inches in diameter in six hours. Dogs will lick or scratch at them, making the condition worse.

The lesions are rare in the colder temperatures of winter. They occur in equal frequency in house and outside dogs. Many dogs develop several of these lesions over their lives. However, this is not a long-term disease. A lesion will suddenly appear, be treated and be gone in less than a week. Another lesion may appear later the same summer, the next year or never be seen again on that dog.

Treatment must be directed at stopping the growth of the hot spot and eliminating the cause. In many dogs it's fleas, but lesions below the ear often indicate an ear infection, those near the hip may be the result of an anal gland infection, and so on. Whatever the cause, if it can be detected it must be treated as the hot spot is being treated.

The first step in treating hot spots is clipping the hair over and surrounding the lesion. This allows air to get into the inflamed tissue and makes it easier to treat. The surface of the lesion is cleaned with non-irritating solutions. Some veterinarians prefer hydrogen peroxide for this, as it also kills any bacteria. To keep the lesion dry, desiccating powders or solutions are often then applied. All of this may be done with the dog sedated or under a general anesthetic because of the great pain associated with hot spots. The dog is also placed on oral antibiotics. Some dogs may be given over-the-counter painkillers such as buffered aspirin. In severe cases, antihistamines or short-acting steroids may be used to suppress the allergic reaction.

Many dogs that have repeated problems with hot spots can have the incidence greatly reduced by keeping their hair clipped short during the summer, giving them frequent medicated baths and following a strict program to protect the dog from fleas and ticks.

ANAL GLANDS

All predators, whether they are dogs in the wild (or your home) or skunks in your backyard, have anal glands. They just use them differently. Skunks discharge the secretion from these glands as a form of defense, while dogs use it primarily for territorial marking or as a form of communication. In dogs, every time a stool is passed, it should put enough pressure on the anal glands that some of the secretion is deposited on the surface of the stool. Other dogs are then able to tell who has been in the neighborhood, just by sniffing the stools they find. Additionally, dogs recognize each other by smelling each other in the general area of the anus, since each dog's anal glands produce a unique scent.

The anal glands.

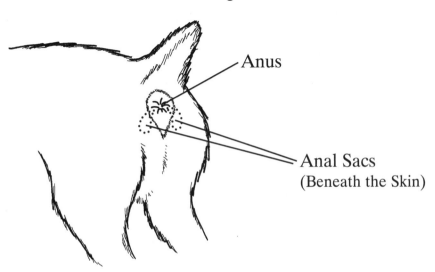

Anus

Anal Sacs
(Beneath the Skin)

As the dog is viewed from behind, these glands are located on each side of and slightly below the anal opening. A tiny duct or tube leads under the skin to an opening directly beside the anus. In dogs that live in our homes, these glands have little purpose. In fact, instead of being a mechanism for communication, they become a medical liability. For various reasons, such as the conformation of the dog, the thickness of the secretions or the hardness of the stool, these glands and their ducts often become clogged, or *impacted*. When this occurs, the dog will sit down on its rear quarters and drag its anal area across the floor or ground. This is called *scooting*. This is a very, very common problem for dogs, especially the smaller breeds.

When the glands become impacted, a veterinarian, groomer or the dog's owner must clean them out, or *express* them. This empties the glands of all material. It is done by applying pressure with the fingers, starting below the gland and then pushing upwards. In some dogs this needs to be done every week or two.

Impacted glands do not affect the overall health of the dog. The problem is that dogs may injure the anal area when scooting across the ground, or discharge the secretion on the carpet or floor. And this material has a terrible odor.

A second problem that can commonly occur with anal glands is abscesses. Bacteria make their way into the glands, probably down through the ducts. An infection occurs and soon develops into a large abscess or boil. This must be lanced by a veterinarian, and antibiotics are usually given to the dog for seven to 14 days. Secondary problems sometimes occur with abscesses, as they may cause scar tissue or other damage that may affect the nerves and muscles in this area. This can cause fecal incontinence, meaning the dog cannot retain its stools.

If an individual dog only has an occasional problem with the glands, they can be dealt with as needed. However, for dogs with repeated or chronic problems, it is usually recommended that the glands be surgically removed. This is a simple procedure, and all problems associated with these glands are eliminated for the remainder of the dog's life.

DRY OR DULL COAT

While this may not seem to be a medical problem, many owners bring their dogs to our clinics for help with various coat problems. Their dog sheds excessively, has a dry or thin coat, or a fine dander flakes off the pet's skin. In most dogs these problems can be eliminated, or at least decreased.

Most coat problems are secondary to another condition, such as poor nutrition, parasites, heat cycles in the intact female, disease or advancing age. The skin and hair are the last places where a dog's body spends its energies and nutrients. All other areas are probably more important to the life of the dog, and they receive preferential treatment. When dogs are placed on weight-reduction diets, for example, the overall quality of their coat usually decreases and shedding increases. Parasites that steal food or cause anemia typically cause dry skin and a thin, dull coat. Aging dogs that no longer do a good job of deriving nutrients from their food commonly lose hair and have dry skin with excessive dander. In the winter months, when the humidity level of our homes drops, our dog's skin may dry out just as our own does.

These are just a few of the things that can affect the overall quality of the skin and coat.

When treating these conditions, it is always important to first determine the cause. If there is another problem, it must be addressed first. In most cases this will improve the quality of the skin and coat, at least to some degree.

When we talk to owners about their pet's coat we try to give them a program of care that will significantly affect the problem. Most will be ecstatic if we can just decrease shedding. If the therapy gives more shine to the coat, along with adding moisture to the skin, it is considered an overwhelming success. We usually advise a three-step program similar to the one people with show dogs use to keep their animals looking their very best.

Step one involves bathing the dog and then following up with one of the many coat conditioners on the market. We bathe the dog to clean the coat and also to break down and rid the skin of the flaky dander—which is nothing more than dead skin cells. The conditioner makes the hair fuller and gives it more body, shine and luster. We really haven't changed anything, but what is there looks better.

Step two is to stimulate the coat and skin by frequent brushing. We aren't trying to get rid of hair as much as we are trying to increase the activity of the oil glands found on the skin and within the hair follicles. Any of the gentle combination pin and bristle brushes will work. Any hair that is being shed will be picked up by either side of these brushes. Slicker brushes are

A slicker brush and pin and bristle brushes.

also excellent for removing loose and shed hair from the dog's coat. You can easily get in the habit of brushing your dog 10 to 15 minutes a day while you are watching television or talking with the rest of the family. The dog will love the extra attention.

Step three is to use nutritional supplements that add specific oils, essential fatty acids and substances that encourage growth for the skin and hair coat. There are hundreds of these on the market. Some of our favorites are Vitacoat Plus, Linatone Plus and Lipiderm. These are all liquids that are poured over the dog's dry food at each feeding.

URINARY INCONTINENCE

In dogs, urine is retained or stored in the bladder. When the dog wants to urinate, the urine passes to the outside of the body through a small tube called the urethra. A normal adult dog can easily control this action. Urinary incontinence is involuntary or uncontrollable leaking of urine from the bladder. Small quantities of urine will leak from the urethra while an incontinent dog is resting or sleeping, and it will commonly be seen licking the vagina or penile opening.

Incontinence is more common in female dogs than it is in males. It is also more common in spayed females than in intact ones. Urine is prevented from leaking out of the bladder in normal dogs by a band of muscular tissue at the base of the bladder that forms a valve that the dog consciously controls. We know today that certain hormones are important in this control. In the female, estrogen has a dramatic effect, giving strength to the muscular tissue of the bladder. In the male, testosterone has much the same effect. Anything that affects the levels of these hormones also affects the dog's ability to retain its urine.

As a dog ages, the production of these hormones naturally decreases. Additionally, the main sites of their production, the ovaries in the female and the testicles in the male, are surgically removed when the dog is spayed or neutered. Urinary incontinence is therefore more common in old dogs or those that have been altered. If the cause is old age, the problem is usually not seen until the dogs are eight to nine years of age. In spayed females, this problem usually doesn't occur until they are three or five years of age. Surprisingly, in males, whether they are neutered or not, this condition is rarely seen in dogs younger than 10.

Dogs suffering from urinary incontinence have some common secondary problems. They have a much higher incidence of bladder infections. It is believed that with the more lax opening to the bladder, it is easier for bacteria to migrate up the urethra and colonize the bladder. These dogs may need to be on antibiotics until the incontinence is dealt with. They also frequently suffer from urine scalding. Urine is fairly caustic, and if it remains in contact with the skin for long periods of time, it can cause severe irritations. Scalded areas are usually treated topically with anti-inflammatory salves that also contain antibiotics.

Treatment for incontinence is usually not difficult. Since the cause is generally hormone deficiency, replacements with hormones or hormone substitutes are usually prescribed. Estrogen can be replaced by the compound diethylstilbestrol. After a brief period of daily doses, it is usually given once a week. There was a time when diethylstilbestrol was produced mainly by pharmaceutical firms for human use. But the drug can have unpleasant side effects in humans, and most companies have now discontinued its production. At the minute levels used to treat incontinence in dogs, however, side effects are extremely rare. Diethylstilbestrol is now being produced by independent laboratories for veterinary use.

Over-the-counter drugs developed for human use, such as propanolamine and ephedrine, are also successfully used in male and female dogs to treat incontinence. Most veterinarians however, have had better luck with diethylstilbestrol. Once dogs go on one of these medications, they will remain on it for the rest of their lives.

BLADDER INFECTIONS

Bladder infections are also called *cystitis*. These infections are usually caused by bacteria, and are much more common in female dogs than in males. Bacteria may gain access to the bladder either from the blood system, the kidneys or, most commonly, by migrating up the urethra into the bladder. The urethra, the tube that carries the urine from the bladder to the outside of the dog, is much shorter and larger in diameter in females than it is in males, which is why these infections are more common in females. Cystitis can occur in dogs of any age.

The bladder is lined by nerves that tell a dog when its bladder is full. When there is cystitis, the bladder wall and these nerve endings are inflamed, making the dog feel as if it has a full bladder all the time. Infected dogs will therefore urinate very small amounts frequently throughout the day. Some dogs will remain squatting for long periods of time and strain as if they are trying to force out additional urine. Others will start to urinate but then, because of the burning sensation the inflammation causes, will stop, only to start again a few steps later.

Blood is common in the urine of dogs with bladder infections. Sometimes it looks as if there's a lot of blood, but this is rarely the case. Rather, a small amount of blood is mixed with the urine, turning it red. Bladder infections are usually diagnosed by the signs we've just described, or by an analysis of the urine.

Bladder infections are treated with oral antibiotics. Dogs are usually left on medication for at least 10 days, and it is important that the antibiotics are used for several days to a week after all the symptoms have cleared up. In some cases, the antibiotic will either not be effective at all or the signs will reappear before the medication is finished. This usually indicates that the bacteria are resistant to the specific antibiotic chosen, and either another must be tried or a culture and sensitivity needs to be done (a procedure we explained earlier in the section on ear infections). Bladder infections can also be the result of other conditions, such as bladder stones or kidney infections, and these will have to dealt with in order to clear up the cystitis.

A small percentage of dogs will develop chronic bladder infections that become resistant to medical therapy. The inner lining of the bladder is usually very smooth, but in these dogs with chronic cystitis it is more like a head of cauliflower. It is rough with many tiny folds and crypts that prevent antibiotics from effectively getting to the bacteria in these isolated areas. In these cases, surgery is indicated. The lining of the bladder is scraped in an attempt to turn a chronic situation into an acute one that is easier to treat.

BLADDER STONES

Also known as *urinary calculi* or *urolithiasis*, in dogs these stones are almost always formed in the bladder. The process starts with tiny amounts of sand or grit settling out of solution, much the way sugar does as a cup of coffee cools. Slowly, over a long period of time, these bits grow in size as additional material comes out of solution and builds upon what's already present. In the end, the mass of stones may completely fill the bladder, causing the dog to urinate frequently throughout the day.

There are several different kinds of stones. They vary as to their chemical composition, and different breeds sometimes form different kinds. Some stones form when the pH of the urine is acid and others when the pH is alkaline.

The actual cause of this condition is not completely understood. We know that stones may form more readily when bacterial infections are present. However, in the vast majority of cases it seems that the metabolic pathways of certain dogs predispose them to this problem. Their systems simply produce urine from which stones are more likely to precipitate. Regardless of how we alter their diets or the acidity of their urine, there are a small number of dogs that continue to form stones over the course of their lives.

Dogs with bladder stones may not show any outward signs! The majority of all cases seen in our clinic are diagnosed during routine examinations. While palpating their abdomens we can easily feel the stones in the bladder. When dogs do show signs, they may be similar to those with simple bladder infections. Affected dogs may strain to urinate and may also urinate frequently throughout the day, eliminating only small quantities of urine with each attempt. Sometimes there will be blood in the urine, caused by the irritation of the stones against the bladder wall.

Bladder stones can be treated surgically or medically. The best way to completely remove them is surgically. This is a very easy surgery, usually taking less time than a spay! The bladder is opened up through an abdominal incision, the stones are removed, the bladder is flushed to remove any fine sand and the dog is sutured back up. These dogs are usually placed on oral antibiotics for seven to 10 days.

However, many dogs are not good surgery candidates because of other medical conditions or the financial limitations of the owner. With certain kinds of stones we are able to feed special diets, such as Hill's S/D, that will actually dissolve the stones within the bladder. This takes several months, but with certain types of stones it works very well. Owners are told to watch their dog closely to ensure that no urinary obstruction occurs and that the dog is always able to urinate.

The only life-threatening problem with bladder stones occurs when a stone enters the opening of the urethra and obstructs the outward flow of urine. While uncommon, this is a true medical emergency. Dogs that are prevented from eliminating urine usually die within a few days. Their kidneys stop functioning and the waste products that they normally remove quickly build up to toxic levels within the body. This condition can only be dealt with surgically.

Regardless of how the stones are removed, it is important that their reoccurrence be prevented. Either through urinalysis or examination of the removed stones, their composition is determined. This tells us if they are more likely to form in an acid or an alkaline urine. The urine is then modified, using medication, to decrease the chance of any further stone development. For some stone types we can also use specially formulated diets, such as Hill's C/D, that help prevent new stones from forming. With any affected dog we watch closely for any sign of bladder infections, as we know that these increase the likelihood of future problems.

Pyometra

This is a disease mainly of middle-aged female dogs that have not been spayed. In the past we thought pyometra was simply a uterine infection, but today we know that it is a hormonal abnormality, and a secondary bacterial infection may or may not be present. Pyometra follows a heat cycle in which fertilization did not occur. Typically, within two to four months after the cycle, the female starts showing signs of the disease.

The two main hormones produced by the ovaries are estrogen and progesterone. Pyometra is caused by an excessive quantity of progesterone, or the uterus becoming overly sensitive to it. In either case, cysts form in the lining of the uterus. These cysts contain numerous secretory cells, and large quantities of fluids are produced and released into the interior of the uterus.

This fluid, along with a thickening of the walls of the uterus, brings about a dramatic increase in the overall size of this organ. The uterus is made up of a body with two horns. In the unaffected dog, the horns are smaller than a common pencil. However, in cases of pyometra they become large, sac-like pouches the circumference of cucumbers and 12 to 18 inches long. Normally the entire uterus in a 40-pound dog will weigh two to four ounces, but in cases of pyometra this typically ranges from one to four pounds!

As the disease continues, fluid spills out through the vaginal opening, causing the dog to lick this area in an attempt to keep itself clean. Bacteria commonly colonize the uterus by entering through the cervix. This produces an even greater response by the body, as it showers additional fluid and white blood cells into the affected organ.

After a while, the cervix closes. This effectively traps all of the fluid within the uterus. Still, the body continues to transfer more fluid and white blood cells into the organ, causing even further dilation and growth. The uterus can rupture, spilling its contents into the abdominal cavity. If this occurs, the dog usually dies in less than 48 hours.

A uterus enlarged by pyometra.

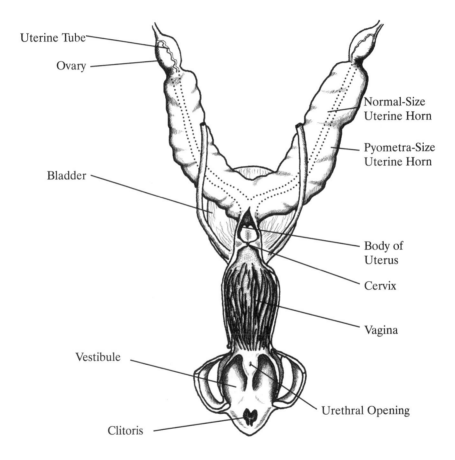

Uterine Tube

Ovary

Normal-Size
Uterine Horn

Pyometra-Size
Uterine Horn

Bladder

Body of
Uterus

Cervix

Vagina

Vestibule

Urethral Opening

Clitoris

In most cases this does not happen. The body will attempt to eliminate the problem by carrying the wastes and excess fluid through the blood stream to the kidneys. However, the amount of material in a dog with pyometra is too great to be eliminated in this fashion, overloading the kidney system. The normal toxins that should be excreted from the body build up, and the dog goes into uremic poisoning. Untreated, the dog dies from kidney failure.

As the body attempts to flush out the build-up of waste products through the kidneys, the dog will drink excessive quantities of water and urinate frequently. She will lick at her vaginal area while the cervix is still open and the uterus is discharging. As the uterus increases in size and weight, the dog shows weakness in the rear legs, often to the point where she cannot rise without help. As the dog enters kidney failure, she stops eating and becomes very lethargic.

In most female dogs the preferred treatment is a complete ovariohysterectomy (spay). This removes the ovaries, oviducts, uterus and all associated blood vessels. These dogs can be a surgical challenge because of their poor overall condition. Most dogs are kept on intravenous fluids and antibiotics for several days.

Ruptured Disc

The dog's spine is made up of numerous small bones called vertebrae. These extend from the base of the skull all the way to the end of the tail. The vertebrae are interconnected by flexible discs made of cartilage. These discs provide cushioning between each bone and permit the neck, spine and tail to bend, allowing changes in position and posture. Above the discs and running through the bony vertebrae is the spinal cord, which is made up of a mass of nerve fibers that run back and forth between the brain and the rest of the body.

As a disc becomes weaker with age or trauma, it may rupture, or *herniate*, causing portions of the disc to protrude upward and place pressure on the spinal cord. This pressure typically prevents or inhibits nerve transmission along the spinal cord. The effect on the spinal cord will depend on the amount and severity of the pressure. In more severe cases, the spinal cord may be damaged. Any injury to the spinal cord can result in pain, weakness or paralysis. The location of the abnormal disc will also affect the cord. A disc herniation in the neck area may affect the entire body, while one in the middle

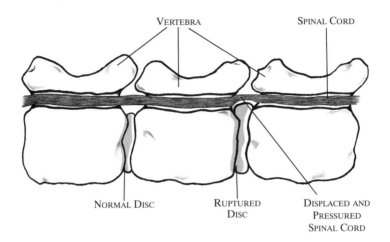

VERTEBRA

SPINAL CORD

NORMAL DISC

RUPTURED DISC

DISPLACED AND PRESSURED SPINAL CORD

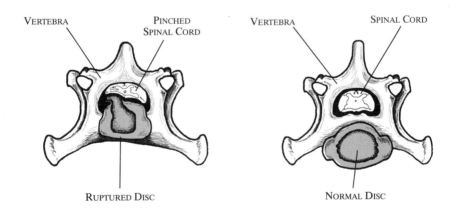

VERTEBRA

PINCHED SPINAL CORD

RUPTURED DISC

VERTEBRA

SPINAL CORD

NORMAL DISC

of the dog's back may only affect the actions of the rear legs and the abdominal organs.

Dogs with very long backs, such as Dachshunds and Basset Hounds, understandably have a greater incidence of disc disease in the middle of the back. In fact, this is the area most often affected in all dogs, regardless of the length of the dog's back. It seems that this area, formed at the union of the chest and abdomen, has an inherent weakness, or at least is more prone to injury. This type of ruptured disc is common, especially in smaller dogs.

In most cases we never find exactly when or what caused the disc to rupture. Surprisingly, this injury is rarely associated with severe trauma such as being hit by a car or falling from heights. In the smaller breeds, many believe it occurs when these dogs jump down off furniture, arching their backs downward.

When a disc first ruptures, it causes intense pain. When this occurs in the middle of the back, the dog will hump its back in response to the discomfort. In severe herniations in this area of the back, the rear legs will be partially or completely paralyzed. This may be temporary or permanent. The nerves affecting the bladder and colon may also be affected, making it difficult if not impossible for the dog to urinate or defecate on its own. This can obviously be a very serious condition, and it is important that if you suspect a ruptured disc, you take the dog to a veterinary clinic immediately—day or night!

Treatment almost always involves the use of anti-inflammatory medications such as cortisone (a steroid). These products help shrink the herniated disc and swollen tissue, and at the same time relieve any inflammation that may have occurred within the spinal cord. Today, more than 90 percent of all ruptured disc cases in this area of the back are handled with medical therapy alone.

Surgery to either remove the protruding disc material or cut away a portion of the bone that surrounds the spinal cord is sometimes necessary. To be effective, however, surgery must usually be done within the first day or so following the injury. Whether medical, surgical or a combination of the two treatments is used, it may be several weeks before the actual outcome of the case can be determined.

KNEE PROBLEMS

Big dogs and little dogs alike suffer problems with the knee joints. The knee on a dog is formed by the union of the femur (the long bone extending down from the hip) and the tibia (the long bone above the dog's ankle).

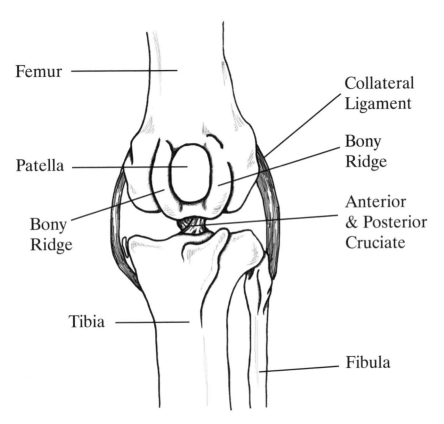

A normal knee joint, showing the patella within the bony ridges.

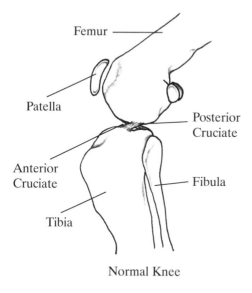

Femur

Patella

Anterior
Cruciate

Tibia

Posterior
Cruciate

Fibula

Normal Knee

Ruptured
Anterior Cruciate

Normal Knee

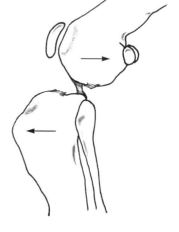

Ruptured Anterior
Cruciate with Drawer
Movement

There are two common problems that can crop up in this joint. The first is luxating patella, predominately a problem of small dogs, and the second is ruptured cruciate ligament, which can occur in dogs of any size. These are very common problems, and in our clinic we see them almost every week.

The bone we call the kneecap is known to doctors as the *patella*. A groove in the lower end of the femur allows the patella to slide up and down when the knee joint is bent back and forth. In so doing, it guides the action of some of the muscles in the upper leg. The kneecap also provides protection for the internal structures of the knee joint. With luxating patella, because of abnormalities in development, the bony ridges forming the groove for the patella are not large enough. This causes the groove to be too shallow, and allows the patella to slide off the side of the femur, usually to the inside of the leg. Sometimes the kneecap gets stuck in this position, causing the leg to lock up with the foot held off the ground. One or both knees may be affected.

Dogs with this condition usually have intermittent lameness on the affected leg. They may be running through the yard when one leg suddenly locks up. The dog may or may not show any evidence of pain when this happens. After a while, the muscles relax, permitting the patella to slide back to its correct position. The dog shows no further signs until the next time the patella slides out of place.

The most serious part of this condition is the long-term effect of the kneecap sliding repeatedly over the bony ridge on the femur. After a while, arthritis usually develops, making all use of the joint painful. These dogs have difficulty getting up after lying down, or in severe cases, even walking. Anti-inflammatories and painkillers such as buffered aspirin can be used to treat the arthritis, and glucosamine-containing products such as Joint Care can help slow its progression.

Only surgical treatment can correct a luxating patella. While it may not be necessary in mild cases, the dog can never truly improve without it. Additionally, it prevents arthritis from developing if it is corrected early enough. If arthritis has already appeared, often during surgery arthritic areas are surgically removed.

The second common problem of the knee joint, ruptured cruciate ligaments, is the same knee injury that is so common in human athletes. A dog's knee has an anterior and a posterior ligament. These two ligaments attach the femur to the tibia, and thereby stabilize the knee joint. The anterior is the one most commonly torn or ruptured.

When either ligament is ruptured, the two bones move back and forth independently of each other, preventing the joint from functioning correctly. This is called *drawer movement,* because the movement of the upper femur bone in relation to the tibia is similar to pulling out and pushing in the drawer in a cabinet. Common causes of this injury are slipping on a wet or icy surface, falling, twisting the knee, obesity or trauma from being hit by a car.

Immediately after the injury, an affected dog will limp, usually holding the foot of the affected leg off the ground. The knee may swell. After time, the dog will use the leg a bit more, but most will still have bouts of limping as they continue to irritate the knee. If the condition goes untreated, the abnormal interaction of the two bones will usually result in severe and painful arthritis. When the dog attempts to favor this leg, it also will put excess weight on the other side, and it is not uncommon for the same injury to then occur to the opposite knee.

The only treatment is surgery. Even dogs that only occasionally limp should have the condition surgically corrected to prevent life-long arthritis problems. There are several different procedures, and all do an excellent job of correcting this condition.

SUMMING UP

The majority of adult dogs that veterinarians see have the same few problems, and most are readily treatable. As with all health problems, the earlier you seek treatment for your dog, the better the prognosis. That's why routine visits to the veterinarian are so important. It's also important for you to know your dog, so you know what is and isn't normal. That way, you can spot problems early on.

Chapter 13

THE NINE MOST COMMON VETERINARY EMERGENCIES

When most pet owners think about an emergency, they think about a high-speed trip to the veterinary hospital in the middle of the night. Obviously, any office visit at that time is an emergency. But we aren't going to discuss the cases in which the dog has been sick for three days and the owner finally decides at two in the morning that the dog must be seen. No, here we want to discuss the emergencies that mean you need to get your dog to the clinic immediately.

Whatever has happened, don't panic. No matter how bad the dog looks, more than 98 percent of all emergency cases we've seen in our veterinary hospital recovered, rarely the worse for wear. Animals, and especially dogs, are amazingly resilient creatures. They can recover from severe injuries quickly, and usually without any long-lasting effects. They also have an advantage over us in that they probably don't realize how badly they are hurt. Dogs have a much higher pain tolerance than we do. When cut they will whine or yelp, but in just a few minutes they're off chasing the next rabbit or trying to jump over another barbed wire fence.

We have a true story to tell you, and we will let you draw your own conclusions about dogs and their ability to withstand pain and live through what would seem to be certain death. It took place in our clinic a few years ago. We call this story *The Dog Who Never Thought About Dying*.

We have two clients, a husband and wife, who moved to the Northwoods of Wisconsin where we practice. They have recently retired and are enjoying it very much. At the time of the events of this story, their Golden Retriever, Ben, was five years old. He was an average patient, came in for his yearly vaccinations and check up and also came in about every five to six weeks to have his nails trimmed. He would always walk into the exam room and stand in front of a cookie jar waiting to get his treat.

As you can tell, this dog had a rough life. He was and is a very calm dog that would not harm a fly. Kids in the waiting room would always encircle him, petting every part of his body. He loved it and would have stood there for hours if his owners would let him. He spent every waking moment with his owners, and the rest of the time he slept at the foot of their bed.

In our part of Wisconsin, a favorite pastime is picking wild raspberries in late summer. The man and his wife ventured into the woods one day to pick their share. Of course, Ben went along. All was going well until the man, up to his waist in briars, spotted a black bear cub next to him in the berry bushes. Now black bear cubs are no worry at all, but their mothers are. These 350-pound critters can cause major damage to just about anything. The man calmly told his wife that they should get back to their car as soon as possible. Just as they were opening the doors, the mother bear charged them from about 20 yards. Ben, reacting on his instincts, returned the assault in an effort to protect his humans.

We received a frantic call at 5:45 p.m. asking if we were still at the clinic. They told us to wait, as they were on the way in with Ben. From the tone of their voices we had a pretty good idea that this wasn't for a nail trim. Thirty minutes later their car screeched into the parking lot.

The sight as they walked through the front door was dramatic. Ben was somehow walking but had a severe limp. All the skin from the right side of his face was pulled away, exposing his eyeball as it moved back and forth. A long cut extended from the midpoint of his neck back across the right side of his chest. From this laceration, a lobe of his lung stuck out from between two broken ribs. The woman was holding Ben's intestines up against his abdominal wall. This was because there was also a huge gash across and all the way through the muscles of the lower abdomen. The bones above and below the elbow on his right front leg were broken, as was the upper bone in his right rear leg. His coat was matted and covered with blood and dirt.

Before we could get to him, Ben somehow dragged himself into the exam room and stared at the treat jar! The physical exam was even more amazing in that we could honestly find no evidence that Ben showed any signs of being in shock.

Imagine your own feelings if you looked at your body and it was in this condition. You might just take one quick glance and die of a heart attack. Think of the pain you would be in! This is an excellent example of the difference between dogs and people.

Don't worry—Ben recovered and did fine. He was put on intravenous fluids and antibiotics. We treated him for shock, just in case his mind caught up with his body. That night we removed the irreparable lung lobe. The ribs had pinched down on this section of the lung so tightly that the blood supply was cut off and it was literally dead. We went through the intestine, cutting out the bad sections and cleaning up and saving the good parts. Their ends were sutured back together to make a complete, albeit much shorter, intestinal tract. We also cleaned and tacked the cuts over his face, neck, chest and abdomen.

Nothing much was done the following day. The day after that we fixed the broken bones of the front leg and worked on the cuts some more. The following day we took care of the broken rear leg. Two days later, Ben walked back out our front door, got into the car with his owners and went home. Please don't get the wrong idea: It was a very easy case. The dog was not saved by two brilliant and superhuman veterinarians. We just put the parts back together, just like you would with an erector set.

Ben's story should tell you something. For starters, things are usually not as bad as they look. Any veterinary clinic will have similar stories to tell. Would Ben have died without veterinary care? Of course he would have, but that doesn't mean the dog was in much danger once he got to our hospital alive. Medicine is a lot like baking a cake: You follow the recipe and in the vast majority of cases everything turns out okay.

In the rest of this chapter are what we believe are the most common canine emergencies. Assuming your dog ever has an emergency, it will most probably be one on this list. These are not necessarily the most serious emergencies; they're just the most common. Some are not life-threatening, but if treatment is to be successful, the dog must be treated immediately. For others, it is a matter of life or death that your dog be seen immediately.

Severe Trauma

Severe trauma obviously includes a very wide variety of injuries. Among these would be car accidents, broken bones, gun shots, dog fights, porcupine quills, fish hooks or lures caught in the lips or skin and lacerations. These types of injuries really are emergencies. Even small cuts that may not seem like emergencies will always heal better if they are cleaned and sutured immediately.

With any of these injuries, your first thought should be to do no harm. In other words, don't make things worse than they already are. Don't even worry about trying to figure out what is wrong. It doesn't make any difference if one bone, two bones or seven bones are broken. The dog needs to be seen by the veterinarian. You shouldn't waste any time. If you know the dog is injured, just get it to the clinic and let the vet decide what needs to be done.

If there are large cuts, or bones are broken, you may not be sure how to get the dog in the car. You don't want to get bitten, nor do you want to hurt the dog any further. If the dog can walk, don't try to carry it. It will hurt the dog a lot less if it goes on its own power. After all, the dog knows what hurts and what doesn't.

If the dog can't or won't move on its own, it needs to be carried. This isn't difficult, and you do not need any special equipment. Slide its body onto a blanket or board, and take the dog that way. If you need to pick the dog up, wrap a couple of blankets around its body and head and simply pick it up. The thickness of the blankets will cushion any pressure you may apply over an injured area. (Make sure your dog can breathe freely!)

If the dog is continuing to bleed, take a towel or cloth and apply pressure over the cut. You can put a layer of tape over that to hold it in place. Any clean towel and any kind of tape will do—don't worry about real medical supplies.

If there is obviously a broken bone, don't worry about stabilizing it. In our combined 35 years of practice, we have never had a client further injure a broken bone. Many books talk about how a simple fracture can turn into a compound one as the dog is moved (with compound fractures, the end of the broken bone is exposed as it sticks out through the skin). This has never happened to our clients, and anyway, we've fixed lots of compound fractures that were caused by cars, trucks and boats.

Just use common sense and don't panic, because it won't make any difference to the outcome of the case. Don't even worry about how bad things are. Remember, of all the emergencies that got to our clinic alive, over 98 percent left the same way a few days later. Dogs make great patients. They make veterinarians look good, because they are tough and heal so well.

SEIZURES

There may be nothing more frightening than seeing your dog go into a seizure. The dog will usually fall down on its side. Its legs will paddle as if it were swimming, and it may bang its head against the floor. The dog will usually drool, possibly vomit and may lose urinary and/or fecal continence. This can last for one to five minutes, and in some cases even longer. Throughout the seizure the dog does not recognize you and probably seems totally unaware of the surroundings or its own actions. There is no question in your mind this is an emergency.

You call the veterinarian, carry the dog to the car and drive like a maniac to the hospital. You are there in less than three minutes. As the car comes to a stop, you look in the back seat to see what is happening to your dog, only to realize that it is sitting up looking at you. You lead the dog into the clinic and you and the veterinarian watch as the dog walks around the waiting room sniffing for evidence of which of its friends was there today. A physical exam and blood tests reveal nothing abnormal. We have lived through experiences identical to this hundreds of times.

Even though most of these dogs are behaving normally by the time they reach the clinic, at the very least you should call your veterinarian when the seizure begins. He or she will undoubtedly want you to bring the animal in immediately. Until the dog develops a pattern for its seizures, no one can be sure of the cause or severity, and it is important to get the dog checked as soon after the seizure as possible. However, to help you put this in perspective, with a combined 35 years of experience behind us and after literally thousands of seizure patients, we have seen only two of these dogs die on their initial seizure, and both had ingested poison.

In the very rare case that the dog is still in seizure when you reach the vet, intravenous medications will be used. These will have the same effect as placing the dog under a general anesthetic—it becomes unconscious. Usually by the time it wakes, whatever was causing the seizure has passed. The dog wakes up probably not even aware that it had a seizure or was brought to the veterinary clinic.

There are many, many things that can cause seizures. Owners typically worry about poisoning, heart attack or a stroke, but it's rarely any of these. The list of potential causes stretches from low blood sugar to brain tumors— widely disparate conditions that have just one thing in common: They all somehow affect the brain. The brain controls the millions of nerve cells that cause the muscles to contract. During a seizure, the brain is sending out signals for some or all of the muscles in the body to contract, but the signals are not coordinated. These muscles are doing what they are told; it's just that the control center has gone haywire. The dog is unable to stand and its legs paddle uselessly. There is also a loss of control over the involuntary muscles. Those are the ones that do their job whether we are awake or not, whether we think about their action or not. In a seizure, the dog may therefore suddenly lose the ability to retain its urine and stool.

The most common cause of seizures in dogs is a syndrome known as *idiopathic epilepsy*. Most owners and veterinarians simply call it epilepsy. Idiopathic means that we are not able to determine the true cause of the seizures. This condition usually starts when the dog is between two and three years of age. The seizures typically start out fairly short and mild, with the dog showing few abnormalities. As the dog gets older the seizures grow more severe until, in the untreated dog, they become violent and may last for 30 minutes or more.

While some cases of epilepsy may result from trauma or infections, most dogs are thought to have inherited this condition from their parents. There is a much higher incidence of seizures in certain breeds.

In idiopathic epileptics, the seizures will vary in severity and are usually described using one of three terms: petit mal, grand mal or status epilepticus. *Petit mal* seizures are mild. The dog may simply develop a blank stare, shake one leg or cry out as if in pain. The seizure usually lasts less than one minute. The *grand mal* seizure is the most common. The dog will fall to one side, urinate or defecate uncontrollably, paddle its feet as if swimming, froth at the mouth and may cry out. It will be unaware of its surroundings. Grand mal seizures usually last five minutes or less. *Status epilepticus* is the most severe form. It appears exactly like a grand mal seizure, but it may last for hours or more. Or, as soon as the dog seems to recover, it immediately degenerates back into the seizure.

The petit and grand mal seizures are not life threatening in most cases, unless they occur at a time when the dog could be in danger. For instance, a dog that is swimming when it has a seizure may drown. Status epilepticus, on the other hand, is a very serious seizure state. With the body convulsing violently for hours, the internal body temperature will become critically high. Organ damage and death can result.

All seizures, when first noted, should be reported to your veterinarian; however, medical intervention is not always indicated. In most instances epilepsy is not life threatening unless status epilepticus develops.

We always ask clients to keep a record of all known seizures their dog has. Generally, anticonvulsant drugs are not given unless the animal has more than one seizure per month or the seizures last more than 10 minutes. This is a general guideline only. The dosages for all the anticonvulsant medications vary widely from dog to dog, and if the seizures do not occur with some regularity, it is difficult to determine the quantities a dog will need. The goal of therapy is to stabilize the nerves and membranes within the brain, but not to a point where the animal appears or acts sedated.

Anticonvulsant medications are therefore used in chronic cases. It must be completely understood that drug therapy is not a total cure, but rather controls the severity and frequency of the seizures. Anticonvulsant drugs include phenobarbital, Dilantin, Primidone and others. These drugs have a sedative action on the nerves in the brain.

Since idiopathic epilepsy is an inherited condition and is genetically transmitted, epileptic dogs should not be bred.

POISONING

In our homes and businesses, there are many substances that can poison a dog. If dogs eat certain houseplants or too much chocolate, they can be fatally poisoned. Many household cleaning products can have the same effect. Some of the common over-the-counter medications that humans use, such as ibuprofen and others, can also poison a dog if enough is ingested. Many of our prescription drugs can cause problems, too, but usually only if the dog eats a lot of them. Today, veterinarians also see cases in which their patients have consumed illegal drugs, and these situations can obviously be quite serious.

Still, as far as true poisoning goes, in canine medicine, more than 90 percent of all serious or life- threatening cases are caused by two substances: antifreeze (ethylene glycol) and rat or mouse poisons (Warfarin).

Antifreeze

Ethylene glycol is the active ingredient of many antifreezes. It prevents water from freezing until exceptionally low temperatures are reached. In many households or buildings that are not heated in the winter, it is also used to prevent drains and toilets from freezing. Unfortunately, it has a taste that dogs and cats really like, and they will readily drink it because of its flavor.

Dogs can be exposed to antifreeze if it is accidentally spilled, when the radiator of a car overflows or from drinking out of drains or toilets where it has been used to prevent freezing. Only a minute quantity is needed to fatally poison an animal. The amount that would collect in a crack in the garage floor after the radiator has overflowed is more than enough to kill a 50-pound dog!

Antifreeze is deadly to dogs, even in tiny amounts. That's why you must clean up spills quickly and completely.

Once ingested, ethylene glycol is absorbed unchanged from the intestines and is carried to the liver. There it is metabolized almost instantly to various toxic compounds that affect the brain and kidneys. Surprisingly, some dogs that consume fatal quantities of antifreeze never show any outward clinical signs for three to four days. However, once they are affected, dogs stagger, vomit, have a seizure, slip into a coma and die within 12 hours. These are all due to the toxic effects on the dog's brain.

Some dogs show few outward signs of poisoning until their kidneys fail. It takes about four days for the tiny crystals of glycolate and oxalic acid to grow large enough to destroy most of the normal functional kidney tissue. When this happens, the dog develops uremic poisoning. It becomes lethargic, depressed, nauseous, stops eating, and soon slips into a coma and dies.

If the dog receives medical treatment immediately after the ethylene glycol is ingested, it can sometimes be saved. The dog must be started on antidote therapy in the first eight hours after the poison was consumed. To counteract the action of the antifreeze, either ethanol or a product known as 4-methylpyrazole is given intravenously over several hours or even a few days. These preparations prevent ethylene glycol from being metabolized by the liver. The ethylene glycol that was consumed is then excreted unchanged in its nontoxic form.

To be honest, antidote therapy is successful in only a few cases. Even when treatment is started in the first few hours, only a small percentage of dogs are saved. One major problem is that owners often do not know the dog has ingested antifreeze. Others do not realize how toxic this substance is to dogs. Most animals are not taken to a veterinary clinic until there are signs of uremic poisoning, and by then it is too late to save the dog. The kidneys have already been destroyed.

Prevention is, without a doubt, the best cure for antifreeze poisoning. Store all containers where dogs and children cannot get to them. If your car radiator overflows in the garage or near the home, immediately flush the area with large quantities of water and clean everything up. If you see or even suspect your pet has consumed any antifreeze, regardless of how small the quantity may be, take the dog to a veterinary clinic immediately.

Rat Poison

The second most common cause of poisonings in dogs is rat and mouse poisons. Their active ingredients are coumarin and indanediones. These substances affect the blood clotting mechanism of animals that ingest them. They prevent clots from forming, thereby causing these dogs to bleed to death internally. Hundreds of tiny blood vessels break in our bodies every day. This is normally not a problem, because a clot quickly forms and very little blood is lost. However, with these poisons, the bleeding continues until the animal dies.

Clinical signs are usually not seen for three to 10 days after ingestion, depending on the amount consumed. At that time, the dog will become lethargic and may have nose bleeds, bloody vomiting, black tar-like stools, bruises, hemorrhages on the skin or membranes of the mouth and difficult respiration. Untreated, it can die.

Rat and mouse poison can pose a real danger if they are easily accessible.

There is little danger from dogs eating the bodies of mice that have been poisoned; these products must be eaten directly for the dog to be affected. The toxin is broken down in the mouse's body and is not passed on to the dog.

Rat poison cases are much easier to treat than antifreeze poisoning. They usually respond quickly to therapy with no permanent damage done to the body. These rat and mouse poisons prevent the liver's metabolism of vitamin K1, a substance that is necessary for clots to form. Therapy involves administering vitamin K1 by injection, and possibly following up with more K1 in tablet form. This quickly reestablishes the body's ability to form blood clots. In some dogs that have lost a lot of blood, blood transfusions are also required. Once a diagnosis is made, treatment is usually successful.

AURICULAR HEMATOMA

This condition, a blood-filled swelling on the dog's ear, is not life threatening. We've included it in emergencies because it does need to be treated quickly, and because it often looks so bad that your natural inclination will be to take your dog to the clinic immediately. In all honesty, it matters little if these cases are seen immediately—but they should be treated within the first 24 hours.

A dog's earflap is similar to a bologna sandwich. Two layers of skin lie on each side of a piece of cartilage. They are attached to each other only by a thin layer of connective tissue. This structure allows the flap to bend easily but still be able to take considerable punishment. However, sometimes due to trauma or simply from the dog shaking its head, the tiny blood vessels that lie between the cartilage and the skin break. Blood flows out into the surrounding tissue with enough pressure to separate the skin from the cartilage. A pocket of blood starts to pool, forming a *hematoma*. (A hematoma is a localized swelling filled with blood, resulting from a break in a blood vessel.) Because the dog now feels this extra weight on its ear, it shakes its head more and more, trying to remove whatever is attached to its ear. This causes additional blood flow, and the small pocket can grow to the size of a golf or tennis ball!

In shorthaired breeds the hematoma will be obvious from the start, but in longhaired ones it may go for quite a while before it is noticed. Owners are understandably disturbed when they see this mass growing in the flap of their dog's ear. Few realize what the problem is—at best it could be an insect bite, at worst a tumor. But in fact, it is not that difficult to treat.

It is possible to simply insert a hypodermic needle into the area and drain the blood off with a syringe. This can usually be done under mild sedation or by using a local anesthetic. However, in most cases at least a portion of the blood has clotted and it is difficult to withdraw through a needle. A second problem is that the bleeding inside the earflap is likely to continue, which means there will be another hematoma in a few days. That's why most veterinarians prefer to place the dog under a general anesthesia and make an S-shaped incision over the area. The blood, including any clots, is removed, and if need be any vessels that are still bleeding are tied off. The skin is then sutured back to the cartilage, and the sutures are passed all the way through to the skin on the other side of the ear. This holds the skin on both sides tightly against the cartilage. Then, as scar tissue forms (which always happens after the tissues of the body have been cut), it holds the three layers tightly together so a hematoma cannot recur in this spot. The only real problem with the surgical method is that the scar tissue may somewhat disfigure the earflap. In longhaired breeds this would not be noticed, but in the shorthaired ones it may cause the skin of the earflap to look a bit wrinkled. The dog is usually placed on antibiotics for seven to 14 days following surgery.

With auricular hematomas, it is always important to take care of any underlying cause. Most of these cases are actually caused by the dog shaking its head due to the irritation or itching from an ear infection. If this is the case, while the dog is being treated the ear canal is cleaned and medication started. If this isn't done, the problem may recur in either ear.

MISMATING

It is very important, if you have an unspayed female dog, to keep her under close supervision the entire time she is in heat. That includes not leaving her outside unattended. We strongly believe that every litter of puppies should be carefully thought out and well planned. Dog breeding should not be left to random chance. However, there are times when you may not realize your dog is in heat, or when an amorous neighborhood male ambushes her, despite your best efforts. What can you do?

It is possible for a female that has just been bred to receive an injection that prevents the pregnancy. This is known as a *mismate shot*. These are usually injections of the hormone estrogen. If given within the first 24 to 72 hours after breeding, the hormone causes the fertilized eggs to pass on through the uterus without attaching to its inner wall. The microscopic eggs then die and are reabsorbed by other cells within the uterus.

This seems like an easy method to prevent pregnancy, and it is, but there are problems associated with estrogen injections. They extend the heat cycle, and the female dog may be able to breed for an additional two to three weeks. During that time, the injections cannot be given again, so the dog must be supervised very closely.

Additionally, the injections are not without health risks. In most dogs, the amount of estrogen used should cause no problems. However, in very rare cases it can cause a dangerous uterine disease called pyometra (this condition is discussed in Chapter 12). If pyometra does develop, the dog must be spayed. In a valuable breeding female, this would be a disaster. A second possible side effect, but still very rare at the dosage used in mismate shots, is that the estrogen injection might cause aplastic anemia. This is a condition in which the body stops making new blood cells. If this effect becomes permanent, the dog would die without repeated blood transfusions.

Newer products are now being used, with mixed results. Some use hormone-like amino acids called *prostaglandins*. These have some side effects, but not the severe ones occasionally seen with estrogen.

For most dog owners, understanding the heat cycle will help prevent the need for mismating shots. Normal female dogs cycle once every six to eight months. During a normal cycle, the first outward sign is that the vagina will become swollen. This is followed immediately by the dog bleeding from the vaginal area for seven to 15 days. In most cases the bleeding stops after seven to 10 days. At this point the female becomes receptive to the male dog. That is to say, she will let him breed with her. She is usually receptive for four to seven days, and occasionally even longer. Unfortunately, many owners believe that as soon as the dog stops bleeding, the heat cycle is over and they can let the dog out in the backyard unattended. In fact, at this time female dogs attract male dogs from great distances with their *pheromones*. These are airborne scent chemicals that are liberated from the vaginal area. This combination of misunderstanding and fertility causes many unwanted breedings.

Many dogs also have abnormal heat cycles, with a wide variation between when they are receptive to the male and for how long. In some breeds, they may bleed until 21 days after the first signs of vaginal swelling were noticed, and then breed a week later. The best preventive is to spay your female at six months of age if you do not intend to breed her, and be very careful if you do. Through blood tests and vaginal smears, veterinarians can predict when a dog will breed and usually for how long.

DYSTOCIA

The most common problem associated with pregnancy is *dystocia*—difficult labor. For birth to occur naturally, the female dog must work and strain through the process we know as labor. This moves the puppies through the uterus, dilates the cervix and passes them on out through the vagina. How long this takes can vary greatly. It usually takes more time and effort during a dog's first pregnancy. It also varies from breed to breed. Those with square heads and short noses generally have more labor problems.

Once the dog goes into labor, most owners feel uncomfortable determining whether the amount of straining or length of labor is normal. Most veterinarians that work with breeders try to counsel them on what to expect for their dog when the big day arrives. Owners want to know when they need to become concerned and when the dog should be seen by the veterinarian. The veterinarian may only need to help pull out the first puppy, or a cesarean section may be necessary.

How does a vet decide? Similar guidelines are used for most breeds. If the dog has been in consistent labor for more than two hours and the first puppy has not yet been born, we start to get concerned. Remember, we are talking about consistent labor. If the dog seems to strain slightly once every 30 minutes, we wouldn't call that consistent labor. After two hours of consistent labor the veterinarian should be called. It may not be time to come to the clinic yet, but the veterinarian should be informed. After you describe the situation, they may have some helpful hints. Your call also gives the vet a chance to set their schedule and priorities for the next few hours. They may not want to start a three-hour surgery if they think your dog might soon need help.

Once the first puppy is born, if the dog is in labor for more than two hours on any subsequent puppy the veterinarian should be called. The first one is most likely the one to cause problems, but the female should be watched until all the pups have emerged.

Don't be concerned if you don't see an afterbirth after each puppy. They may come much later, or two or more may come together and look like only one. The female will instinctively eat these, but it is not necessary for her to do so. It is probably better if you properly dispose of them.

Also, don't be concerned if one or more of the puppies come rear end first. In dogs this is not considered a true breech birth—nearly 40 percent of all puppies are delivered this way.

Pregnancy and birth can have complications. Make sure you know what to do in an emergency.

Try to get the female checked by the veterinarian within 12 to 18 hours after the last puppy is born. They will be able to determine if any puppies remain within her. They may also give an injection of oxytocin, which will cause the uterus to shrink and expel any unwanted products, such as blood and placental fragments.

CESAREAN SECTION

Sometimes, for a wide variety of reasons, female dogs are unable to give birth to their puppies. The pups may be too large to move through the birth canal, a puppy may be positioned in such a way that it cannot make it through the cervix or pelvis, the mother's uterus may not have the muscular strength to expel the pups or the shape of the puppies' heads or bodies may be so blunt that they cannot dilate the cervix correctly. For whatever reason, if the combined efforts of the dog, owner and veterinarian cannot get the puppies out of the uterus through the vagina, a cesarean section must be done.

This is usually a fairly easy surgery for the veterinarian, but the follow-up care for the owner may be difficult. The female will be placed under a fast-acting and often reversible anesthetic. The surgery is then usually done as an incision through the midline of the belly. The veterinarian will take the pups out one by one from the uterus. Thirty minutes or less after the mother's incision is closed with sutures, she will walk out the door of the clinic with her puppies carried in a box behind her.

It would seem that all should go well after the puppies are out into the world, and it usually does. However, in some cases the mother dog, for whatever reason, ignores or rejects litters that were born by c-section. The owners then have to take over the task of round-the-clock feedings using a commercial milk replacement. They will also have to stimulate the pups to urinate and defecate for the first 10 to 16 days, and keep the puppies warm, dry and clean at all times. This is a lot of work!

When female dogs are bred, they usually have their puppies within 61 to 65 days. This is fairly predictable, but can vary among breeds and from dog to dog. It is important to keep track of the dates the dog was bred. This allows the breeder and the veterinarian to manage the final stages of pregnancy. If a cesarean section is necessary, if it is done too early or too late it could result in the unnecessary death of the puppies or their mother.

HYPERTHERMIA

Hyperthermia, also known as *heat prostration*, is a common canine emergency. Dogs can overheat from too much exercise or when they are confined to sunny areas on hot days. There are a number of ways dogs can get stuck in the heat, including being in a dog run with insufficient shade, but the most common by far is being left in a vehicle on a hot day. The car does not even have to be parked in the sun! A car parked in the shade when outside temperatures are high can quickly become a death trap, especially for dogs that get excited and bark at people or other dogs that go by. Often someone will leave their dog in a car during hot weather for only a few minutes and return to find the dog near death. Our clinic is near the parking lot of a shopping center, and we have seen this happen too often.

Being stuck in a hot car can be a death sentence for a dog. Make sure there is plenty of ventilation and that your dog is protected if it must wait even a moment in your car.

The normal body temperature of a dog is 101.5° to 102° F. This is a wider range than in humans. A dog that gets excited in the waiting room of our clinic looking or barking at other dogs or cats can easily drive its temperature up to 103°. This is not abnormal, nor does it cause a problem. But once the body temperature reaches 105° to 106°, the dog is suffering from hyperthermia.

When a dog gets hot, its only method of cooling itself is by panting. This moves air back and forth through its body, and that, along with the cooling effects of evaporation, can significantly lower their temperatures in most situations. Dogs with short, flat faces have more problems cooling down. Because of the restrictive way the throat and mouth are formed, they cannot ventilate as well as other breeds. Dogs in poor health or those with medical conditions involving the lungs or heart also have problems cooling their bodies through panting. And even a healthy dog in an environment where the air taken in by panting is just too hot will suffer.

A dog with heat prostration will pant rapidly and its gums will often turn brick red. Its heart rate will increase dramatically and it will usually become extremely agitated. If untreated, it will have increasing difficulty breathing. Its gums will turn a bluish color and it may even slip into a lethargy that is close to coma. Vomiting and diarrhea may occur. After this point, the dog usually dies within one to two hours.

The immediate goal of treatment is to reduce the body temperature. This must be done carefully but quickly. The preferred course of action would be to get the dog to a veterinary clinic immediately. If this isn't possible, you can attempt to start lowering the temperature with a cold water bath. Submerse the dog up to its neck and run more cold water over its head. Once the dog is wet, you can use fans to evaporate some of the water and further drop the dog's temperature.

In a clinic situation, we do pretty much the same thing, but in a controlled setting. We try to get the temperature down to 103° quickly and then drop it an additional degree per hour until it is back to between 101° and 101.5°. Hyperthermic dogs almost always go into shock—another good reason to get to a vet. To counter this, we place these dogs on intravenous fluids and treat for shock when the cooling process is started. Short-acting steroids are administered with these fluids.

Affected animals must be observed closely for several days. After they have stabilized, some of these dogs will lose the ability to maintain their body temperature within the normal range. Their temperatures may go too low, sometimes below 98°. Others may have their temperatures go back to 106° or higher, even if they are maintained in a cool room. In some dogs, their blood starts clotting within the blood vessels all over their bodies. This is obviously very serious.

The prognosis for dogs that have suffered hyperthermia is never good, and varies according to how high their temperature went, how long it was elevated and whether they regain the ability to maintain their own temperature correctly.

Obviously, preventing hyperthermia is much easier than treating it. There are many variables that keep us from giving you an exact outside temperature that is safe for your dog. These variables include the amount of cloud cover, shade, wind and humidity. The bottom line is that on hot or humid days, *never* leave any pet in a vehicle with the windows rolled up. Don't assume because your car is parked in the shade that the dog cannot suffer from hyperthermia. It happens all the time. Don't think, either, that because the window is rolled down part way on a hot day, your dog cannot suffer from hyperthermia. It happens every summer in our area, and we are in the far northern reaches of Wisconsin where the temperature seldom gets out of the low 80s. Be very, very careful, and think twice about taking your pet along if it would mean a wait in the car.

BLOAT

The medical term for bloat is *gastric dilation volvulus*, but by any name, whenever this happens it is a life-threatening emergency. The stomach of the dog dilates with gas, and may also twist on itself (called *torsion*). Bloat with torsion is one of the most dangerous intestinal disorders known in canine medicine.

The exact cause of canine bloat is unknown. However, it is believed to be brought on by abnormal stomach motility (that means the stomach can move more easily within the abdominal cavity). Somehow the stomach becomes excessively dilated with gas, causing it to expand—occasionally to three to four times its normal size. As the stomach swells with gas it may "float up" on other organs, and can actually rotate or twist on its axis. When the stomach twists, it causes the esophagus (at the entrance) and the small intestine (at the exit) to also twist, preventing passage of gas, liquids or food. With no release of gas possible, the stomach expands further.

Also as the stomach twists, veins and arteries within the stomach walls and other organs such as the spleen and liver become twisted, and blood is no longer able to flow through them normally. The spleen, closely associated with the stomach, may also twist, completely obstructing the blood flow. The trapped gas, foods and blood form a deadly combination. Not all cases of gastric dilation result in torsion. However, it is our experience that the majority do.

Large breeds, especially those with deep chests, develop bloat more frequently than small breeds. Additionally larger chest cavities and abdomens in dogs such as Labrador Retrievers, Greyhounds, Afghan Hounds, Great Danes and similar breeds have enough space within the abdominal cavity to more readily allow the stomach to bloat and twist.

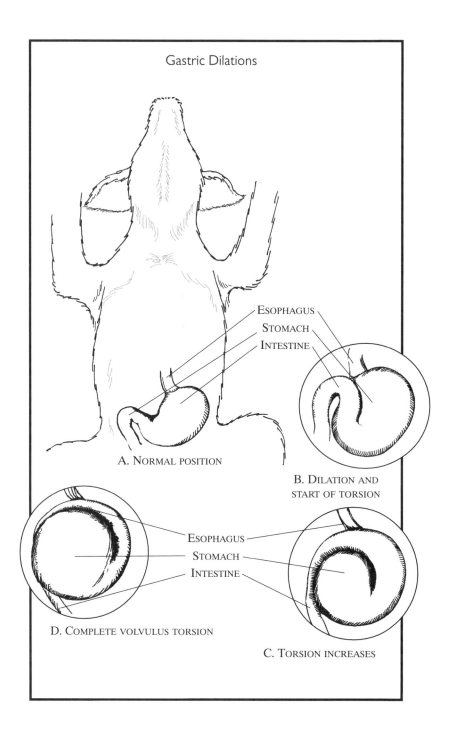

Gastric Dilations

A. Normal position

Esophagus
Stomach
Intestine

B. Dilation and
start of torsion

D. Complete volvulus torsion

Esophagus
Stomach
Intestine

C. Torsion increases

The initial signs of bloat are usually seen within the first few hours after eating. Generally, the dog acts nervous and cannot get comfortable. It may try but be unable to vomit, and may have a tight, bloated abdomen. When torsion occurs, the dog may try repeatedly, but unsuccessfully, to vomit; since torsion involves the esophagus, it is not possible to bring anything up from the stomach. Along with the bloated appearance, there is excessive panting, probably due to pain and the fact that enlarged stomach is pushing the diaphragm against the chest cavity. Any dog that tries to vomit and cannot should always be treated as an emergency!

Left untreated, virtually all bloat victims will die. Once the stomach twists, death will result within hours. Treat every case of suspected bloat as a medical emergency. Do not wait!

To be successful, veterinary treatment must begin as soon as possible. The first step is to relieve stomach gases and shrink the size of the stomach. This is accomplished by passing a tube through the mouth and into the stomach. Anti-gas remedies such as Di-Gel can be administered through the tube. A dog that can vomit once treatment has been started has a much better chance of survival. But this is not always possible, especially if torsion has occurred where the esophagus and stomach meet. If a tube cannot be passed through, then large needles (called *trocars*) can be placed directly into the stomach through the left abdominal wall to relieve the pressure. Occasionally an incision can be made into the stomach through the abdominal wall to relieve the gas and drain the stomach contents.

Dogs suspected of having torsion must undergo surgery at once. The abdomen is opened up and the stomach, spleen and intestines are rotated back to their original positions. The stomach is sutured in place against the ribcage to help prevent another twist. It must be pointed out that even with prompt surgical correction, not every patient survives. Many dogs go into shock or develop infections after surgery. Careful postoperative care and monitoring are important, especially for the first 72 hours after surgery.

Dogs that survive bloat are generally put on a modified diet. Although diet has never been definitely proven to be a contributing cause to bloat, several theories that link the two show promise. It is best to avoid feeding large amounts of food at a single meal to the recovered patient. Many smaller meals may help lessen the stomach's gas production. Many authorities believe cereal-based diets should be avoided, as these foods tend to expand once they meet the stomach fluids. Antacids and anti-gas preparations, such as

Di-Gel or others containing simethicone, can be useful in preventing bloat, as well.

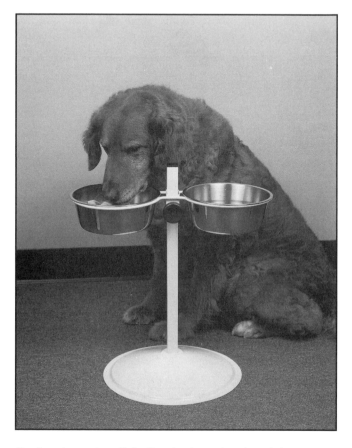

Feeding a larger dog off the floor has been thought to help prevent a recurrence of bloat.

There are many theories about bloat. However, abnormal stomach motility is still the prime suspect, not diet, and we, the authors, have never been able to detect a propensity to bloat based on diet. We do think that giving two or three small meals a day rather than one large meal is a good idea for dogs with deep chests that are prone to bloat. Additionally, exercise should always be limited immediately after a meal. Hopefully, future research will yield better information.

SUMMING UP

These are the most common emergencies you'll see in adult dogs. In previous sections of the book we have discussed other potential emergencies that are more likely to occur with young dogs. In Chapter 5 we talked about acute vomiting and diarrhea and how you can decide if the dog should be taken immediately in to the veterinarian. In that chapter we also discussed insect bites and how to determine if a dog that has suddenly injured a leg and is limping needs to be seen by the veterinarian. In Chapter 9 we discussed gastrointestinal foreign bodies and obstructions and what to do if your dog is hit by a car.

Do everything possible to protect your dog from situations that could result in medical emergencies, but understand that some may still occur. When it happens, don't panic! Remember, it is not your job to determine exactly what is wrong or what should be done. Your only job is to get the dog to the veterinarian. The rest is their responsibility.

Chapter 14

OLD AGE AND YOUR DOG

Just as people age at different rates, so do dogs. However, the variation is much greater in dogs than it is in people. Most of this variability in dogs is related to their size. The smaller breeds live much longer and therefore age slower than do the large or giant breeds. Many Yorkshire Terriers live to be 14 or 15 years old, while nine might be very old for an Irish Wolfhound. Regardless of the breed, however, aging affects all dogs in similar ways. After all, they are the same species. As the years go by, the same systems are prone to failure whether the dog weighs 10 pounds or 100.

As dog owners, we all want the best for our dogs, especially as they get old. We will strive to add as much comfort and enjoyment as we can to their later years. Anything we can do to extend their lives, we generally do, even though in some cases what is best for us is not necessarily what is best for them. We may also have to rethink what role an older dog plays in our lives. When we first got the dog, we wanted a hunting partner, a guard dog or maybe just a companion. However, an old dog may no longer be able to meet these needs. The time when the dog always wanted to do more for us may be past. Now it is our turn to take care of our beloved friend.

EXERCISE

As dogs age, their needs and desires change. Sometimes what they need is not what they want, and what they want is not what they need. Older dogs often become more sedate and are happier to spend more and more time lying at your side or in front of the fireplace. Their activity level decreases. Unfortunately, this can cause problems, and in fact, may take years off their life. When older dogs, through their own choice, decrease their activity levels, they often start a process that limits their ability to participate in many activities with us. The less they use their muscles, the weaker they become. This becomes a vicious cycle: The less they do the weaker they become, the weaker they are the less they can do. This lifestyle is a disaster for our older pets.

It is very important that you encourage your canine senior citizens to exercise. They need it, and they also need your encouragement and participation. They won't respond if you tell them to go walk around the block a few times. In some cases you may need to almost force them, but usually they will happily join in what you are doing. For some dogs this may be fetching a ball or playing with a Frisbee. For others, just a routine daily walk will be perfect. Older dogs should be started on regular exercise before they get to the point where a 10-minute walk is taxing. In fact, it's probably good for both of you.

Exercise will do more than keep their muscles strong. It will also help maintain good cardiac and respiratory function. Older dogs do not suffer the same heart problems we do, but stimulating the heart helps to keep it functioning longer. Exercise also keeps the weight down, which in itself takes a huge burden off the body. Excess weight in the younger dog may be uncomfortable, but in the older dog it shortens life. Later in this chapter we will discuss common kidney and heart diseases of senior dogs. These systems simply wear out in dogs. Excess weight forces these organs to care for a larger mass of tissue, thereby shortening the length of time that they are capable of functioning normally. The liver gets more fat deposited in it as the dog becomes overweight. This fatty infiltration of the liver crowds out normal functioning cells, thereby diminishing the liver's ability to take care of the body's needs.

In our practice we have consistently observed that active older dogs enjoy these years more. They are often spared from a long, lingering demise, marked by poor health. In most cases, the added years that active dogs gain are of better quality, allowing them to do more things. Then, as if some automatic clock had ticked away, they are suddenly gone. If dogs could choose, this would seem to be their choice.

Older pets still need to be active, and can enjoy life
with people of all ages.

DIET

We do not believe that special diets are needed for older dogs unless they
suffer from specific conditions. There are specific foods for those with failing
kidneys or hearts. We always prefer that all dogs be on a dry food and believe
that it should be fed dry. The calorie level is easy to regulate, and the abrasive
action of eating dry food helps keep the teeth clean while at the same time
massaging the gums. We usually leave older dogs on the same diet they are
used to and only change the amount if it is necessary.

The one factor about the dog's diet that does concern us is how it relates
to weight. Even with exercise, some older animals tend to gain weight. As

we mentioned before, this can be very hard on older dogs. When their weight increases, the best thing to do is simply cut back on how much they're fed. We don't like the reducing diets or the senior diets. They are usually very bland with little flavor. Our feeling is that older dogs should at least get to eat something they enjoy. Almost every client we know that has put their dog on either of these special diets has complained that the dog didn't want to eat them. When we look at the ingredients, we think they probably taste a lot like cardboard. Our recipe for overweight dogs is simply to start out by decreasing the amount of food you give them by about 10 to 15 percent. Try the smaller amount for four to six weeks, and then adjust again, if needed. Smaller and more frequent meals throughout the day may help. And of course, no or very few treats, as these tend to be high in calories. Increased exercise should also be part of any weight reduction plan.

Some older dogs are placed on bland senior diets due to problems with constipation. Again, in most cases we would try to stick with the food they like, but add a small quantity of Metamucil to each meal. This causes no side effects, but adds bulk and fiber to the diet and often will eliminate constipation problems.

GROOMING

Grooming is even more important for older dogs than it is for younger ones. The skin and hair in older dogs typically lose vitality. The hair often becomes dry, brittle and thin, and the skin gets very dry with dander. Much of this can be lessened, if not reversed, by frequent brushing. This stimulates the hair and skin. Regular bathing is also recommended, and will help to rid the body of built-up dander, oils and other debris. Dogs with excessively dry coats or skin or that have shedding problems can be helped with nutritional supplements formulated for these conditions. Linatone or Vitacoat are two brands that are frequently used.

DENTAL PROBLEMS

We covered dental problems in adult dogs in Chapter 11. For canine seniors, these become much more common and can cause more serious problems. The teeth and gums are like any other part of the body, and slowly wear out over a dog's life. If not attended to regularly, the thin film known as plaque hardens into tartar. This mineralized substance works its way between the teeth and gums, allowing bacteria to reach the deeper regions of the jaw. In older dogs, changes in these areas can occur rapidly, and what seemed like a normal, healthy mouth can suddenly be filled with tiny abscesses and loose teeth.

It is important that the teeth of these older patients be cleaned regularly. This can be done at home using dental cleansers and canine toothpastes used with dental sponges, brushes or pads. The bacteria you eliminate from the dog's mouth will then not get the chance to cross over into its bloodstream and spread to the rest of its body. These bacteria can lead to heart, kidney and liver problems in many older dogs. Don't assume that your older dog should have bad breath. Bad breath is a sign of a problem, and your cleanings will help eliminate it, as well as heading off many other problems.

ROUTINE VETERINARY CARE

Many dog owners believe their older canines no longer need routine veterinary care. This is not true. Yearly vaccinations are probably more important for dogs in this age group, as their immune systems are not as capable of defending against infections. Vaccinations do no harm to older dogs, and they provide protection against life-threatening diseases.

Your dog should still have yearly stool checks for parasites and be on a heartworm preventive. We strongly recommend that senior dogs also be on one of the monthly products that protect against fleas. Dogs gain no special immunities as they age. Rather, they are affected more by things like flea bites than are younger dogs. As an example, a moderate hookworm or flea infestation that might only mildly affect a younger dog frequently causes severe anemia in an older dog.

One thing few dog owners think about is spaying or neutering their older pet. Many of these dogs were bred in their younger years. Now their breeding days are long gone, but the reproductive organs are not. As we mentioned in Chapter 9, the estrogen produced by females and the testosterone produced by males does more harm than good in most of our pets. This is true at any age. As soon as you know there is no chance that a dog will be used for breeding, it should be spayed or neutered. You will reduce or eliminate problems such as breast, uterine and testicular cancer, prostate disease and common uterine problems such as pyometra and endometritis. These problems are serious in any dog, but for older dogs they may be fatal. Even if your dog is a senior, ask your veterinarian about spaying or neutering. In most cases, this simple procedure will add years to the dog's life.

THE COMMON MEDICAL PROBLEMS OF OLD AGE

We are not unique in the problems of aging. Dogs' bodies have some of the same limiting factors that ours do. Our old dogs also get little aches and pains, and some more serious conditions. In this section we will discuss some of the specific medical problems commonly encountered in the older canine patient. Take some time to look over the other chapters, too, especially Chapter 12, which deals with the medical problems of adult dogs. Older dogs often suffer from the same conditions that affect their younger relatives.

For dogs, just as their lifespan is shorter, so is the course of some of these diseases. Older dogs can go downhill quickly. One day they seem to be perfectly fine, and the next day an organ system has completely failed. This is very common in dogs. Remember, they cannot tell us how they feel. We usually have no indication that one of their body's structures has in some way been compromised until there is a radical change. Then, without any apparent warning, the dog is near death.

Most diseases progress slowly but consistently. As certain functionality is lost, other structures of the body are able to compensate. But eventually, enough damage is done that no compensation is possible. The bit of functional tissue within the eye is gone or the heart muscles can no longer keep up with the amount of blood returning from the rest of the body. Don't be surprised when these things happen to your dog. Regretfully, you should expect them.

Hearing and Vision Loss

The loss of vision and hearing are changes that all older dogs experience to some degree. While these losses can be caused by many different things, from infections to tumors, they are usually just normal aging changes. In most dogs they occur over a long period of time. You must remember that these are even more important senses for canines than they are for us. Some experts believe hearing, along with scent, may be more important for dogs than sight. Any loss of their ability to smell is difficult for us to detect.

However, when our dogs do not hear us as we arrive home or see the squirrel on the window sill, we know what has happened.

In some dogs this sensory loss seems to have occurred overnight, but this probably is not what happened. We simply haven't noticed the slow, progressive loss. To us it appears that one day the dog was fine, and the next day it was blind or deaf. In most cases, these dogs lost their senses over an extended period of time. However, they compensated for the loss by relying on other senses. The blind dog probably relied heavily on its scenting ability and hearing, along with its memory of the location of the furniture, doors and trees. But when its ability to smell further degenerated, or someone moved the furniture, the problem became obvious.

Dogs that have lost one or more of their senses actually do very well. We always have several blind dogs in our practice, and many that apparently hear nothing. They learn to get around in their world and suffer little because of their problem.

Prostate Disease

The function of the prostate gland is poorly understood by most dog owners. It is the only accessory sex gland in the male dog. Its primary function is to add fluid as the dog ejaculates that is important for the life and nutrition of the sperm. For most dogs, except during breeding periods, the prostate is more of a liability, as it serves no function important to daily life but is a common site of disease. In most veterinary texts it states that at least 75 percent of all unneutered male dogs over the age of eight years will have prostate trouble.

Three prostate diseases are most commonly encountered. While they can occur in any mature dog, they are most common in older dogs.

Cystic hyperplasia of the prostate is brought on by the lifelong effects of the male hormones produced by the testicles. The disease is characterized by an overall enlargement of the prostate. The tissue may simply grow, but in most cases the gland develops numerous internal cysts, further expanding its size. These are benign growths and are not cancerous.

The second common condition is prostate infections. Bacteria usually enter from the urinary tract, where they cause an inflammation and increase the size of the gland. In many of these cases, the prostate develops numerous small internal abscesses.

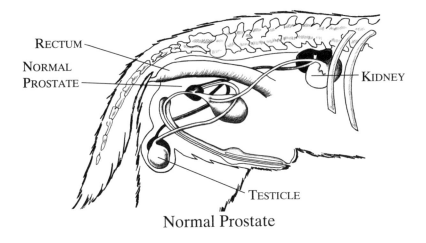

Normal Prostate

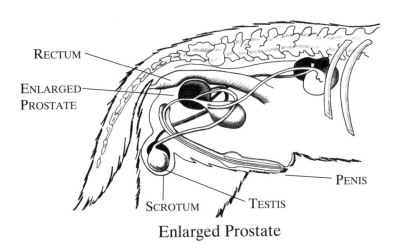

Enlarged Prostate

The third, but much less common problem, is cancer. In many types of animals, tumors of the prostate are very common, but this is not so in dogs. When they do occur in dogs, they are usually malignant changes of the glandular cells and are therefore referred to as *adenocarcinomas*.

All of these prostate diseases are predominantly problems of unneutered dogs. The testosterone produced by the testicles is necessary for the maintenance of the prostate. Without this hormone, the gland shrinks to a fraction of its normal size and does not tend to cause problems later in life. This is one of the main advantages of neutering male dogs.

All of these prostate diseases increase the size of the gland. The most common symptoms are therefore the result of this change in size. The prostate surrounds the urethra directly below the rectum. As it enlarges, it places pressure on and constricts the rectum. This leads to constipation and/or straining to defecate. If the prostate is painful, and it often is in these disorders, defecation will also be painful, further aggravating constipation. Because of the pain associated with prostate disease, either from the gland itself or through the spread of infection or cancer, affected dogs frequently walk with an abnormal gait.

The urinary tract will also be affected. Dogs may have difficulty passing their urine if the gland constricts the urethra, while others may be unable to hold their urine. Prostate infections can easily spread into the bladder, causing cystitis. Whether from the bladder or the prostate, blood and pus are often seen in the urine of affected dogs.

As we said, prostate disease is very common. Many dogs live with the problem for quite some time before they show any outward signs. Prostate disease can be very serious, however, as it may spread to or affect other areas and organs of the body. The bacteria found in prostate disease can spread throughout the body. Cancer of the prostate is malignant and spreads, both by local invasion to the immediately surrounding structures and via the bloodstream, throughout the body. In either case, this cancer is usually untreatable.

In the early stages of prostate disease, dogs will usually need enemas and will be placed on stool softeners. These help overcome the problems caused by constriction of the rectum. If the urinary tract is blocked, inserting a catheter may also be necessary.

To exist and maintain itself, the prostate gland needs to be consistently supplied by the male hormone testosterone. Since this hormone is produced by the testicles, the first step in treating most forms of prostatitis is neutering. In cases of cystic hyperplasia where bacteria are not present, this in itself may be a cure. But when infections are present, antibiotic therapy is indicated. It is often difficult to get adequate concentrations of antibiotics into the prostate, so antibiotic therapy goes on for a long time after the dog is neutered.

In some cases of prostate disease, estrogen treatments are also used. This female hormone helps to override the effects of its male counterpart. However, estrogen therapy is not without risk, and is only used when absolutely necessary.

Unfortunately, neutering has little effect on prostate cancer. It is possible to surgically remove the prostate gland, but this, too, may have little effect on prostate cancer if it has spread.

Dr. Marty Smith's 14-year-old Golden Retriever.

Prostate disease should be avoided if at all possible by neutering your dog as early as you can. If the animal is to be used for breeding, it should be neutered as soon as its reproductive days are over.

Kidney Disease

Kidney disease, also called *chronic renal disease*, often has no identifiable cause. Remember that the primary purpose of the kidneys is to filter out waste products from the body. Most of these are urea-based compounds, which is why dogs or humans suffering from kidney disease are said to be *uremic*. These compounds are toxic, and their effect on the body is what kills a patient that has lost significant kidney function.

Kidney disease is generally related to aging and is simply a deterioration and loss of filtration area within the kidney. The cells responsible for this primary renal function are called *glomeruli*. When a significant portion of the glomeruli die or are injured, there may not be enough left to remove normal wastes from the bloodstream. Toxic levels of waste materials build up in the body.

The signs of chronic renal disease emerge slowly over time. Because the kidneys cannot conserve water, you will usually notice increased urination, both in frequency and volume. To compensate and in an attempt to keep the body hydrated, the dog will drink more and more water.

In the early stages of the disease, nitrogen levels may or may not be elevated in the bloodstream. The kidneys can lose more than 75 percent of their normal function before they are no longer capable of detoxifying the body. If nitrogen is elevated in the blood, mouth ulcers may develop, as well as weight loss, poor appetite, vomiting, bleeding disorders and possible seizures. In severe cases, due to a lack of the hormone erythropoietin, there may be a decrease in the production of red blood cells, causing anemia.

Many older dogs have some degree of kidney disease. Mildly affected animals will live relatively normal lives. They compensate for their loss of kidney function by drinking more water to flush their system. More severely affected dogs will not be able to cope with the loss of kidney function and may die from renal failure. Renal failure is the number one cause of "death from natural causes" in dogs. Unlike humans, the canine heart generally outperforms the kidneys.

Most cases of chronic renal disease are not reversible. The kidneys have simply worn out. If the early signs of disease (increased thirst and urination) are recognized before the kidneys actually fail, there are treatments to help slow down the degenerative process. Low-protein diets will reduce the intake of nitrogen and therefore decrease the workload on the kidneys. Commercially prepared diets are available from veterinarians. Hill's K/D and U/D are examples of diets low in protein that are manufactured just for kidney patients. While low-protein diets do help manage kidney disease, high-protein diets do not cause it. And there is certainly no reason to put a dog on a low-protein diet simply because it is old.

Heart Valve Disease

There are many diseases that affect the heart in older dogs, and most affect the valves. The primary function of all heart valves is to prevent blood from flowing backward into the chamber it just left. This maintains the flow of blood in one direction—always forward through the entire circulatory system. When a valve does not function properly, the blood flows backward, putting additional stress on the valves and muscles in that portion of the heart. These malfunctioning valves are usually smaller, which is why they are unable to block the blood from flowing backward. This may be due to an infection in a valve, heartworm infestation, or simply a deterioration of the valves generally associated with aging.

The disease that is by far the most common affects the valve between the upper (atrium) and lower (ventricle) chambers on the left side of the heart, called the left atrioventricular or *mitral valve*. This mitral valve is by far the most likely to fail. This condition is called *mitral insufficiency*. Because the left ventricle is the strongest chamber in the heart, when a mitral insufficiency occurs, blood is forced all the way back into the lungs, elevating blood pressure there. Due to the high pressure, the smaller blood vessels push fluid through their walls into the lungs, creating a build-up of fluid in the lungs referred to as *pulmonary edema*. The most common sign of this condition is a dry, hacking cough as the lungs try to expel the fluid. Initially, the dog may only cough at night or after exercise, but the condition will progress to the point where it coughs throughout the day. As the disease continues, the dog will become weak and may even faint.

Most dogs with mild mitral valve insufficiency can live relatively normal lives. They simply learn not to exercise too much and to live with the cough. In more severe cases, the fluid accumulates in the lungs and causes serious labored breathing. Once this stage is reached, none of the body's tissues can get an adequate blood supply. This leads to other organ system failures. The heart muscle also becomes overworked trying to meet the demand. It can fail, resulting in sudden death, but in mitral insufficiency this is very rare.

Medical therapy can be very successful in eliminating the clinical signs and slowing the progression of heart valve diseases. Medications are used to strengthen the heart and diuretics help eliminate the edema within the lungs and their tissues. Activity should be restricted and the pet should not be allowed to become overweight. Less activity and less body weight means less work for the heart. Special low-salt diets can also be fed to keep blood pressure down. With this type of therapy, most dogs can return to a normal routine, at least for a significant period of time.

There is no way to prevent heart valve disease. You can only hope to minimize its effects on the body by recognizing the signs early and getting the dog on medications that ease the symptoms and slow the progression of the disease.

Arthritis

Arthritis, more properly referred to as osteoarthritis, is an inflammation of the bone and cartilage structures within the joints. Many things, such as injury or infections, can cause arthritis; however, most cases are simply due to aging. This discussion is about osteoarthritis due to the normal aging process.

As a dog ages, the normally smooth cartilage surfaces on the joints erode and wear thin. The body attempts to repair this erosion, but the repair job is never as good as the original, and the new cartilage often has irregular surfaces. These rough surfaces within the joint cause pain and inflammation when the bones rub against each other as the joints flex. The large joints, such as the shoulder, elbow, hip and ankle, are the ones most likely to develop osteoarthritis, but every joint, including those of the spine, can be affected. Some days the pain is worse than others, depending on the stress placed on the joints. Obese dogs tend to be affected the most, as the excess weight places a greater strain on their joints.

Virtually every old dog will have some degree of osteoarthritis, although some will never show signs. As in humans, stiffness and pain in the affected joint areas are the most common signs. The pain may be chronic or intermittent, mild or severe. Arthritic joints may swell, but this is relatively rare in dogs. Osteoarthritis is progressive, and the symptoms usually get worse with age.

This very old Collie still finds enjoyment in life.

Osteoarthritis and its accompanying symptoms are not life threatening. Many dogs simply live within the limitations caused by the arthritis. Overweight patients should be placed on a diet. Dogs with more severe pain may need some treatment to improve their quality of life. Various anti-inflammatories have been successfully used. Buffered aspirin controls mild arthritis, while more advanced cases may require cortisone, phenylbutazone, carprofen or other products. Nutritional products containing glucosamine and chondroitin sulfate have been found to be very helpful for many osteoarthritis patients. One example is Joint Care, a nutritional supplement designed to slow the advancement of the disease.

Occasionally, in very severe cases of osteoarthritis of the hip, a total hip replacement can be done. This is similar to the procedure performed in humans. This is a very expensive procedure. Fortunately, most dogs respond well to medical therapy, ensuring a decent quality of life with minimal symptoms.

Diabetes

The medical term for diabetes is *diabetes mellitus*, a disease in which the pancreas does not produce enough insulin, a hormone needed to move glucose from the bloodstream into most of the body's cells. Most of the body's tissues need glucose for energy. However, with diabetes the glucose simply builds up in the bloodstream, causing an elevated blood sugar level, and the tissues do not get the energy they need to function. Genetics play a role in diabetes, with a higher incidence of diabetes seen in Beagles and Poodles. In all dogs, it is most common in females over six years of age.

Elevated blood sugar can affect many systems of the body. Blood sugar will be filtered out through the kidneys and excreted, causing increased urination and thirst. Elevated blood sugar also alters the lens of the eye, leading to diabetic cataracts. Weight loss is a common symptom, as the body burns muscle for energy to help compensate for the inability to make use of glucose. A loss of muscle mass, combined with inadequate energy levels within the cells, leads to generalized weakness. The most common signs of diabetes are weakness, weight loss and increased thirst and urination.

The elevated blood sugar is toxic to many body systems and organs, including the blood vessels, nervous system, brain and liver. Uncontrolled diabetes can be fatal. That's why as soon as you even suspect diabetes could be a problem, a blood test should be performed by a veterinarian to determine the dog's blood sugar level. The earlier treatment is started, the better.

Unlike with some humans, canine diabetes cannot be controlled simply with diet management. Similarly, tablets designed to lower blood sugar are not usually effective in pets. The diabetic canine requires daily insulin injections. At first, the dog must be carefully monitored with blood and urine sugar tests to help determine the proper amount of insulin to be given and how often. When the dosage is set, monitoring will be less frequent, but still ongoing. Daily feeding should be a consistent amount on a regular schedule to provide a consistent supply of glucose, so that insulin requirements remain the same. Activity levels should also be as consistent as possible from day to day.

Most dogs with diabetes can live relatively normal lives with proper care. The insulin injections are not difficult to administer, and your veterinarian can teach you how to do it. Maintaining a diabetic pet requires great owner dedication, but the rewards are well worth it.

Breast Cancer

Breast cancer is the most common malignant tumor of the female dog, especially the older ones. It is responsible for the death of many dogs each year. However, breast cancer rarely, if ever, occurs in females that have been spayed at an early age. It is thought that the tumor is stimulated or brought on by one or more of the female hormones associated with heat cycles—probably estrogen. These hormones are produced and released by the ovaries, which are removed when a female dog is spayed. Thus, early spaying totally prevents breast cancer.

Mammary tumors are not usually seen in dogs less than six years old. A tumor can be either *mixed mammary* (in which many different cell types are present), or *adenocarcinoma* (a tumor rising from glandular cells). Regardless of the type, they may spread via the lymph glands to other parts of the body. Many dogs will have several different tumors developing at the same time within various glands. They develop slowly but exhibit rapid periods of growth, both in size and number, immediately following heat cycles.

Mammary tumors are easily felt through the skin. They are very hard, round masses with irregular or bumpy surfaces. Sometimes they are lying just under the skin. On a dog with white or very light-colored skin, such tumors can be seen and have a light yellow color. Although they can be found in any of the mammary glands, they are most frequently noted in the two rear glands. Sometimes these tumors grow rapidly, rupture through the skin over the mammary gland and drain a pink-tinged fluid.

Usually there are no clinical signs associated with mammary tumors, unless they drain or spread. These are highly malignant tumors that spread to other parts of the body, and usually signs can be seen from the effects they cause elsewhere. For example, they often spread to the lungs and cause a cough or difficult respiration. Whatever organs they spread to, they replace or destroy tissue that is necessary for life.

The vast majority of all mammary tumors are malignant, and if untreated they are life threatening. The preferred treatment is prevention by spaying.

Once tumors have developed, the only treatment is surgery. If this is done early in the course of the disease, the cancer will probably be eliminated before it has a chance to spread. At this point in time, chemotherapy is not considered to be a valuable weapon in the fight against canine breast cancer.

SUMMING UP

Old age is a time when dogs need extra attention and care. The problems of the older dog are not unlike those of older humans. Most are simply part of a long, slow process of organs and systems wearing out. Many can be prevented, and some can be eliminated if caught early. Early recognition always increases the chances of successful treatment. These conditions may not be cured, but their progression can be slowed and the dog spared from suffering.

Chapter 15

WHEN IT'S TIME
TO SAY GOOD-BYE

Sometimes our older pets pass away in their sleep. This makes it easier for both of us. They do not have to suffer any longer or deal with the anxiety that is often brought on by our reactions as we learn of a medical problem that will take them from us. For us, while the mental pain may be severe, we are not forced to be responsible for saying when they must die. For some of us, this final act of requesting the euthanasia of our pet washes away all of the memories of the good times we had over the long years we enjoyed with our dog. Somehow, being responsible for the death of this dog makes us forget the love and respect we felt for each other.

Part of the responsibility you take on in the relationship of "owning" your dog is deciding when the most humane thing you can do for your pet is to end its life. This is never easy. And each person who reaches this point lives through those final few moments with their dog, and then deals with the grief later.

We wish as veterinarians that we could give you some secret that makes this decision easier. Together, we have over 35 years of practice experience and have put thousands of dogs "to sleep." We wish, or maybe we don't, that we had been able to develop some sort of a callus that made this process easier. So far it hasn't happened, and we doubt if it ever will. For veterinarians there is also a sense of loss. We consider most of our clients to be our friends, but in all honesty, we can usually remember the names of the dogs more easily than those responsible for the bills. With many cases we are left alone with the dog, treating it in our hospital. With others, because of a chronic medical condition, we see the dog on a regular schedule. Additionally, just as owners wonder if they could have done more, those same questions run through our minds.

Once you have decided that the appropriate time has come to euthanize your dog, things will be a bit easier if you make some decisions beforehand. Think about whether you want to be present when the dog is actually "put to sleep." Do you want a friend or family member to be there with you? Do you want to save the dog's collar? Will you want your pet buried or cremated, and how will you arrange that? In some cases you may want to have your dog's favorite blanket or bed on hand to make the experience more comfortable.

Many clients who couldn't stand the thought of being in the room with the dog as it was euthanized later ask us about the procedure. What is actually done? Does the dog feel any pain? How long does it take? These questions don't bother us—after all, the dog has probably been one of their closest friends for several years.

Euthanasia is done by overdosing the dog on an anesthetic agent. The same product we would use when doing a spay or suturing a cut is prepared in a concentrated form and given intravenously with a syringe. With most of these products, the dog dies during the first pass the substance makes through the blood vessels of the brain. This usually only takes three to four seconds. While other organs of the body might continue to function for a few moments longer, the dog's brain is dead and it is oblivious to everything that occurs after those first few seconds. People who stay in the room with the dog sometimes notice that the heart continues to beat. That's normal, but the dog is already gone. The body may twitch or move slightly, but these are just reflexive movements. The euthanasia agents are very dependable and consistent in their action. Even if we tried, we could not save one of these dogs after the drug's initial passage through the brain.

Many owners do not want to bring their dog to our clinic at the end. This is understandable, and we often go to their homes. We are sometimes asked by these same people if there is something they could use at home to put their dog to sleep. There isn't. The common household items that might be used would poison a dog slowly. This would usually cause considerable pain and suffering over a prolonged period of time. There are stronger sedatives and medications used in human medicine, but for the veterinarian the laws and liabilities associated with dispensing these potentially abusable substances make it impossible. The action of these medications is not always dependable, either.

The one question we are asked most by clients of sick or older dogs is how to know when it is time to have the dog euthanized. While this would seem to be a very difficult thing to determine, it rarely is. You, of course, have your veterinarian to help you decide when the dog has reached this point. However, in most cases we aren't needed. You will know and you will have no question about it.

The decision is usually made in long-term, chronic cases involving a terminal illness. The owners understand that we are all doing our best to make the dog as comfortable as possible for as long as possible. That is the owner's job and it is our job. In at least half of these cases, some time along the way the clients ask how they will know when to step in and put the dog out of its misery.

In the early part of Chapter 14 we described the teeter-totter phenomenon, where dogs seemed to compensate for injuries or the loss of one of their senses. For example, if a dog slowly goes blind, the owner may notice no changes at all until the other senses can no longer compensate for the loss. The same usually happens with terminally ill dogs. They may not feel well, but they are happy to see us, are eating well and are getting around fairly well. Then, suddenly they become lethargic, stop eating and show some outward sign like nausea. Their behavior and actions usually make the decision for us. Many people do not believe this, but it is true. The veterinarian, by his or her actions, and often without words, usually lets you know that what you are thinking is correct.

The problem that can arise at this point is that the dog's owners may not be willing to believe what they are seeing, or won't admit the inevitable. This is understandable—no one wants to believe a friend is suffering or is about to die.

Another problem is that some people don't want to let go of their companion. This is the single hardest thing for some owners to deal with, and it causes them, the dog and the veterinarian more problems than any other aspect of caring for the dog. They are more concerned with their own feeling of loss than they are with the dog's suffering. While they genuinely do not want to see their dog—or any dog—suffer, they cannot deal with their own grief or see the situation in a realistic perspective. Every pet owner has to guard against allowing this thinking to affect the well-being of their animal. For those of us who have chosen to live with dogs, it becomes part of our responsibility to be able to do what is right for the dog at the end of its life, just as it was to make sure it received its vaccinations, food and love.

When the dog is gone, there is still the grief to deal with. There are no easy solutions, but we must always remember the good times we had with our dog and not let our minds be clouded by a small and final portion of its life. If you had to make the hard decision to euthanize the dog, remember that the relief from suffering was probably the greatest gift you could give.

Don't try to rush the grieving process. It takes time. And don't feel that rushing out and getting a new puppy or dog will always make it easier. For some people, it may be good therapy. For others, the idea of another dog will have to wait awhile. Just don't expect the new one to replace the one that has passed. That will never happen.

Don't let your last memory of your dog be your only memory. Take time to recall all the fun you had together throughout the dog's life.

BREED PREDILECTIONS FOR HEALTH PROBLEMS

This is a list of breed predilections for a variety of diseases and defects. You should ask your dog's breeder if their dogs, or puppies they have produced, have had problems with these conditions. Good breeders breed away from these problems, and their dogs should not be affected. But it's important to ask before you acquire a dog. Remember, almost all of these disorders can affect any dog. We've listed the breeds in which they have the highest incidence.

BREED	DISEASE OR DEFECT
Brachiocephalic breeds	Upper respiratory problems, facial fold dermatitis, exophthalmos, predisposition to dystocia
Large and giant breeds	Elbow and hip dysplasia, bone cancer
Large, deep-chested breeds	Bloat
Miniature breeds	Tracheal collapse, luxating patella, Legg-Calvé perthes disease, predisposition to dystocia

BREED	DISEASE OR DEFECT
Afghan Hound	Cataracts, demodicosis, hypothyroidism
Airedale	Eyelash abnormalities, umbilical hernia, progressive retinal degeneration
Akita	Eyelid abnormalities
Alaskan Malamute	Zinc-responsive dermatosis, clotting factor abnormalities, progressive retinal degeneration
American Staffordshire Terrier (Pit Bull)	Cataract eyelid abnormalities
Basset Hound	Glaucoma, interdigital dermatitis, primary seborrhea, eyelid abnormalities, inguinal hernia, luxating patella
Beagle	Intervertebral disc disease, congenital heart defects, atopy, demodicosis, epilepsy, clotting factor abnormalities
Bedlington Terrier	Chronic progressive hepatitis
Belgian Sheepdog	Epilepsy, hip dysplasia
Bernese Mountain Dog	Hip dysplasia, bloat
Bichon Frise	Epilepsy, luxating patella, cataracts
Borzoi (Russian Wolfhound)	Bloat, elbow hygroma
Boston Terrier	Hyperadrenocorticism (Cushing's disease), atopy, demodicosis, luxating patella, inguinal hernia
Boxer	Cancer (all types), demodicosis, hypothyroidism, atopy, hyperadrenocorticism (Cushing's disease), congenital heart defects
Brittany	Cataracts

BREED	**DISEASE OR DEFECT**
Bulldog (English)	Demodicosis, facial fold dermatitis, congenital heart defects, atopy, canine acne, hypothyroidism, keratitis sicca, elongated soft palate
Bullmastiff	Bloat, hip dysplasia, eyelid and eyelash abnormalities
Bull Terrier	Congenital heart defects, hernias, deafness
Cairn Terrier	Craniomandibular osteopathy, clotting factor abnormalities, inguinal hernia
Chihuahua	Clotting factor abnormalities, demodicosis, alopecia (congenital), hydrocephalus, congenital heart defects, luxating patella
Chinese Shar-Pei	Otitis, atopy, primary seborrhea, demodicosis, eyelid and eyelash abnormalities, body fold dermatitis, hip dysplasia
Chow Chow	Hypothyroidism, hip dysplasia
Cocker Spaniel	Atopy, glaucoma, lipfold dermatitis, otitis, primary seborrhea, epilepsy
Collie	Congenital heart defects, "Collie eye," Grey Collie syndrome, nasal solar dermatitis, lupus erythematosis, epilepsy
Dachshund	Intervertebral disc disease, epilepsy, demodicosis, hyperadrenocorticism (Cushing's disease), primary seborrhea, acanthosis nigricans, diabetes mellitus, hypothyroidism

BREED	DISEASE OR DEFECT
Dalmatian	Uric acid bladder stones, atopy, demodicosis, hereditary deafness
Doberman Pinscher	Cardiomyopathy, congenital heart defects, atopy, demodicosis, hypothyroidism, von Willebrand's disease, wobbler syndrome, primary seborrhea, canine acne, acral lick dermatitis, abnormal copper storage in liver
English Cocker Spaniel	Glaucoma, progressive retinal degeneration, cryptorchidism, atopy
English Setter	Progressive retinal degeneration, hip dysplasia, deafness
Fox Terrier	Congenital heart defects, atopy, Legg-Calvé perthes disease
German Pointer	Eyelid abnormalities, congenital heart defects
German Shepherd	Congenital heart defects, epilepsy, degenerative myelopathy, hip dysplasia, nasal dermatitis, perianal fistula, demodicosis, panosteitis, pancreatic insufficiency, seborrhea
Golden Retriever	Hypothyroidism, atopy, cataracts, progressive retinal degeneration, hip dysplasia, acral lick dermatitis, hot spots, congenital heart defects
Gordon Setter	Hip dysplasia
Great Dane	Bone cancer, demodicosis, hypothyroidism, wobbler syndrome, congenital heart defects, canine acne, bloat
Great Pyrenees	Hot spots, hip dysplasia, demodicosis

BREED	DISEASE OR DEFECT
Greyhound	Drug sensitivities
Irish Setter	Atopy, acral lick dermatitis, epilepsy, deformed tail, hypothyroidism, seborrhea
Irish Wolfhound	Bloat, hypothyroidism, elbow hygroma
Keeshond	Congenital heart defects, hypothyroidism, epilepsy
Labrador Retriever	Cataracts, progressive retinal degeneration, hip dysplasia, atopy, hypothyroidism, congenital heart defects, primary seborrhea, hot spots
Lhasa Apso	Atopy, abnormal eyelashes, luxating patella
Newfoundland	Congenital heart defects, hip dysplasia
Norwegian Elkhound	Progressive retinal degeneration
Old English Sheepdog	Demodicosis, hip dysplasia, wobbler syndrome
Pekingese	Intervertebral disc disease, facial fold dermatitis
Pomeranian	Tracheal collapse, luxating patella, congenital heart defects
Poodle (Miniature and Toy)	Congenital heart defects, progressive retinal degeneration, epilepsy, atopy, epiphora, hyperadrenocorticism (Cushing's disease), hypothyroidism, intervertebral disc disease
Poodle (Standard)	Hyperadrenocorticism (Cushing's disease) in black Standard Poodles, bloat, epilepsy

BREED	DISEASE OR DEFECT
Pug	Facial fold dermatitis, elongated soft palate, corneal irritation
Rottweiler	Hip dysplasia, congenital heart defects
Saint Bernard	Bone cancer, epilepsy, bloat, eyelid and eyelash abnormalities, clotting factor abnormalities, lipfold dermatitis
Samoyed	Congenital heart defects, sebaceous cysts, hip dysplasia
Schnauzer	Cataracts (Miniature Schnauzer), Schnauzer comedo syndrome, congenital heart defects
Scottish Terrier	Scottie cramp, atopy, skin tumors, craniomandibular osteopathy
Shetland Sheepdog	Lupus erythematosis, congenital eye defects, congenital heart defects
Shih Tzu	Luxating patella
Siberian Husky	Zinc-responsive dermatosis, lupus erythematosis
Vizsla	Sebaceous adenitis
Weimaraner	Congenital heart defects, skin tumors, bloat, hip dysplasia, eyelid abnormalities
West Highland White Terrier	Legg-Calvé perthes disease, atopy craniomandibular osteopathy, epidermal dysplasia, primary seborrhea
Yorkshire Terrier	Eyelid and eyelash abnormalities, luxating patella

ABOUT THE AUTHORS

Dr. Race Foster is a practicing veterinarian with a special interest in canine and feline medicine and surgery. He has practiced in northern Wisconsin since receiving his DVM from Michigan State University. In addition to his veterinary practice, he is co-owner of Drs. Foster and Smith, Inc., a leading catalog supplier of products for pets and their owners that is known throughout the world.

Dr. Foster is a member of the Michigan and Wisconsin Veterinary Medical Associations. He lives in Minocqua, Wisconsin, with his wife and four children.

In his free time, Dr. Foster writes veterinary articles and books and, of course, enjoys being with animals. He has a special interest in consulting and working with professional dog and cat breeders, especially in the area of animal health, and is a consultant on pet health nationwide.

Dr. Marty Smith's interests in veterinary medicine include canine and feline medicine and surgery, along with many hours devoted to wildlife treatment and rehabilitation. He received his DVM from Iowa State University and is a member of the Wisconsin Veterinary Medical Association.

Dr. Smith, his wife and their five daughters enjoy a wide range of outdoor activities, including camping, hiking, boating, wildlife photography and skiing. Today he is co-owner of one of America's largest pet supply mail order catalog companies, Drs. Foster and Smith, Inc. He divides his time between his family, his veterinary practice, writing and consulting with other writers, organizations and pet breeders across the United States.

INDEX

T

U–Y